19+
X -1

LESSONS IN
SCHOLASTIC PHILOSOPHY

A *first* (or *direct*) intention is the apprehension of an object as it is in itself. A *second* (or *reflex*) intention is the apprehension of an object as it exists in the thinking mind—a concept of our direct concept of an object.

ARTICLE II.—CLASSIFICATION OF IDEAS.

Ideas or concepts may be classified according (a) to their *origin,* (b) the objects represented by them, (c) the *perfection* with which they represent their objects, (d) their *relations* to one another.

10. **According to their origin,** ideas are either *intuitive* or *derivative.* *Intuitive,* if they are directly and immediately derived from the objects they represent or are such as if they had been so derived from their objects.

Derivative, when they are not determined by the objects which they represent, but are formed by synthesis or analysis or other modifications of intuitive concepts. Thus our concept of a man is *intuitive,* while our concept of an angel or of God is *derivative.*

Intuitive concepts are *direct* or *reflex* according as their objects are *without* or *within* the thinking mind.

Derivative concepts are *arbitrary or discursive,* according as the synthesis of intuitive ideas by which they are formed, is arbitrary, or the result of strict logical reasoning.

11. **In regard to the objects represented,** ideas may be classified according to their *comprehension and extension.*

(i) According to their *comprehension,* ideas are *simple* or *complex* according as they represent one or several notes. *Concrete* or *abstract* according as they represent a subject as affected by a form or determination; or a form or determination apart from its subject.

NOTE.—An abstract idea is said to be *positively* abstract when the subject of the form or determination is positively excluded from the concept; *negatively* abstract when the

A. M. D. G.

Or, according to *common usage,* 'President is the head of the executive in a Republic.'

Or *arbitrarily,* i. e., when a word is ambiguous, and one settles the particular sense in which he uses it, *e. g.,* 'By President we mean the one whom the class chooses to represent it in regard to class matters with the authorities of the College.'

(b) A *real* definition declares what the thing, signified by a word, is, by giving a clear and distinct account of it. It is either:

Causal, if it assigns the extrinsic causes of the object, i. e., its efficient, final, exemplary cause; or

Essential, if it gives the essential or constitutive parts of the object, regarded as a physical or metaphysical whole, *e. g.,* 'Man is composed of a spiritual soul and an organic body'; 'Man is a rational animal'; or

Descriptive, if it gives the properties of the object, or such of its accidents as serve to distinguish it from all other objects; or finally

Genetic, if it gives the *manner* in which a thing is produced.

24.   A Definition should be clearer and more distinct than the object defined.

It should embrace neither more nor less than the object defined, and apply to none but it.

It should not be *tautological,* i. e., it should not contain the name of the object to be *defined,* or any of its derivatives, or of such correlatives of the thing to be defined as cannot be explained unless the thing itself is already known.   This is called Defining in a Circle.

It should not be *negative,* for the purpose of a definition is to declare what a thing is, not what it is not.   However, an exception to this law is allowed in the case of contradictory opposites.   When one has been positively defined, the other may be defined negatively, *e. g.,* 'knowing what parts

PART ONE.

LOGIC

DEFINITION AND DIVISION OF LOGIC.

1. **Logic** is the science of the laws by which reason must be governed in order to act conformably to its nature, and so to form *correct* and *true* judgments.

2. There are, then, **two sets of laws to be considered:** the one set, that our thought may be *correct* and *consistent* or conformed to the *necessary laws of thinking;* the other, that our thought may be *true* or conformed to the *objective reality of things.* Hence the division of Logic into *Dialectics* or Formal Logic, and *Critics* or Material Logic.

NOTE.—Logic may be called an *art,* inasmuch as it gives us the practical rules by which we must be guided in order to reason correctly ourselves, and to judge correctly about the reasoning of others. It is a *science* inasmuch as it gives us the fundamental reasons of the laws it propounds.

The importance of the study of Logic is evident from its purpose, which is to secure exact, correct, true thought, and to avoid deception by fallacy or error.

Published 1905
Copyright 1912
Reprinted 1915
Reprinted 1916
Reprinted 1918

Common, when the term expresses a note or character common to many individuals, *e. g.,* 'a President.'

(d) Common supposition is

Absolute, when the term signifies the common note found in different individuals prescinded from individuation, i. e., neither including nor excluding individuation, but simply not considering it. It simply expresses the contents or *comprehension* of a direct universal idea.

Relative or *personal,* when the term signifies the individuals included under the *extension* of the universal idea, *e. g.,* 'Presidents are fallible.'

(e) Common personal supposition is

Collective, when the words stands for all the individuals to which it applies, *taken together, e. g.,* 'The President of the United States has had certain rights for over a hundred years.'

Distributive, when the word stands for the individuals to which it applies *taken severally.*

NOTE.—Distributive supposition is *complete,* when a generic or specific term is used for *each* and *every individual* under its extension; *incomplete,* when a generic term is used to express *some* individuals of *every species* under its extension, *e. g.,* 'all terrestrial animals were in the Ark'; i. e., some of each species.

Particular, when the common name expresses but *some* of the objects to which it can be applied, *e. g.,* 'Saints have erred'; and this either *indeterminately, e. g.,* 'ships are necessary to cross the ocean'; or *determinately, e. g.,* 'ships carried Columbus to America.'

ARTICLE VI.—LOGICAL DIVISION.

Logical definition and division are the test of, and the means of acquiring, clear and distinct ideas.

Logical division is the mental analysis or resolution of a

PART ONE.

LOGIC

DEFINITION AND DIVISION OF LOGIC.

---

1.   **Logic** is the science of the laws by which reason must be governed in order to act conformably to its nature, and so to form *correct* and *true* judgments.

2.   There are, then, **two sets of laws to be considered:** the one set, that our thought may be *correct* and *consistent* or conformed to the *necessary laws of thinking;* the other, that our thought may be *true* or conformed to the *objective reality of things.*   Hence the division of Logic into *Dialectics* or Formal Logic, and *Critics* or Material Logic.

NOTE.—Logic may be called an *art,* inasmuch as it gives us the practical rules by which we must be guided in order to reason correctly ourselves, and to judge correctly about the reasoning of others.   It is a *science* inasmuch as it gives us the fundamental reasons of the laws it propounds.

The importance of the study of Logic is evident from its purpose, which is to secure exact, correct, true thought, and to avoid deception by fallacy or error.

5

BOOK ONE.

DIALECTICS.

3. **Dialectics** or Formal Logic treats of the laws by which our mental acts must be governed in order that our thinking may be *correct* and *consistent* or conformed to the necessary laws of thought.

4. The principal acts of the human mind are Simple Apprehension, Judgment and Reasoning; these are the primary subject-matter of Dialectics. But as speech is so closely connected with the exercise and expression of thought, the forms of speech by which these mental acts are expressed will also need to be considered here.

5. This Book, therefore, will comprise three chapters, viz.:

1st. Simple Apprehension, and its verbal expression, the Verbal term.

2d. Judgment, and its verbal expression, the Proposition.

3d. Reasoning, and its verbal expression, the Syllogism, etc.

CHAPTER I.

Article I.—Simple Apprehension.

6. **A Simple Apprehension** or Notion or Idea or Concept or Mental Term, for all mean the same thing, is a simple intellectual representation of an object.

Explanation.—*Simple* because it merely represents the object without affirming or denying anything of it. *Intellectual* to distinguish this representation from those of the *senses* or *imagination.* *Representation,* that is, a physical entity existing in the intellect whose essential function it is to cause the mind *immediately* to *perceive the object* of which it is a representation; or, technically speaking, a *natural formal* sign which leads to the immediate perception not of *itself,* but of the *object signified.*

7. **The object of an idea** is that which it represents. Every object has certain attributes or characters peculiar to itself, by which it is what it is and is knowable or capable of manifesting itself to the mind. These characters we may call the *notes* of the object. When, then, the mind represents an object, it does so by representing some or all of these notes.

8. The object, as it really is, with all its notes, is called the *material object* of the idea. The same object considered only in those notes, which are here and now represented in the thought, is called the *formal* object of the idea.

9. The *Comprehension* of an idea is the sum of the notes represented in that idea.

The *Extension* of an idea is its capacity of representing more or fewer objects.

The greater the *Comprehension* of an idea, the less its *Extension,* and vice versa.

NOTE.—Attention is a special application of the mind to one object among many simultaneously presented to it. It may be *involuntary,* in which case its direction and intensity are determined by the interest or attractiveness of the object; or *voluntary,* and then it is determined chiefly by motives which influence the will.

Abstraction is an act of simple apprehension in which the mind represents one note or character or aspect of an object, *prescinded* from other notes of the same object, with which it is actually united or even identified.

Reflection is an apprehensive act whose object is the mind's own acts or states.

The act of simple apprehension is often called an *intention.*

A *first* (or *direct*) intention is the apprehension of an object as it is in itself. A *second* (or *reflex*) intention is the apprehension of an object as it exists in the thinking mind—a concept of our direct concept of an object.

ARTICLE II.—CLASSIFICATION OF IDEAS.

Ideas or concepts may be classified according (a) to their *origin,* (b) the objects represented by them, (c) the *perfection* with which they represent their objects, (d) their *relations* to one another.

10. **According to their origin,** ideas are either *intuitive* or *derivative. Intuitive,* if they are directly and immediately derived from the objects they represent or are such as if they had been so derived from their objects.

Derivative, when they are not determined by the objects which they represent, but are formed by synthesis or analysis or other modifications of intuitive concepts. Thus our concept of a man is *intuitive,* while our concept of an angel or of God is *derivative.*

Intuitive concepts are *direct* or *reflex* according as their objects are *without* or *within* the thinking mind.

Derivative concepts are *arbitrary or discursive,* according as the synthesis of intuitive ideas by which they are formed, is arbitrary, or the result of strict logical reasoning.

11. **In regard to the objects represented,** ideas may be classified according to their *comprehension and extension.*

(i) According to their *comprehension,* ideas are *simple* or *complex* according as they represent one or several notes. *Concrete* or *abstract* according as they represent a subject as affected by a form or determination; or a form or determination apart from its subject.

NOTE.—An abstract idea is said to be *positively* abstract when the subject of the form or determination is positively excluded from the concept; *negatively* abstract when the subject is neither excluded nor included, but simply prescinded from.

(ii) According to their *extension*, ideas are *singular, universal, particular, transcendental*.

(a) A *singular* idea represents one definite individual object, i. e., a sum of notes so defined and determined that all taken together can only be realized in and predicated of the individual thing, *e. g.,* 'Cleveland,' 'California,' *'this* family.'

NOTE.—The peculiar incommunicable characters of such an *individual* being are called *individuating notes*.

(b) A *universal* idea represents a note or sum of notes which may be realized in and predicated of many distinct objects (which are called its *inferiors* or *subordinates*), *e. g.,* 'man,' 'state,' 'family.'

(c) A *particular* idea is a universal idea restricted to an indeterminate portion of its extension, *e. g.,* 'some men,' 'most families,' 'many states.'

Classification of Universal Ideas.

If I draw a circle on the blackboard and explain to you how it is formed, you will have first, a concept of *that* particular circle, then, a concept of what constitutes *a* circle (a *direct* universal idea) ; lastly, you can conceive that sum of notes (represented in your *direct* universal idea) as realized in or capable of being realized in and predicated of innumerable individuals (a *reflex* universal idea).

Hence a *direct* universal idea represents its object as *negatively abstract* or *prescinded* from individuation. What it represents really exists independently of the thinking mind, though it does not and cannot exist in the *manner* in which it is represented, i. e., as prescinded from individuation; individuation is neither included nor excluded in the contents of the concept, it is simply neglected.

A *reflex* universal idea, on the contrary, represents its object as *positively* abstract, as positively *excluding* individuation. Such an object does not and cannot exist outside the thinking mind; it is a logical entity with a foundation in reality.

What is common to many and predicable of each and all of them distributively must be referred to its subordinates in one or other of the five following ways, viz.: as species, genus, difference, property, or accident.

For what is thus conceived as common to and predicable of many, either belongs to each and all of them necessarily and constantly, or not; in the latter case, it is an *accident*. If it belongs to all its subordinates necessarily and constantly, it must be either a constituent, or a necessary concomitant of their essence; if the latter is a *property*. If the common predicate is a constituent of the common essence, it either expresses the *whole* of that essence, and then we have a *species;* or it expresses that element of the essence which is common to several different species, and we have a *genus;* or finally, it expresses that essential element which distinguishes different species of the same genus from one another, in which case we have a *specific difference*.

A *species* is that sum of notes which constitutes a complete *essence* or *nature* conceived as common to and predicable of many distinct individuals.

A *genus* is that note or sum of notes which constitutes an essential element common to and predicable of many different species.

A specific *difference* is that peculiar essential note or character by which each species of the same proximate genus is distinguished from other species of the same genus. It is common to and predicable of each individual of the given species.

A *property* is a note which, though not an essential constituent of a given species, is yet a necessary concomitant of that species and is found in every individual of that species and of that species only.

An *accident* (logical) is a note which is neither an essential constituent of a given species, nor a necessary concomitant of its essence, but may be absent or present in individuals without affecting their essence.

(d)   A *transcendental* idea represents a note which is common to and predicable of all beings.

12.   **In regard to the various degrees of perfection with which they represent their objects,** ideas may be classified as *clear, obscure, distinct, confused, complete, incomplete, comprehensive, proper, analagous.*

(a)   A *clear* idea represents its object so as to distinguish it from all other objects, *e. g.,* 'our idea of man.'

(b)   An *obscure* idea does not so represent its object, *e. g.,* 'an ignorant man's idea of bismuth.'

(c)   A *distinct* idea is a clear idea in which, moreover, some at least of the characteristic notes of the object represented are distinguished from one another.

(d)   A *confused* idea is one in which the notes are not so distinguished

(e)   A *complete* idea is a distinct idea in which *all* the characteristic notes are distinguished from each other.

(f)   An *incomplete idea,* if not all the notes, are so distinguished.

(g)   An idea is *comprehensive* when the mind so represents an object as to conceive not only all its notes distinctly and completely, but also all that is knowable about it.

(h)   A *proper* idea represents its object according to the latter's own proper nature and character.

(i)   An *analagous* idea represents its object, not according to the latter's own proper nature, but by a modification of the proper concepts of other less perfect objects, in some way similar to it or otherwise related to it. It is only in this way that we can form our idea of God.

NOTE.—The word proper is sometimes applied to ideas in the sense of *singular* (12-11-a). In this sense a *proper* concept is opposed to a *common one* (universal or transcendental). In this sense of the word, we have undoubtedly a *proper* concept of God, i. e., one whose contents can only be verified in and predicated of the one infinitely perfect God.

13. **Considered in regard to their relation to one another,** ideas are classified as *identical* or *different, congruent* or *repugnant, associated.*

(a) Ideas are *intrinsically identical,* when their contents or comprehension is the same (the same formal object).

Intrinsically different, when their comprehension is different (different formal objects).

Objectively identical, when they represent the same *material* object, i. e., when their contents are verified in the same material object.

Objectively different, when they represent different *material* objects.

(b) Ideas are *congruent,* when they represent notes which *can be* united to form one complex idea.

Repugnant, if the notes represented cannot be united in one and the same material object, i. e., if they mutually exclude one another.

NOTE.—The objects of repugnant ideas are called *opposites.* There are four classes of opposites, viz.:

Contradictories, when one is a positive note, and the other its *simple negation,* e. g., 'man, not man'; 'black, not black.' Here there is no mean. Everything that is or is thinkable, is either man, or not-man, etc.

Privatives, when one is a positive note, and the other its privative negative, *e. g.,* 'sight and blindness in man.'

Contraries, when both are the positive notes farthest apart under the same genus, *e. g.,* 'simple, compound'; 'virtue, vice'; 'beauty, ugliness.' Here there is a mean.

Correlative opposites, when each necessarily implies the other—'father, son'; 'Creator, creature.'

(c) Ideas are said to be *associated,* when, on account of some intrinsic or extrinsic connection between them, one recalls the other, *e. g.,* 'the ideas of *whole* and *part'*; 'of *home* and the *persons living there.'*

ARTICLE III.—VERBAL TERMS.

14. A **sign** is that which conveys to a cognitive faculty the knowledge of something besides itself, *e. g.,* 'smoke is a sign of fire.' Two relations may be considered in a sign: one to the thing signified, the other to the faculty to which it conveys the knowledge of the thing signified.

(a) When the relation to the thing signified is founded in the nature of things, the sign is *natural, e. g.,* 'smoke is a natural sign of fire.'

(b) When this relation arises, not from the nature of things, but from the will of man, the sign is *arbitrary* or *conventional, e. g.,* 'a barber's pole.'

In regard to its relation to the faculty to which it represents the thing signified, a sign is:—

(a) *Instrumental,* if it leads to the knowledge of the thing signified only *mediately,* i. e., through the previous knowledge of itself. It is itself the immediate object of cognition; and, once known, it leads to the knowledge of the object it signifies.

(b) A *formal* sign, on the contrary, *immediately* and without being perceived itself as a sign, represents the thing signified.

15. **Words** are articulate sounds of the human voice, having a signification fixed by convention, or arbitrary instrumental signs manifesting ideas and standing for the objects which those ideas represent.

The chief words considered in logic are nouns (substantive and adjective), pronouns and verbs. They are called verbal terms because the logical analysis of speech terminates in them.

NOTE.—In logic every *grammatical* verb is equivalent to the present tense of the verb *to be* and an attribute, *e. g.,* 'I have written a letter is equivalent to 'I am one-who-has-written-a-letter.' Hence the verbal terms to be considered are chiefly the *subject* (that of which something is affirmed or denied), and *predicate* (that which is affirmed or denied of something).

ARTICLE IV.—CLASSIFICATION OF VERBAL TERMS.

Verbal terms may be classified in the same way as concepts, viz.: according to their perfection as *signs;* and according to the comprehension, extension, and mutual relations of the ideas they signify.

16. **According to their perfection as signs,** terms are

(a) *Fixed* or *Definite,* if their sense is constant.

Vague, if their sense is variable, *e. g.,* 'nature.'

(b) *Univocal,* if the note signified is verified completely and independently in all the objects to which the term is applied.

Equivocal, when the same term is used to signify objects altogether different and in no way related to each other, *e. g.,* 'bank.'

Analogical (1) when the note signified by the term is found in all the objects to which the term is applied, but not *equally* and *independently* in all; (2) when the note signified belongs in reality to but one of the objects, while the term is applied to other objects on account of some relation they bear to it, *e. g.,* the word 'healthy' as applied to man, food, color, etc.; the word 'foot' as used of a man, a mountain, etc. The various objects to which the common name is applied are called *analogates*. That object to which the note signified belongs absolutely, completely and independently, is called the *primary analogate*.

17. **If we consider the comprehension of the idea signified**, a term is

(a) *Positive*, if it expresses a positive note.

Negative, if it expresses the negation of some positive note.

Privative, if it expresses the negation of some positive note or perfection in an object which *ought* to possess it, *e. g.*, 'blindness in man.'

(b) *Simple*, when it is expressed in *one word*, whether the idea signified be simple or complex.

Complex, when the idea signified is expressed in many words which give the object and some of its notes or attributes distinctly. The word which expresses the object itself is called the *principal* term; those which distinctly express its notes or attributes are called *incidental* terms, *e. g.*, 'a learned eloquent man.'

NOTE.—When an incidental term belongs to the whole extension of the principal term, it is said to be *explicative*, *e. g.*, 'mortal man'; when it is applicable only to a part of the extension of the principal term it is said to be *restrictive*, *e. g.*, 'a wealthy man.'

(c) *Absolute*, when it expresses a subject directly according to its own proper nature, *e. g.*, 'man.'

Connotative, when it signifies directly some attribute or qualification, and indirectly the subject to which this attribute belongs or in which it inheres, *e. g.*, 'the poor,' 'a scholar.'

(d) *Concrete*, or *abstract*, according as it signifies an abstract or a concrete idea.

(e) *Of first intention* (*real*), or of *second intention* (*logical*).

18. **According to the extension of the idea signified,** a term is

(a) *Proper,* when it signifies the object of a singular idea.

Common, when it signifies a note common to many distinct individuals, i e., all that the word expresses is found in each of the individuals to which the word is applied.

NOTE.—A common term may become *singular* by the addition of the demonstrative pronoun, *e. g., 'this* pen'; or of some singular incident, *e. g.,* 'the man who assassinated Carnot.'

It may become *particular* by prefixing 'some,' 'many,' etc.

ARTICLE V.—SUPPOSITION OR USE OF VERBAL TERMS.

Almost all words may have different senses.   The supposition or *use* of a term is the precise meaning it has in a given context.

19. Supposition is

(a) *Material,* if the word merely stands for itself and not for any object signified by it, *e. g.,* 'President is a word of three syllables.'

Formal, if the word stands for the object is signifies, *e. g.,* 'Cleveland is President.'

(b) Formal supposition is

Logical, if the word stands for the object as it exists only in the mind, or as conceived by a Second Intention, *e. g.,* 'President is a universal idea.'

Real, if it stands for the object as it is in itself, independently of the thinking mind.

(c) Real supposition is

Singular, when the term expresses a singular concept, or a definite individual object, *e. g.,* 'The first President.'

Common, when the term expresses a note or character common to many individuals, *e. g.,* 'a President.'

(d) Common supposition is

Absolute, when the term signifies the common note found in different individuals prescinded from individuation, i. e., neither including nor excluding individuation, but simply not considering it. It simply expresses the contents or *comprehension* of *a* direct universal idea.

Relative or *personal,* when the term signifies the individuals included under the *extension* of the universal idea, *e. g.,* 'Presidents are fallible.'

(e) Common personal supposition is

Collective, when the words stands for all the individuals to which it applies, *taken together, e. g.,* 'The President of the United States has had certain rights for over a hundred years.'

Distributive, when the word stands for the individuals to which it applies *taken severally.*

NOTE.—Distributive supposition is *complete,* when a generic or specific term is used for *each* and *every individual* under its extension; *incomplete,* when a generic term is used to express *some* individuals of *every species* under its extension, *e. g.,* 'all terrestrial animals were in the Ark'; i. e., some of each species.

Particular, when the common name expresses but *some* of the objects to which it can be applied, *e. g.,* 'Saints have erred'; and this either *indeterminately, e. g.,* 'ships are necessary to cross the ocean'; or *determinately, e. g.,* 'ships carried Columbus to America.'

ARTICLE VI.—LOGICAL DIVISION.

Logical definition and division are the test of, and the means of acquiring, clear and distinct ideas.

Logical division is the mental analysis or resolution of a

whole as represented by one idea, into its parts as represented
by many ideas.

20. (a) An *actual* whole really contains in itself the
parts which are distinguished and enumerated in it, i. e., the
notes of its comprehension. It is

Metaphysical, if the parts distinguished in it, though real,
are not really, but only in concept, distinct and separable,
e. g., the notes of substance, life, animality and rationality in
man. Such parts are called metaphysical parts. They are
said to be *virtually* distinct from one another.

Physical, if the parts are not only real, but also really
distinct and separable. These parts are either: (1) *essential,
e. g.,* body and soul in man; (2) or *integral, i. e.,* those into
which a body is divisible, with respect to its quantity, *e. g.,*
'hand,' 'foot,' 'head,' etc. These again may be either *homogeneous* or *heterogeneous.*

NOTE.—Under the head of *physical* whole, we may place
the *moral whole, e. g.,* 'an organized community'; the *artificial*
whole, *e. g.,* 'a watch,' 'a house,' etc.; the *accidental* whole,
e. g., the composite of a substance and its various accidental
modifications.

(b) A *logical* or *potential* whole is a reflex universal in
regard to its inferiors, i. e., in regard to all that is covered by
its extension; these are called *subjective* parts.

NOTE.—An *actual* whole may be affirmed of all its parts
united together.

A *potential* whole may be affirmed of each of its parts
taken separately.

An actual whole may be called a Whole of Comprehension; a potential, a Whole of Extension. The two are in
inverse ratio—the larger the potential whole the smaller the
actual, and vice versa.

Hence an *actual* whole is divided by mentally *separating*
the various parts or notes of its comprehension; a *logical*

whole, by *adding* to the notes of its comprehension. Hence division by *analysis,* or by *synthesis.*

21. Logical division is either

Division of a *verbal* term. This is called *distinction.* It consists in assigning the different senses of an ambiguous word, phrase or sentence; or

Division of the *object* signified by a verbal term. It is the resolution of the thing signified into its parts, and varies according to the character of the whole to be divided, *e. g.:*

An *actual* whole may be divided into its metaphysical, essential or integral parts;

A *potential* whole, *e. g.,* 'a genus, may be divided into its species'; a 'species, into its individuals';

A *subject* may be divided accordinig to its different accidents, an accident according to its different subjects, or according to the accidents with which it is found united.

22. The division should be adequate, i. e., all the parts taken together should be equal to the whole, neither more nor less.

(a) No part should be equal to the whole.

(b) One part should not include another.

(c) Division should be, first into proximate and immediate parts; and then, if need be, each of these should be subdivided into its approximate parts; else we shall have confusion, and not clearness and distinctness of ideas.

NOTE.—See Clarke, p. 225, seqq.

ARTICLE VII.—DEFINITION.

A **definition** declares brieflly and distinctly what a thing is. It is either Verbal or Real.

23. (a) A *verbal* or *nominal* definition gives the meaning of a word. It is formed either:

According to the *etymology* of the word, *e. g.,* 'President is one who sits at the head.'

Or, according to *common usage,* 'President is the head of the executive in a Republic.'

Or *arbitrarily,* i. e., when a word is ambiguous, and one settles the particular sense in which he uses it, *e. g.,* 'By President we mean the one whom the class chooses to represent it in regard to class matters with the authorities of the College.'

(b) A *real* definition declares what the thing, signified by a word, is, by giving a clear and distinct account of it. It is either:

Causal, if it assigns the extrinsic causes of the object, i. e., its efficient, final, exemplary cause; or

Essential, if it gives the essential or constitutive parts of the object, regarded as a physical or metaphysical whole, *e. g.,* 'Man is composed of a spiritual soul and an organic body'; 'Man is a rational animal'; or

Descriptive, if it gives the properties of the object, or such of its accidents as serve to distinguish it from all other objects; or finally

Genetic, if it gives the *manner* in which a thing is produced.

24. A Definition should be clearer and more distinct than the object defined.

It should embrace neither more nor less than the object defined, and apply to none but it.

It should not be *tautological,* i. e., it should not contain the name of the object to be *defined,* or any of its derivatives, or of such correlatives of the thing to be defined as cannot be explained unless the thing itself is already known. This is called Defining in a Circle.

It should not be *negative,* for the purpose of a definition is to declare what a thing is, not what it is not. However, an exception to this law is allowed in the case of contradictory opposites. When one has been positively defined, the other may be defined negatively, *e. g.,* 'knowing what parts are and that a compound consists of parts, we may define a simple being as one which does not consist of parts.'

NOTE.—See Clarke, p. 193.

25. All things known to us can be more or less accurately *described;* but not all need or can be *defined,* partly on account of their simplicity or obviousness, partly owing to the imperfection of our knowledge.

26. We may form a strict definition either by

(a) The method of *synthesis,* i. e., by starting with a notion more universal than the object to be defined, and gradually *descending* to it by the addition of different notes; or

(b) The method of *analysis,* i. e., by starting with the individual, and gradually *ascending* by the elimination of individual or accidental characters to a specific or generic concept.

CHAPTER II.

ARTICLE I.—JUDGMENT.

27. A Judgment is an intellectual act which affirms or denies the objective identity of two ideas upon comparing them with each other. The *material* object of a judgment are the two objective ideas, inasmuch as they are simultaneously present and compared with a view to discover their identity or non-identity. The *formal* object is the objective identity of those ideas, mentally affirmed or denied.

NOTE.—(a) A judgment is *elicited* by the intellect, not by the will; though the judgment may be determined by the *command* or influence of the will.

(b) A judgment considered in regard to its *material* object may be called a compound or composite act, for it represents two simple concepts in regard to their objective identity or diversity. Considered, however, *formally,* i. e., in regard to its formal object, it is necessarily a simple act, being the simple affirmation or denial of objective identity between two ideas.

(c) To perceive this relation of identity or diversity it is necessary to have compared the ideas with each other. Therefore, all judgments are *comparative,* and there is no such thing as merely instinctive judgment.

(d) The comparison of ideas required in a judgment regards not their intrinsic but their objective identity.

(e) The relation between subject and predicate in a judgment may be considered in three ways, viz.: In an affirmative proposition, for instance.

A. The predicate contains the subject *under* its *extension.*

B. The subject contains the predicate *in* its *comprehension.*

C. The subject and the predicate are *objectively identical,* that is, are verified of one and the same *material object.*

28. Judgments are:—

(a) *Analytical,* if the mere consideration of the ideas compared, suffices to make it clear that they are objectively identified or different, *e. g.,* 'The whole is greater than any of its parts.' Such judgments are also called *pure, rational, absolute, necessary, metaphysical.*

(b) *Synthetical,* if we gather the objective identity or diversity of the ideas compared, from internal or external experience. Such judgments are also called *empirical* or *experimental, physical, contingent.*

NOTE.—Hence a judgment is *analytical* when the predicate represents something which is either the essence, or of the essence, or necessarily required by the essence of the subject; otherwise it is synthetical. Sometimes, however, the predicate is the essence or of the essence, etc., of the subject, yet owing to the relative or absolute imperfection of our mental grasp, this is not perceived by us. In such cases the proposition is said to be analytical in *itself,* but *not so with regard to us.*

A judgment is *synthetical,* when the predicate is not apprehended as an essential note or property of the subject, i. e., as not *necessarily,* but only accidentally or *contingently* required by it. Hence as the relation of predicate to subject is either necessary or not-necessary, the so-called *"synthetic a priori* judgment of Kant can have no place among our mental operations.

(e) *True* or *False,* according as the mental affirmation or negation corresponds or conflicts with the objective reality. Other divisions of judgments will be noticed when we speak of Propositions.

NOTE.—See Clarke, p. 245, seqq., also p. 58, seqq.

ARTICLE II.—PROPOSITIONS.

29. A proposition is an *indicative* sentence, or *enuncia-tion* in which something is affirmed or denied of something else. The *subject* is that of which something is enunciated; the *predicate,* that which is enunciated of the subject; that which unites or separates them, i. e., affirms or denies their objective identity is called the *copula.* The subject and predicate are the *matter* of the proposition, the copula is the *form.* Every proposition therefore may be reduced to the formula 'S is P'; or , S is not P';—whether it be expressed in three, or more, or fewer verbal terms.

NOTE (1)—The copula is always the *present indicative* of the verb 'to be.' It does not signify the *existence* of the terms which it unites (which would be its *verbal* sense) ; *but merely* affirms their objective identity (which is called its *substantive sense*).

(2)—The *subject* is so called either because it is conceived as the possessor or *sustainer* of the note expressed by the predicate, or because it is conceived as coming *under* the extension of the latter. Hence the *natural* order of the terms is *subject-copula-predicate.* When the predicate is placed first, the proposition is said to be *inverted.*

ARTICLE III.—CLASSIFICATION OF PROPOSITIONS.

30. If we consider the *matter* of a proposition, i. e., subject and predicate, it will be either *simple* or *compound,* according as it contains *one* or *many* statements or enunciations.

If we consider the *form* or copula or *quality* of the proposition, it is either *negative* or *affirmative.*

If we consider the *quantity,* i. e., the extension of the subject, it is either *universal, particular, singular* or *indefinite.*

Lastly, if we consider the *relations* between propositions we shall find that they may be *opposed, equivalent,* etc. In the following article we shall consider only the division of propositions according to their *quality* and *quantity.*

ARTICLE IV.—DIVISION OF PROPOSITIONS ACCORDING TO THEIR QUALITY AND QUANTITY.

31. With regard to its **quality** or *form,* a proposition is either *affirmative* or *negative.* S is P; S is not P.

(a) In an affirmative proposition,

The predicate in the whole of its comprehension, distributively or collectively taken, is affirmed of the subject—in other words, it is affirmed that the subject has all and each of the notes that make up the predicate; thus when I say, "man is an animal," I mean that "man is a sentient, living, corporeal substance."

The Use of the predicate is, generally speaking, particular; in other words, no more is affirmed than that the subject is one or some of the things contained under the extension of the predicate, *e. g.,* 'man is an animal,' i. e., man is one of the objects to which the term animal applies. We said above, 'generally speaking,' for in cases where the predicate is a singular term, or a strict definition, or a property in the strict sense of the word, it is taken in the whole of its extension.

Hence, if we call the subject S and the predicate P, the formula of an affirmative proposition is 'S is P'; and it signifies that if we consider the extension of the ideas expressed by both terms, S is contained under the extension of P; while, if we consider the comprehension of the ideas, P is contained in the comprehension of S.

(b) In a negative proposition,

The predicate, in the whole of its comprehension taken collectively, is denied of the subject, though not necessarily in regard to *each* of its notes, *e. g.,* when I say 'a stone is not an animal,' I mean that a stone has not that sum of notes which constitutes the essence of animal. It lacks the notes of life and sensibility, though it has those of body and substance in common with an animal.

The Use of the predicate, except in cases where the predicate is a singular term, is distributively common or universal. In other words, it is denied that the subject is any of the things contained under the extension of the predicate, *e. g.,* 'man is not a stone,' i. e., man is not one of those objects to which the term stone is applied. Hence the formula of a negative proposition is 'S is not P,' i. e., S is not contained under the extension of P; all the notes of P, collectively taken, are not contained in the comprehension of S.

32. The **quantity** of a proposition depends upon the extension of the *subject*. Hence, according as the subject is singular, or particular, or universal, or indefinite, the proposition is (a) *singular, e. g.,* 'Washington was President of the United States'; (b) or *particular, e. g.,* 'Some Presidents were great scholars'; (c) or *universal, e. g.,* 'All Presidents are

heads of the executive'; or *indefinitely, e. g.,* 'Presidents are men of executive ability.'

As, in a *singular* proposition, the subject is taken in the whole of its extension, it may be treated in practice just as a universal.

NOTE.—With regard to universal propositions, we may observe here that there are three kinds of universality, viz.:

(a) *Metaphysical universality,* when the predicate necessarily agrees or disagrees with all and each of the inferiors of the subject, so that an exception is absolutely impossible, *e. g.,* 'Man is a rational animal'; 'A circle is not a square.'

(b) *Physical universality,* when, according to the ordinary laws of nature, the predicate agrees or disagrees with all and each of the inferiors of the subject, *e. g.,* 'A man who tries to walk on water will sink.'

(c) *Moral universality,* when, according to the ordinary laws and motives by which human action is governed, the predicate agrees with each and all of the inferiors of the subject, *e. g.,* 'All parents love their children.'

In an *indefinite* proposition the subject is taken, at least in a *morally* universal sense; for this is the ordinary sense in which men understand such propositions, *e. g.,* no one would admit as true the propositions, 'The Chinese are Christians.'

Thus, omitting the singular and the indefinite proposition as being, at least for all practical purposes of reasoning, reducible to the universal, we may consider all propositions in regard to their quantity as either universal or particular. Each of these classes, again, may be either affirmative or negative. Hence, considering *both* quantity and quality, we have four kinds of propositions.

Universal affirmative (designated by A), 'All men are mortal.'

Universal negative (designated by E), 'No man is a stone.'

Particular affirmative (designated by I), 'Some men are virtuous.'

Particular negative (designated by O), 'Some men are not industrious.'

These distinctions are expressed in the lines:

> *A* affirms of each and all,
> And *E* denies of any;
> I affirms, while *O* denies,
> Of one, or few, or many.

ARTICLE V.—DIVISION OF PROPOSITIONS ACCORDING TO MATTER.

33. (a) A proposition is *Categorical* if it affirms or denies absolutely the objective identity of two ideas, *e. g.*, '*a* is *b*.'

A proposition is *Hypothetical* if it affirms or denies the objective dependence or sequence of one judgment upon another, e. g., 'if *a* is *b*, *x* is *y*.' This may be reduced to the Categorical Form, thus, 'All cases of *a* being *b*, are cases of *x* being *y*.' The negative form *denies* the *connection* between the propositions, in some way equivalent to this: 'Not even if *a* is *b* is *x* therefore *y*'; 'Not all cases of *a* being *b* are cases of *x* being *y*.'

(b) A proposition is *Simple* if it consists of one subject and predicate, i. e., if it expresses a single judgment.

A proposition is *Compound* if it consists of many subjects or many predicates, i. e., if it expresses many distinct judgments. A compound proposition may be either *explicitly* or *implicitly* compound. For clearness' sake, then, we will speak in three distinct paragraphs of *simple, explicitly compound* and *implicitly compound* propositions.

(i) *Simple Propositions.*

34. They may take different forms, provided they only express a single judgment, *e. g.*, 'Man is mortal'; 'Well-organized and skilfully-administered governments are capable of

procuring the happiness of their subjects'; 'As a man lives, so will he die'; 'One admires a man who is not afraid to acknowledge he has been wrong.' In all these propositions it is clear there is but one affirmative or negation.

NOTE.—A phrase which modifies the subject or predicate is called "an Incident." Such incidents are notes of one of the terms of the main proposition here and now enunciated. They may be either *explicative* or *restrictive* (16 c. note).

(ii). *Explicitly Compound Propositions.*

35. These are, chiefly, either *copulative, adversative, or causal.*

(a) *Copulative,* when many subjects or predicates are connected by copulative conjunctions expressed or understood, *e. g.,* 'John and James and Paul were there'; 'Neither John nor James nor Paul was there.'

NOTE.—That such a proposition be true, *each* of the simple propositions into which it is resolvable must be true. If one of these be false, the compound proposition may be denied. It is better, however, in practice, to distinguish what is true and false in the proposition and to concede the true and deny the false.

(b) *Adversative,* when many subjects or predicates are connected by adversative conjunctions, such as *but, however,* etc., *e. g.,* 'Not St. Paul *but* St. Peter was the first Bishop of Rome'; 'Robinson is not a genius, *but* he has a good share of common sense.'

NOTE.—That it be true, each of the simple propositions it contains must be true, as in the preceding case.

(c) *Causal,* if it consists of many simple propositions connected by causal particles, such as *for, because, since, e. g.,* 'Blessed are the pure in heart, for (because) they shall see God.'

NOTE.—That it be true, all the simple propositions contained must be true, and, moreover, that which is assigned as the cause or reason why the others are true, must be really the cause or reason why they are so, *e. g.,* 'The three angles of a triangle are equal to the two right angles, because Paris is the capital of France!' Here, though each single proposition is true, yet the whole compound proposition is false.

(iii) *Implicitly Compound Propositions.*

36. *Exclusive, Exceptive, Restrictive, Disjunctive, Modal.*

(a) *Exclusive,* when the subject or predicate is modified by an exclusive particle, as *only, alone,* etc., *e. g.,* 'God alone is eternal'; 'The senses perceive only material objects.'

NOTE.—Here two things are asserted (a) that God is eternal, and (b) that nothing else is eternal; (a) that the senses perceive material objects, (b) and that they perceive nothing else.

(b) *Exceptive,* when it states the subject universally, yet with a specified exception, to which it is implied, that the predicate as affirmed or denied does not belong, *e. g.,* 'All but one have disappeared.'

(c) *Restrictive,* when the signification of subject or predicate is determined more narrowly by an incidental clause, *e. g.,* 'as a judge he ought not to receive these presents'; 'He was murdered maliciously.'

(d) *Disjunctive,* when disjunctive particles, *either, or,* connect many enunciations which are such that one and only one can be true, *e. g.,* 'All bodies are either in motion or at rest.' Such a proposition affirms or denies two things, (a) that bodies cannot at once be in motion and at rest, and (b) that they must be either.

Hence, that such a proposition be true, it is required, first, that the enumeration of alternatives be complete; second, that the various alternatives enumerated cannot be simultaneously true of the same thing, under the same circumstances; third, or be simultaneously false.

(e) In a *modal* proposition, the *copula* is modified by an adverb which declares in what *manner* the predicate is included in or excluded from the subject. These adverbs are four, viz.: *necessarily, contingently, impossibly, possibly.* All other words which may seem to indicate the manner in which the predicate is related to the subject are either reducible to one or other of the above, or are modifications of the predicate.

> Note.—*Possibly* indicates that A *can* be B.
> *Impossibly* "   " A *cannot* be B.
> *Necessarily* "   " A *must* be B.
> *Contingently* "   " A *may* or *may not* be B.

It is well to remember that each of these words may be taken in either a *metaphysical,* a *physical* or a *moral sense.*

When we say that the relation between S and P is impossible or necessary or contingent we assert two propositions, viz., (a) the existence of a relation between S and P. and (b) the *manner* of this relation; not so, however, when we say that the relation is possible; and, hence, in this latter case, our modal proposition is really a simple proposition.

ARTICLE VI.—OPPOSITION, EQUIVALENCE AND CONVERSION OF PROPOSITIONS.

37. Two propositions are said to be **opposed,** when, having the same object and predicate, they differ in quantity or in quality, or in both.

Opposition is two-fold.

(a) *Perfect,* when one denies what the other affirms; this again is, either (1) of *contradiction, i. e.,* when one affirms or denies just enough to destroy the negation or affirmation of the other, *e. g.,* 'All A is B;' 'Some A is not B'; 'All men are mortal'; 'Some men are not mortal'; 'No man is an animal'; 'Some men are animals.' These propositions, it will be noticed, differ from each other both in quantity and quality;—(2) or of *contrariety,* when one affirms or denies more than enough to destroy the negation or affirmation of the other, *e. g.,* 'All A is B'; 'No A is B'; 'All men are mortal'; 'No man is mortal.' Here the propositions are alike in quantity but differ in quality.

(b) *Imperfect,* when the opposition is only apparent; and this again is two-fold, (1) either of *sub contrariety,* which exists between propositions differing in quality but alike in quantity, *e. g.,* 'Some men are learned'; 'Some men are not learned'; (2) or of *subalternation,* when both propositions are alike in quality but differ in quantity, *e. g.,* 'All men are learned'; 'Some men are learned.'

38. Recalling what we have said above, the following scheme will represent the whole doctrine of opposition:

A	CONTRARIES	E
All *x* is *y*.		No *x* is *y*.

Subalternates	Contra dictories	Subalternates
	Contra dictories	

Some *x* is *y*.		Some *x* is not *y*.
I	SUB-CONTRARIES	O

39. **Laws of Opposition:—**

(a) *Contradictories* can neither be both true nor both false. Therefore, if A is true, O is false; if E is true, I is false, and *vice versa.*

(b) *Contraries* cannot both be true, but both may be false; therefore, if A is true, E is false, and *vice versa;* but if E be false it does not follow that A is true.

NOTE.—Observe that two propositions properly contradict each other only when what is affirmed by the one is denied by the other, (a) in the same degree, (b) in the same respect, (c) at the same time.

(c) *Subalternates may* both be true or both false; but if the universal (A or E) is true the particular of the same *quality* (I or O) is also true; if the particular (I or O) is false, the corresponding universal (A or E) is also false; if the particular is true the corresponding universal may be true or false; if the universal is false the particular may be false or true.

(d) *Sub-contraries* cannot both be false; both may be true, i. e., in *contingent* matters, but not in *necessary.*

40. Two propositions are said to be **equivalent** when they express the same judgment but in a different logical form.

41. A proposition is **converted** when its terms are transposed, so that subject becomes predicate; and predicate subject, without changing the sense of the proposition. The proposition, as it stands before conversion, is called the *convertend;* after conversion, the *converse.*

There are three sorts of conversion, viz.: simple conversion, limited or accidental conversion, conversion by contraposition.

(a) Simple conversion is had when the subject becomes the predicate and the predicate the subject, without changing either the quantity or the quality of the proposition. This is possible in the propositions E and I, *e. g.,* 'No man is a stone'; 'No stone is a man'; 'Some men are white'; 'Some white things are men.'

(b) Conversion by limitation has place when subject and

predicate are transposed, and the quality of the proposition remains the same; but the quantity is changed from universal to particular. In this way A may be converted, *e. g.,* 'All men are animals'; 'Some animals are men.'

(c) Conversion by contra-position. This has place in O, i. e., Transfer the negative particle from the copula to the predicate, and then convert simply, *e. g.,* 'Some men are not industrious; Some not-industrious creatures are men.'

42. Inference in general is the derivation of a judgment from another or others. If the new judgment is derived from a comparison of two previous judgments, the process by which it is derived is called Reasoning, in the proper sense of the word. If the new judgment is derived from one previous judgment, the process is called *Immediate Inference.*

Reasoning will be the subject of the following chapter. Immediate Inference is based on the properties of propositions, which we have just been considering, viz., opposition, equivalence and conversion.

CHAPTER III.

ARTICLE I.—REASONING IN GENERAL.

43. It may happen that on comparing two ideas together we are unable to judge whether they are objectively identical or not. In such cases the obvious way to free ourselves from suspense is to compare both ideas with a third. If both are identical with the third we can conclude that they are so far both identical with each other; while, if one be identical with the third and the other different from it, we conclude that they are different from each other. The mental act with affirms or denies the objective identity of two ideas on account of their relation to a third is called **Reasoning.**

44. Hence, **reasoning comprises three judgments,** one of which affirms or denies the objective identity of two ideas as the *necessary consequence* of two other judgments, in which a common third idea is affirmed to be objectively identical with both or with one only of these ideas. The main judgment is called the *conclusion;* the two subsidiary judgments on which it depends are called the *premises.* The necessary connection between the premises and the conclusion, i. e., that which entitles us to infer the one from the other, is the *consequence.*

The common third term with which each of the terms united or separated in the conclusion was compared in the preceding judgments is called the *middle* term. The predicate of the conclusion is called the *major term,* as having the greater extension; the subject the *minor* term. Of the two preceding judgments, that in which the major term occurs is called the *major* premise or sumption; that in which the minor term occurs the *minor* premise or subsumption.

ARTICLE II.—THE FUNDAMENTAL PRINCIPLES OF REASONING.

45. **All reasoning may be reduced** either to the principle of *identity, i. e.,* Two things which are both identical with a third are identical with each other; or to the principle of *discrepancy, i. e.,* Two things, one of which is identical with and the other different from a third, are different from each other; or, to the more readily applicable Aristotelian *"Dictum de Omni et de Nullo,"* which may be enunciated thus: Whatever may be affirmed of a potential or logical whole may be affirmed of each and all of its subjective parts. Whatever may be denied of a potential whole may be denied of each and all of its potential parts. And conversely: Whatever may be affirmed or denied of all and each of the subjective parts may be affirmed or denied of the whole. Thus: 'All morally responsible agents are free agents. But man is a morally responsible agent. Therefore, man is a free agent.' Or, in general: 'All M is P. But all S is M. Therefore, all S is P.'

Reasoning is *pure, mixed* or *empirical,* according as the two judgments from which the conclusion proceeds are either both analytical, or one analytical and the other synthetical, or both synthetical.

Reasoning is *deductive* or *inductive,* according as it concludes from the potential whole to the subjective parts, or from the subjective parts to the whole.

Article III.—Verbal Expression of Reasoning.

46. The verbal expression of reasoning is called **argumentation.** The simplest and most perfect form of argumentation, to which all others, if legitimate, may be directly or indirectly reduced, is the syllogism.

47. **A syllogism** is an argumentation consisting of three explicit propositions so connected with each other that one of them necessarily follows from the other two.

48. **The correctness of the conclusion** depends on the *consequence,* i. e., the conclusion is correct, if it necessarily follows from the premises. **The truth of the conclusion** regards the proposition as it stands, i. e., according as it affirms or denies of a subject a predicate which really is objectively identical or not identical with it. Hence a conclusion might be correct and yet not true, and *vice versa.*

When the conclusion is both correct and true the syllogism is said to be both *materially* and *formally* true.

49. If the reasoning is *correct,* i. e., if the conclusion is the necessary consequence of the premises, then

(a) From a *true* antecedent you can never have a *false* conclusion. For, if the middle term is really identical with the two extremes, these are necessarily identical with each other; or if the minor term is contained under the extension of the middle and this under the extension of the major, the minor, too, is necessarily contained under the extension of the major.

(b) If the conclusion be false, one at least of the premises is false.

(c) If the antecedent be false, the conclusion may be either true or false. It may not be true to say all M is P, or that all S is M, and yet S may be P for other reasons.

Hence, even if the conclusion be true, it does not follow that the antecedent is true.

Dialectics is not so much concerned with the *truth* of thought as with its *correctness*. It is, therefore, with this that we are chiefly concerned in the present chapter.

Article IV.—Laws of the Syllogism.

50. **The laws which regulate the correctness of the conclusion** are all deduced from the fundamental pirnciples of reasoning. These laws are eight. Four of them regard the *terms* of the syllogism; four, the *propositions*.

(i) A syllogism must contain three terms, neither more nor less; and the Use of each term must be the same throughout the argument. This is clear from the nature of the syllogism.

(ii) No term should have a greater extension in the conclusion than it had in the premises; else we should have in reality more than three terms. A violation of this rule is called *Illicit Process* (of *major* or *minor* as the case may be).

(iii) The *middle* term must not appear in the conclusion. This is clear from the function of the middle term.

(iv) The *middle* term must be *distributed,* i. e., taken universally in at least one of the premises; else we may compare the minor term with one portion of the extension of the middle, the major term with one portion of the extension of the middle, the minor term with another portion, and, thus, we should have four terms. This mistake is called an *Undistributed Middle.*

(v) To have a *negative* conclusion, one of the premises must be a negative.

(vi) From *two* negative premises no conclusion follows.

(vii) Two particular premises can give no conclusion. For if they are I I, we have no place for a distributed middle. If they are I O, then the conclusion is negative and consequently the *major* term *universal*. But as the middle term must be distributed at least once, we shall therefore need to have two universal terms in the antecedent. But obviously there is place only for one. Hence to draw any conclusion from I O would involve either an *illicit process* or an *undistributed middle.*

(viii) The conclusion follows the *weaker* premise. If either premise be *negative,* the *conclusion* clearly must be negative. If either premise is *particular,* the *conclusion* must be particular. For, suppose the premises are A I and a universal conclusion is drawn, we should need place for two universal terms in the antecedent (the middle and minor terms), while there is in fact place only for one. Suppose the premises are E I and A O. In each case we have *two* universal terms in the antecedent; but to justify a universal (negative) conclusion all three should be universal in the premises (*major, minor* and *middle*).

These laws are summed up in the following verses to aid the memory:

Limit both in *word* and *meaning* all the terms you use to *three.*
In *Conclusion* terms must never *broader* than in *Premise* be.
From intrusion of the *Middle* always your *Conclusion* save.
Once at least distribute Middle, else no argument you have.
Two Particulars can never any safe *Conclusion* prove,
Nor from two *Negations* can a logical *Conclusion* move,
Should you twice make *Affirmation,* no *Negation* thence can start.
See that your *Conclusion* ever follows the *inferior* part.

Article V.—Figures of the Syllogism.

51. As we have seen, there are in every syllogism three terms and three propositions. Hence syllogisms may differ (a) according to the *positions* which the *terms* occupy in the Antecedent; and (b) according to the quantity and quality of the *propositions* of which they are composed. The *position* of the terms gives us the **Figures of the syllogism**; the quantity and quality of the propositions, give us **the Moods**.

52. The position of the middle term with reference to the two extremes in the premises constitutes what is called the figure of the syllogism. Now the middle can have only four variations of position, and hence there are *four figures*.

(a) It may be the subject of the major premise and the predicate of the minor; (b) or it may be the predicate of both premises; (c) or it may be the subject of both premises; (d) or it may be the predicate of the major and the subject of the minor premise, thus:

I	II	III	IV
M-P	P-M	M-P	P-M
S-M	S-M	M-S	M-S
S-P	S-P	S-P	S-P

The four figures are expressed in the hexameter: (M is.)

"Sub-pred; then pred-pred; then sub-sub; finally pred-sub.

53. The rules for the validity of these figures, easily deducible from the general laws of the syllogism, are as follows:

I Fig. *Minor* should always affirm, and the *major* should be universal.

II Fig. One premise always denies, and the *major* must be universal.

III Fig. *Minor* should never deny, nor the *consequent* be universal.

IV Fig. Whenever the *major* affirms, the minor must be universal;

Whenever the *minor* affirms, the conclusion is not universal;

Whenever the minor *denies,* the major must be universal.

Article VI.—Moods of the Syllogism.

53. **The mood of the syllogism** is the arrangement of its propositions with reference to their quantity and quality. Now, as on the one hand there are three propositions in a syllogism while on the other there are four kinds of propositions —A, E, I, O, to ascertain the number of conceivable syllogistic moods we have simply to arrange the letters A, E, O, I in all possible combinations of three at a time. Thus, taking A as major premise, we have sixteen moods. But we may also take E, or O, or I, for major premise. Hence, the total number of moods possible is 64. Applying to these, however, the general laws of the syllogism, we find that of the 64 moods only 11 are valid, viz.: Four affirmatives, AAA, AAI, AII, IAI; and seven negatives, EAE, AEE, EAO, AOO, OAO, EIO, IEO.

55. If now we take these moods in each of the four figures, we have 44 moods in all. But again applying the laws of the different figures we find that many moods which are valid in one figure are not so in others.

Examining, thus, each of the 44 moods, we find that only 24 are valid, viz.:

1st F	2d F	3d F	4th F
AAA	EAE	AAI	AAI
EAE	AEE	IAI	AEE
AII	EIO	AII	IAI
EIO	AOO	EAO	EAO
(AAI)	(EAO)	OAO	EIO
(EAO)	(AEO)	EIO	(AEO)

56. Of the above 24 valid moods those in brackets are said to minimize their conclusion, making it particular when it might be universal. Omitting, therefore, those minimizing moods, we have 19 moods left which are valid and useful.

These are expressed in the mnemonic hexameters of Peter Julian (afterward Pope John XXI):
"Barbara, Celarent, Darii Ferio are the *First Fig.*
Cesare, Camestres, Festino, Baroko, the *Second.*
Third Figure: Darapti, Disamis, Datisi, Felapton,
Bokardo, Ferison. To these, *Fourth Figure* finally addeth
Bramantip, Camenes, Dimaris, Fesapo, Fresison."

NOTE.—Of these verses De Morgan says: "They are magic words, more full of meaning than any that were ever made." The *vowels* express the order, quantity and quality of the propositions of the valid moods of the four figures. The *consonants* indicate to what mood of the *first* figure each mood of the other figures may be reduced, and the process by which this reduction is to be made.

ARTICLE VII.—REDUCTION OF THE LESS PERFECT FIGURES TO THE FIRST.

57. Each of the 19 syllogistic forms enumerated above is a valid form of reasoning. Yet those of the first figure are the most perfect, as being immediately reducible to the principle. *"De Omni et de Nullo."* Hence, logicians give rules

for reducing the syllogisms of the three less perfect figures to those of the first. These rules are all indicated by certain consonants of the verses above.

(a) The initial consonants—B, C, D. F—indicate the moods of the first figure, to which the moods of the other figures are to be reduced, *e. g.*, 'Cesare and Camestres of the second figure are reducible to Celarent'; 'Darapti, etc., to Darii'; 'Fresison to Ferio.'

(b) *m* indicates that the premises are to be transposed.

(c) *s* indicates that the proposition denoted by the preceding vowel is to be converted *simply*.

(d) *p* indicates that the proposition preceding is to be converted by *limitation*.

(e) *k* denotes that the mood must be reduced by a distinct process called *indirect reduction,* of which we shall speak presently.

We will now take an instance of the application of these rules: 'All stars are self-luminous bodies. No planets are self-luminous bodies. Therefore, no planets are stars.' This is a syllogism in Camestres; it is reducible to Celarent. The first *s* indicates that the minor is to be simply converted; the *m* that this new minor is to change places with the former major; the last *s* that the conclusion is to be simply converted, thus, 'No self-luminous bodies are planets. All stars are self-luminous bodies. Therefore, no stars are planets.'

58. **Indirect reduction** is like the indirect proof often employed in geometry. It consists in supposing the conclusion false, and therefore its contradictory true; and thence forcing the one who denies the conclusion to deny one of the premises, which he had granted, *e. g.*, 'All virtue is rational. Some zeal is not rational. Therefore, some zeal is not virtue.' This is in Baroko. The contradictory of the conclusion is, 'All zeal is virtue.' Now, letting the previous major stand, put this new

proposition in place of the minor, and we have, 'All virtue is rational. All zeal is virtue. Therefore, all zeal is rational.' Here the conclusion is the contradictory of the minor before conceded.

In like manner with Bokardo: Take the contradictory of the conclusion, put it in place of the *major premise,* keep the minor and deduce the contradictory of the previous major.

ARTICLE VIII.—CLASSIFICATION OF SYLLOGISMS ACCORDING TO THE PROPOSITIONS OF WHICH THEY ARE COMPOSED.

59. A syllogism is **hypothetical** when the major premise is a hypothetical proposition, and the minor either (a) the affirmation of the condition, in which case the conclusion will be the affirmation of the conditioned, and the syllogism is called *constructive;* or (b) the denial of the conditioned, in which case the conclusion will be the negation of the condition, and the syllogism is said to be *destructive, e. g.,*

Constructive, 'If man is an animal, he is sensitive. But he is an animal. Therefore, he is sensitive.'

Destructive, 'If man is an animal he is sensitive. But he is not sensitive. Therefore, he is not an animal.'

NOTE.—You cannot conclude from the denial of the condition to the denial of the conditioned, nor from the affirmation of the conditioned to the affirmation of the condition; *unless* the condition is the *only* one on which the conditioned proposition can be true, *e. g.,* 'If a man dies in mortal sin he goes to hell. But X did not die in mortal sin. Therefore, he did not go to hell'; or 'X went to hell. Therefore, he died in mortal sin.'

60. A syllogism is disjunctive when the major premise is a disjunctive proposition, and the minor, either (a) denies all the alternatives but one, in which case the conclusion affirms

that one; or (b) affirms one of the alternatives, in which case the conclusion denies all the others.

NOTE.—The major must be *really* disjunctive, *i. e.*, such that *one*, and only one, of the alternatives is true, *e. g.*, 'The time of the year is either spring, summer, autumn or winter. But it is neither spring, summer nor winter. Therefore, it is autumn.'

'The time of the year, etc. But it is autumn. Therefore, it is neither spring, nor summer, nor winter.'

61. **Reduction of hypothetical and disjunctive syllogisms to categorical.**

(a) It is plain that the disjunctive may be reduced to the hypothetical, *e. g.*, 'If the angle A is neither greater nor less than B, it is equal to B. But it is neither greater nor less than B. Therefore, it is equal to B.'

(b) The hypothetical may be reduced to the categorical, thus, 'All angles which are neither greater nor less than B are equal to B. But the angle A is neither greater nor less than B. Therefore, it is equal to B.' Or, in general, 'All the cases of *x* being *y* are cases of *z* being *m*. But the present case is the case of *x* being *y*. Therefore, the present case is the case of *z* being *m*.'

NOTE.—If it be affirmed that the present case is a case of *z* being *m*, it will not follow that in a case of *x* being *y;* nor, again, if it be denied that the present is a case of *x* being *y*, can it be concluded that it is not a case of *z* being *m*.

ARTICLE IX.—OTHER FORMS OF ARGUMENTATION REDUCIBLE TO THE SYLLOGISM.

62. The **Enthymeme** is a syllogism in which one of the propositions is suppressed.

(a) It is said to be of the *first* order, and this is the commonest form, when the major premise is suppressed, *e. g.*, 'Air has weight, because it is a corporeal substance.' Here the missing premise is 'All corporeal substances have weight.' and the complete syllogism runs thus, 'All corporeal substances have weight. Atmospheric air is a corporeal substance. Therefore, it has weight.'

(b) It is said to be of the *second* order if the minor premise is suppressed, *e. g.*, 'Robinson is mortal, for all men are mortal.'

NOTE (1.)—If the *subject* of the conclusion is found in the expressed premise, the *major* premise is suppressed; if the *predicate* of the conclusion is found in the expressed premise, then the *minor premise is suppressed*.

(2.)—If *neither* term of the conclusion is found in the antecedent, the whole syllogism is *hypothetical*, *e. g.*, 'The men are at dinner, therefore it is mid-day.'

63. The Epicheireme is a syllogism in which one or both propositions are *causal,* and, consequently, each implies a suppressed syllogism, *e. g.*, 'Every simple being is of itself incorruptible; because it does not consist of parts into which it is resolvable. But the human soul is simple. Therefore, it is of itself incorruptible.'

Here the major is equivalent to
'That which does not consist of parts into which it is resolvable is of itself incorruptible. A simple being does not consist of parts into which, etc. Therefore, a simple being is of itself incorruptible.'

NOTE.—To test the validity of such arguments it is enough to express them in full syllogistic form.

64. The Sorites is a syllogism, consisting of many propositions so arranged that the predicate of the preceding proposition of the series is the subject of the following, until the conclusion, in which the *subject* of the *first premise* is com-

bined with the *predicate* of the *last.* 'The human soul is a thinking substance. A thinking substance is a simple spiritual substance. A simple spiritual substance is independent of matter. That which is independent of matter is indestructible except by annihilation. That which is indestructible, except by annihilation, is immortal. Therefore, the human soul is immortal.' Or, generally, A is B, B is C, C is D, D is E. Therefore, A is E.

NOTE (1).—The Sorites really contains a series of syllogisms incompletely expressed, the predicate of each proposition being a middle term. The safest way to be sure of its validity is to resolve it into its component syllogisms.

(2.)—No premise can be *negative,* except the *last,* i. e., the one immediately preceding the conclusion.

No premise can be *particular* except the first.

65. The **Dilemma** is a syllogism in which each of the alternatives of a disjunctive proposition is shown to prove or refute the same conclusion, *e. g.,* (St. Augustine's Argument) 'The Catholic Church was either propagated by miracles or it was not. If it was, then it is divine; if it was not, then its propagation without miracles, in the face of so much opposition, was the greatest of all miracles; and, therefore, it is divine.'

NOTE (1.)—The enumeration of alternatives should be complete. See, too, that your dilemma cannot be retorted by showing that whichever alternative is chosen the conclusion opposite to yours can be deduced, *e. g.,* 'You will administer your office either well or ill. If well, you will displease your enemies. If ill, you will displease your friends. Therefore, you should not accept the office.' This may be retorted thus, 'I shall administer my office either well or ill. If well, I shall please my friends. If ill, I shall please my enemies. Therefore, in either case, I may accept the office.'

(2.)—Many apparent dilemmas are fallacious. To detect the fallacy, reduce the dilemma to syllogistic form, thus:

If A is *x*, M is *n;*
If A is *y*, M is *n;*
If A is *z*, M is *n*.
But A is either *x, y* or *z*.

Therefore, in any case, M is *n*.

66. **Induction** is an argument in which a universal is inferred from an enumeration of inferiors. It is

(a) *Complete,* if it infers the universal from a *complete* enumeration of the inferiors contained under it. Such an induction is thus reduced to syllogistic form:

In all right-angled, obtuse-angled, acute-angled plane triangles the three angles are equal to two right angles. But all plane triangles are either right-angled, obtuse-angled, or acute-angled. Therefore, in all plane triangles, the three angles are equal to two right angles. This is rather an immediate inference than a syllogism.

(b) *Incomplete,* if from an *incomplete* enumeration of the inferiors, it infers the universal. That the consequence be legitimate the argument must be capable of reduction to some such formula as this:

(1). An effort which is constant and uniform amid all manner of different circumstances has a constant and uniform cause. But the effect A, which we observe in the individual *x,* is constant and uniform in all manner of different circumstances. Therefore, this effect comes from a constant and uniform cause.

(2). What is constant and uniform in different individuals differently circumstanced pertains to the nature of those individuals. But to cause the effect A is something which is constant and uniform in the individuals *x.* Therefore, to cause the effect A, pertains to the *nature* of the individuals *x*.

(3). What pertains to the *nature* of an individual is common to *all* who have that nature. But to cause the effect A, pertains to the nature of the individuals *x*. Therefore, to cause the effect A, is common to *all* the individuals of the nature or species *x*.

NOTE (1).—Hence the incomplete enumeration of inferiors, which logically justifies the inference of a universal, does so only in virtue of analytical principles, *e. g.,* 'the principle of sufficient reason' or 'causalty,' etc., which render it really equivalent to a complete enumeration. Hence, induction is of value as an argument, only inasmuch as it is reducible to a syllogism of the third figure where M is the enumerated parts, S the logical whole of which they are inferiors, and P the predicate common and constant in each and all of them, in all circumstances.

(2). To be able to say that a certain phenomenon is in some way *necessarily* connected with the *nature* of a given antecedent, often requires much careful observation and experiment. As a general rule we may say that there is such a connection when, wherever the antecedent is, the phenomenon is; wherever the antecedent increases, the phenomenon increases; wherever the antecedent decreases or ceases, the phenomenon decreases or ceases. This simple rule seems to sum up all that concerns us here about the various methods of induction, viz., the method of *agreement,* the method of *difference,* the method of *residues, concomitant variations,* etc. (See Clarke, Logic, p. 389 seqq.)

(3). The *necessary* connection between antecedent and consequent may be moral, physical or metaphysical (32 N. B.)

67. **Analogy** is a form of argument which denies or affirms something of an individual or class because it is denied or affirmed of other *similar* individuals or classes. It is reducible to a syllogism thus, *e. g.,* Similar things have similar properties; causes, effects, ends, are ruled by similar laws,

etc.: But A and B are similar things; therefore they have similar properties, etc. But A has the property, etc., *x*. Therefore, B has the property, etc., *x*.

NOTE (1).—If A and B are shown to have perfectly similar *natures*, and *x* is shown to be a constant and uniform concomitant of that *nature* in A, of course it will be so in B. Otherwise the argument can only serve to render the conclusion more or less probable.

(2). From what has been said of the last two forms of argumentation, it is clear that great caution is needed in accepting conclusions based upon them. It is very easy to mistake an *accidental* for a *necessary* connection, between antecedent and consequent; an *occasion* or *condition* for a *cause*, etc.

ARTICLE X—CLASSIFICATION OF ARGUMENTS ACCORDING TO THEIR VALIDITY.

68. Supposing the laws of reasoning so far considered to be strictly observed, our argumentation will be *demonstrative* if both premises are *certainly true; probable,* if either premise or both are *probably true; fallacious* or *sophistical,* if either premise or both are *only apparently true;* and our conclusion will be, respectively, a *certainty,* an *opinion,* an *error.*

(i). *Demonstrative Reasoning.*

69. It is the deduction or induction of a *legitimate* conclusion from *evident* premises. It is

(a) *Direct,* when it is shown that S is, or is not, P, on account of their relation with M.

Indirect, when the truth of a conclusion is shown by proving the *falsity* of its *contradictory.*

NOTE.—A *negative* argument shows that no valid reason can be assigned for a given proposition. *Of itself,* it does not

prove the proposition false, but it puts the 'Burden of Proof'
on the one who asserts it. But when the reasons which would
justify the given proposition are such that they would be apparent if they existed, then their absence *disproves* the proposition, *e. g.*, the proposition 'plants feel' is disproved by showing that they exhibit no signs of sensation.

(b) *A priori*, when the premises contain truths *prior* in
the *nature of things* to the truth contained in the conclusion,
e. g., 'when we conclude from the existence and nature of a
cause to the existence and nature of its effects, or from a
universal law or principle to a particular application of it.'

A posteriori, when, on the contrary, the truth of the antecedent is in the nature of things, or *ontologically*, posterior to
and dependent on the truth of the conclusion, *e. g.*, when we
conclude from the existence and character of an effect to the
existence and character of its cause, or from particular instances to a general law.

70. The end of demonstration is **Science** in its strict
and only accurate sense. Hence we may define scientific
knowledge as true and certain knowledge acquired by demonstration; and a *complete* science as a complete *system* of *certain* truths in regard to a given subject, *derived by demonstration* from *certain* principles.

NOTE.—Sciences are distinguished according to their *formal objects*, i. e., the particular aspect in which the subject-
matter is viewed. Thus, one subject, *e. g.*, 'man,' may be the
material object of many distinct sciences, *e. g.*, 'of physiology,
anatomy, ethics, etc.' Again, the science, *e. g.*, of human morals, is twofold, according as we regard man, inasmuch as his
duties, rights and destiny are manifested to us either by mere
unaided human reason, or by divine revelation and faith, i. e.,
human sciences are distinguished, not only according to their

formal objects, but also according to the light in which the formal objects are presented.

(iii.)   *Probable Reasoning.*

71.   **It is the deduction or induction of a legitimate conclusion from one or more probable premises.** The probability of the conclusion will be of course proportionate to that of the whole antecedent from which it is inferred.

NOTE.—An *hypothesis,* in science, is a proposition whose truth has not been demonstrated, but which, for the time being, is assumed as true, because it seems to assign a satisfactory cause of known phenomena.   It is a probable proposition giving not what actually *is,* but what *may be* the unknown cause or antecedent of a given known consequent.   It may be reduced to this formula: 'If *x* existed *y* would exist; but *y* exists; therefore *x* exists.'

As to the laws which govern the formation of an hypothesis; neither the proposition itself, nor any legitimate inference from it, should contradict any known truth.   The antecedent assigned should account satisfactorily for all the facts it proposes to account for.

If, finally, it is the *only* antecedent that can account for the given consequent (59 N. B.), it ceases to be an hypothesis, and is demonstrated to be actually true.

(iii)   *Sophistical Reasoning.*

72.   An open violation of any of the laws of *correct* reasoning is called a **paralogism.**   When a false premise is introduced, or a false *sense* given to a premise, we have a *sophism;* the latter we may call a *verbal* sophism, the former a *real* sophism.   Of paralogisms nothing further need be said.

(a)   Verbal Sophisms.

Equivocation.   An equivocal (16 c.), or vague (16 a.) *term* is taken in different senses.

Amphibology. An ambiguous *proposition* is taken in different senses.

Composition or Division. A predicate is attributed to a *qualified* subject, which really belongs to it only when without the qualification, or *vice versa*. Or again, a predicate true of each individual subject *separately,* is attributed to all taken *collectively;* or *vice versa*.

(b) Real Sophisms.

Accident. A predicate which is only *accidental* and occasional in a given subject, is represented as constant and *essential* to it; and vice versa. Or again, what is true of a few instances only, is represented as true of a whole class; and *vice versa*.

Missing or Evading the Question. *Ignoratio elenchi.* Attention is turned away from the real question to something like it, or in some way connected with it. Under this head will also come the *Argumentum ad Hominem, ad Invidiam,* etc.

Begging the Question. The conclusion to be proved is in some way or other covertly assumed as true in the premises.

False Cause. A mere antecedent or concomitant is represented as cause: *Post Hoc, Cum Hoc; ergo, Propter Hoc.*

NOTE.—Of all these forms of sophistical reasoning we have numerous instances in current literature and oratory, as well as of many others which a logician will easily recognize, *e. g.,* 'hasty induction,' 'false analogy,' 'unverified and impossible hypotheses,' 'citation of untrustworthy authorities,' etc., etc.

ARTICLE XI—METHOD.

73. By method, we mean orderly procedure in the acquisition, exposition or defense of truth in regard to a given subject matter. The subject-matter is supposed to be presented

in the form of a question, *e. g.*, 'Is the human soul immortal?' Hence the general laws of method are:

(a)   *Let the question be clearly determined (status quaestionis)*—This implies

That there is no ambiguity in the terms; therefore, *definition* of terms.

That the subject be properly *divided* into the parts which it contains.

That the truths *assumed*, in starting to resolve the question, be clearly recognized.

It also helps greatly to a clear understanding of the question, to recall the doctrines of others on the subject, and their principal reasons for holding them.

(b)   In the process of argumentation, advance from that which is better known to that which is less; from that which is easily grasped and admitted, to that which is more difficult.

(c)   Advance *gradually*, i. e., so that each new step connects with and is justified by what has gone before.

74. (26). **Methods of analysis and synthesis.** Having determined the status questions as above, we need to find a middle term which shall show us the relation between the subject and the predicate of our questions. This we can do in two ways:

(a)   If the predicate belongs to the subject, it must be found among the notes of the *comprehension* of the subject, or at least be *required* by one of these notes. We therefore *analyze* the subject. If the predicate is one of the notes, or required by any of the notes which this analysis gives us, it must be *affirmed* of the subject. If, on the contrary, the predicate is incompatible with any of these notes, it must be *denied* of the subject. This is the *analytic method;* and when there is question of discovering for ourselves what predicates are to be affirmed or denied of a given subject, it is obviously the safest and simplest way to proceed.

(b)   If the predicate belongs to the subject, it must contain the subject under its *extension*.   We, therefore, by *synthesis*, divide the predicate as a *logical whole* into its subjective parts.   If the subject is found among them, the predicate is affirmed of it; if not, the predicate is denied.   When there is question of *explaining* or *proving* a doctrine, it is generally the shortest and clearest way to proceed.

NOTE.—Hence, the synthetic method proceeds from that which is simpler in comprehension and more universal to that which is more complex and particular.   The analytical method, on the contrary, starts with the complex and particular, and proceeds to the simple and universal.   Which method should be adopted, or rather which should predominate in our treatment of a subject, will depend on the nature of the subject-matter, and the occasion and purpose of our dealing with it. Some sciences are primarily synthetic, *e. g.,* 'geometry,' 'ethics,' etc., which proceed from most simple and universal principles to gradually more and more complex applications of them. Others, on the contrary, as chemistry and physics, are primarily analytical.   They begin, so to say, with concrete complex facts, and work their way laboriously back to general laws and principles.   In general, we may say that a *mixed* method is the one most suited to the human mind.   Theory regardless of fact, is dangerous.   Mere knowledge of facts without an effort to understand the general laws and principles which govern them, is unnatural and unworthy of man.

75.   *Method of Discussion.*—The **Circle.**

One undertakes to defend, another to attack a given proposition or *thesis*.   Both are supposed to understand and agree upon the *status quaestionis*.   All arguments and objections are proposed clearly and briefly in strict syllogistic form.

(a) The *Defender*—

(i) Proposes the thesis, explains the *status quaestionis* (70 a), proves each part of his proposition by one or two short, solid arguments, and then awaits the attack of his opponent.

(ii) When the first argument against his thesis is proposed, he first repeats it faithfully word for word, then repeating each proposition, he says whether, and how far, he admits it, or denies it, *e. g.,* '*y* is *z*, I grant the major. But *x* is *y*, I deny the minor. Therefore, *x* is *z*, I deny the conclusion.' Or '*y* is *z*, I distinguish the major; in the sense *m*, I grant the major; in the sense *n*, I deny the major. But *x* is *y*, I contra-distinguish the minor; in the sense *n*, I grant the minor; in the sense *m*, I deny the minor. Therefore, *x* is *z*, I deny the conclusion.'

NOTE.—If the syllogism fails in logical form, he lets major and minor pass, and denies the conclusion and the consequence, i. e., that it follows from the premises, *e. g.,* '*y* is *z*, let the major pass. But *x* is *y*, let the minor pass. Therefore, *x* is *z*, I deny the consequences and the conclusion.'

NOTE (2).—As either S, P or M may be ambiguous, each proposition in which the ambiguous term occurs must be distinguished. Thus, if M is ambiguous, both major and minor premises must be distinguished, and M denied of S in the sense in which it was admitted to belong to P. If S or P is ambiguous, the premises in which it occurs must be distinguished, and also the *conclusion;* for S and P will agree with each in the conclusion, only so far as they agree with M in the premises.

NOTE (3).—If one of the premises of the objection rests on a false supposition, the defender says, *e. g.,* '*x* is *y*, I deny the supposition.' If the enumeration of alternatives is incomplete, a *disjunctive* proposition is denied. If an analogy is false, he denies the parity.

(b) The *Objector* may attack either the thesis directly or the argument by which it was proved.

(i) If he attacks the *thesis,* he simply asserts the contradictory of the thesis, *e. g.,* 'Against the proposition which asserts that S is P, I say, S is not P, and I prove it thus;' etc. If he attacks the *argument,* he asserts, and attempts to prove the contradictory of either major or minor premise.

(ii) As the defender has proved the main proposition, of course the 'Burden of Proof' lies with him who would assert its contradictory. Hence the objector is obliged to prove his contradictory; and if the defender denies any premise of his argument, he is obliged to prove that premise. If one of his premises is distinguished, he may show that the difficulty remains even with what is granted, or he may prove what is denied in the distinction.

(iii) If the defender denies something *supposed* in one of his premises, the objector may ask him to say distinctly what that supposition is. If the completeness of his enumeration of disjunctive alternatives denied, he may ask the defender to assign the alternatives omitted.

(iv) When an objection has been fully solved by the defender, he should not urge it further, but take up a new objection. Hence, he should have studied his subject carefully and be familiar with the objections urged against the thesis, know how to urge them strongly, and recognize a satisfactory solution when it is given.

BOOK TWO.

CRITICS.

76. So far we have considered merely the *correctness* of thought, i. e., its conformity with the laws of *consistent* thinking. We now go on to consider the *Truth of thought*, i. e., its conformity with the *objects* which it represents. This book will comprise three chapters, viz.:

I. Conceptual Truth and the Possibility of attaining it.

II. The Trustworthiness of the Faculties we possess for attaining Conceptual Truth.

III. The Criteria or Motives of Certitude.

CHAPTER I.

CONCEPTUAL TRUTH AND THE POSSIBILITY OF ATTAINING IT.

77. Words, as we have said, are arbitrary signs. Hence, to understand what is meant by the word *truth,* let us consider in what sense or senses this word is ordinarily used by men. Now, men commonly speak (1) of true and false *things, e. g.,* 'diamonds'; (2) of true and false *knowledge, e. g.,* 'as to historical facts'; (3) of true and false *statements, e. g.,* of witnesses. That is, they speak of the *truth of things,* of the *truth of thoughts,* of the *truth of speech.* Further, by a *true* diamond, they mean one which corresponds with the idea of diamond; by *true* knowledge of a fact they mean knowledge in conformity with the fact as it really took place; by *true* speech they mean speech which is in conformity with the inner

secret thought of the speaker. Hence we see that in all cases truth implies a relation to thought. In the first case, we have the relation of conformity between things and thoughts; in the second, between thoughts and things; in the third, between speech, or its equivalent, and thought. Hence **truth in general** is defined, conformity or correspondence between thoughts and things.

NOTE.—From what has been said we can understand the reason of the division of truth into ontological, moral and conceptual.

(a)   *Ontological* truth, or the truth of things, i. e., their conformity with their archetypes or ideals, is the object of *metaphysics.*

(b)   *Moral* truth, or truth of speech, or its equivalent, e. g., 'gesture,' 'writing,' etc., i. e., its conformity with the speaker's thought, is the object of *Ethics.*

(c)   *Conceptual* truth, or the truth of thought, i. e., its conformity with its object, is the object of *Critics.*

78.   When we define **conceptual truth as the conformity of a concept with its object**, of course, we refer, not to the *material,* but to the *formal* object (8) of the thought.

Again, when we speak of *conformity* between a concept and an object we do not mean *entitative* likeness, but such a *re-presentation* of an object in a spiritual faculty, as results from the action of an object on the faculty and the perceptive reaction of the faculty apprehending the acting object; "Cognitum est in cognoscente secundum modum *cognoscentis.*"

79.   **Conceptual truth is of two kinds, formal and material,** or as others say, complete and incomplete.

(a)   *Material* conceptual truth consists in the simple conformity between the mental representation and the object, without any cognizance of affirmation by the intellect of the conformity.

(b) *Formal* conceptual truth consists in conformity between the mental representation and the object, and includes, besides, the perception and affirmation of this conformity by the intellect.

80. **Hence, material conceptual truth is inseparable from the act of simple apprehension.** For every simple apprehension or idea is conformable, as a representation, to the formal object represented.

NOTE (1).—It must be borne in mind that simple apprehensions *merely represent,* and neither affirm nor deny anything of what they represent.

(2) Can one concept of an object be *truer* than another of the same object? If there is question of the same *material* object, of course one concept can represent it more completely than another, i. e., re-present more of its notes. If there is question of the *formal* object, one proper concept (12 h) *cannot* be truer than another, as both represent the same notes, i. e., both are equally conformed to their object; both are *absolutely* true of the object they represent. Hence to speak of the *relativity* of conceptual truth in regard to the formal object of the concept is a contradiction in terms.

81. **Formal conceptual truth is found only in the act of judgment.** For formal conceptual truth implies conformity between thought and its object, and, moreover, the perception and affirmation of this conformity by the mind.

Now, it is only in the judicial act by which, after comparison, predicate and subject are united, that the mind, while directly affirming, *e. g.,* 'all men are mortal,' implicitly perceives and affirms that its concept of *mortal* represents a note common to *all men,* and that its judgment is therefore in conformity with the object. In other words, the Subject of the judgment holds the place of the thing judged of, as it is itself; the Predicate expresses some of the notes of the same thing affirming the conformity of predicate and subject, the mind implicitly perceives and affirms the conformity of its own concept with the thing as it is in itself.

The two preceding assertions are confirmed by the common usage of men. One must *affirm* or *deny* something before his words can be said to express either truth or falsehood.

82. **Falsity** is the opposite, the contradictory of truth, the *non-conformity* of a concept with its object. It is clear that it can, properly speaking, be found only in the judgment in which the mind affirms or denies, contrary to the fact, that a certain predicate belongs to a certain subject. Simple apprehensions, on the other hand, cannot be in themselves false, for they represent what they represent, and nothing else.

Note (1).—Simple apprehensions and sense-perceptions may be called false, but only analogically, when they give occasion to or are the results of false judgments.

(2).—A judgment (27) is a mental affirmation of the objective identity or non-identity of two concepts. This *comparative* apprehension, and affirmation, if motived by *objective evidence,* cannot, of course, be false. If not motived by evidence, then it is not a *purely* intellectual act. For the intellect of its own nature apprehends and affirms only what is evident, i. e., what *is.* But it may happen that, comparing two objective ideas together, the intellect perceives a sort of confused and imperfect similarity between them, which really exists from the point of view in which they are regarded, and then the *will* desirous of identifying them, or impatient of suspense, inclines the intellect to affirm their absolute identity, attending only to the apparent identity, and neglecting the grounds for hesitation.

Hence the *occasion* of false or erroneous judgments is generally to be found in want of attention or obscure and confused ideas on the part of the *intellect;* the ultimate *cause* is the *will* desirous of some good, or impatient of suspense.

(3).—The occasions of false judgments are classified by Bacon under four heads:

(a) *Idols of the tribe,* i. e., Errors to which the human mind is liable from its own finite and limited nature, *e. g.,* the difficulties it finds in acquiring clear, distinct, complete ideas of a great many objects, and on the other hand, its eagerness for knowledge.

(b) *Idols of the den,* i. e., Errors which arise from the peculiar character and disposition, education and prejudices. of each individual.

(c) *Idols of the market place,* i. e., Errors which are almost imposed upon us by the tyranny of public opinion and our own innate love for novelty. Our newspapers and reviews or pet authors do our thinking for us.

(d) *Idols of the theatre,* i. e., the various systems of false and fashionable philosophy current in our times.

Add to these the influence of passion, negligence, lack of logical training, inaccurate use of language, etc., and we have abundant occasion of false judgments all the day long, unless we are constantly on our guard.

83. Objections.

NOTE.—In answering objections the following abbreviations are used: c. (concedo, I grant), n. (nego, I deny), d. (distinguo, I distinguish), cd. (I contradistinguish), sd. (I subdistinguish), t. (transeat, let it pass), maj. (major), min. (minor), concl. (conclusion), neg. sup. (I deny the false supposition implied).

(a)　Conceptual truth is conformity of concept with object. But there can be no conformity between concepts and objects. Therefore, there can be no truth in our ideas. *Answer.*—D. maj.; entitative conformity, n. maj.; representative conformity, c. maj. Cd. min.; no entitative conformity, c. min.; no representative conformity, n. min.; and hence, n. concl.

(b)　All our concepts are primarily derived from material objects. But from material objects you cannot derive concepts conformable to spiritual objects. Therefore, our concepts of spiritual objects are not true.

Answer.—T. maj. D. min.; you cannot derive intuitive (10) and *proper* (12 h.) concepts of spiritual objects, c. min.; you cannot form *derivative* (10) and *analogous* (12. h. note) concepts of spiritual objects, n. min.: and hence in this sense, n. concl.

Note.—Analagous and derivative concepts are *less perfect* than intuitive and proper ones, but they are *true* as far as they go.

(c)　If truth is characteristic of the judicial act, it must be either an *essential* or an *accidental* character of the act. But it cannot be an essential character; else a false judgment would be impossible. Nor can it be an accidental character; else the intellect could not be said to tend necessarily to truth. Therefore, truth is in no way characteristic of the act of judgment.

Answer 1.—N. maj.; for truth may be essential to one class of judgments (i. e., those motived by *evidence*), accidental to another (i. e., those elicited under command of the *will*).

Answer 2.—T. maj. D. min. As to First Part: a false judgment necessitated or motived by evidence would be impossible c. min.; a false judgment elicited under command of the will would be impossible; sd. without any *apparent* identity (or non-identity) between subject and predicate, c. min.; where there is some apparent identity (or non-identity), n. min. As

to Second part of min. D. the intellect could not be said to
tend necessarily to truth if it erred in a judgment necessitated
or motived by evidence, c. min.; if it erred in a judgment
elicited under command of the will; sd. without any *apparent*
truth, c. min.; with some apparent truth, n. min.

NOTE.—The intellect is not a free faculty. Hence, in
presence of its formal motive, objective evidence, it is compelled by its nature to assent. If there be no objective evidence there can be no *necessitating* motive for judging. But
in a false judgment there can be no objective evidence. Hence
the mind is not forced to a decision; and, as its acts are either
spontaneous and necessary, or under the control of the will,
it follows that a false judgment is elicited at the command
of the will. Hence, while admitted that there must be *apparent* motives which allure the mind to a false judgment,
we deny that *they can be sufficient* motives to compel intellectual assent without the intervention of the will. Hence
purely intellectual judgments, i. e., motived by objective evidence, are *essentially* true; those elicited under command of
the will, may or may not be true, i. e., they are *accidentally*
true.

ARTICLE II.—THE VARIOUS STATES OF MIND POSSIBLE IN
REGARD TO TRUTH.

84. The mind is said to attain and possess truth when it
pronounces judgments in conformity with things. **Now, in
regard to the attainment and possession of truth, the mind
must be in one or the other of these five states.** Either it
pronounces a false judgment; or it has no knowledge of the
object; or it has some knowledge, but hesitates to judge; or it
judges, yet not with firmness and security; or, finally, it judges
without any hesitancy or insecurity. In the first case, we have
error; in the second, *ignorance;* in the third, *doubt;* in the
fourth, *opinion;* in the fifth, *certitude.* Of Error we have

spoken in the preceding article, and of Opinion and Certitude we shall speak presently in separate articles. A word here on Ignorance and Doubt.

85. **Ignorance** is lack of knowledge, i. e., a state of mind in which one has neither ideas nor judgments in regard to a certain matter. It may be universal, as, e. g., 'in the case of infants'; or more or less partial, according as it extends to fewer or more truths. If the unknown truths are such as one *can* and *ought to know,* ignorance of them is called *privative* ignorance. In other cases, it is said to be merely *negative.*

There are many things of which the mind of man, left to itself, can know nothing, either because they are above its natural capacity, e. g., 'the mystery of the Godhead,' or because it has not sufficient data to proceed upon, e. g., 'the number of the stars.' But apart from these, there are many subjects upon which the human mind can acquire more or less full and perfect knowledge. Ignorance in such matters is to be attributed to lack either of ability or of opportunities, or of application and industry, or of order and method in study.

86. **Doubt,** we have said, is a state of mental hesitancy or suspense, so that the mind, on comparing two ideas together, finds itself unable to pronounce whether they are objectively identical or diverse. Hence, it is defined, hesitation or suspense of mind between two contradictory judgments. The doubt is *positive* when there are, or seem to be, good reason on both sides. It is *negative* when there is, or semes to be, no good reason for either side. Daily experience shows us that there are a multitude of judgments, in regard to which, under the present circumstances, it is rational to remain in doubt. There are some, however, who maintain that we must doubt about everything, or, at least, about many things of which our own reason and the common sense of mankind declare we are certain. These are called *sceptics.* **Scepticism,** in general, is a state of

doubt in regard to those things which are known with certainty by means of our natural faculties, properly disposed and applied.

NOTE.—The word *belief* is used in many senses. In strictness it means, Assent to a proposition on sufficient *testimony*. In the language of the Church it means, Absolute certainty on the supreme authority of God.

ARTICLE III.—CERTITUDE.

We will divide this article into two parts. In the first we will treat of the *nature,* in the second, of the *existence* of certitude.

(i). *Nature of Certitude.*

87. **Certitude** is defined, Firmness of mental assent, or of adhesion to a truth, from a motive which manifestly excludes all rational fear of error. Hence certitude includes three essential elements, two of which are *subjective,* and the third *objective,* viz.: (1) firmness of adhesion, (2) exclusion of all rational fear of error, and (3) an objective motive manifestly and really sufficient to exclude all fear of error.

NOTE (1).—By a *motive* of assent we mean the *reason why* we give internal mental assent to a given proposition. By an *objective* motive, we mean something independent of our own views and feelings, something in objects themselves, or in their surroundings, which justifies and compels our assent, and to which we can appeal as justifying and compelling assent in any rational being who perceives it. By an objective motive *which excludes all reasonable fear of error,* we mean a motive which shows clearly that, in the given case, the contradictory of the proposition we assent to, is not merely *improbable,* but *impossible.* Hence, a *certain* judgment is always true.

(2).—It is one thing to see clearly that a given predicate

belongs to a given subject, and that the contradictory proposition, in the given case, expresses an impossibility; it is quite another thing to be able to answer all the arguments that may be urged against our proposition, and in favor of the contradictory. Hence, as Newman says, "ten thousand difficulties do not make one doubt."

(3).—It is clear that of the two subjective elements of certitude one may be described as *positive,* i. e., the firmness of adhesion (this is *variable,* and may be greater or less, according to the force of the motive); the other may be called *negative,* i. e., the exclusion of all rational fear of error (this is *invariable,* and must be equally found in all certain judgments; for, if there be any, even the smallest rational fear of error. the judgment ceases to be certain).

88. Kinds of Certitude.

(a) Certitude is *metaphysical, physical* or *moral,* according as the manifest objective necessity of uniting or separating subject and predicate is metaphysical, physical or moral, i. e., according as this necessity is based upon the essential natures of things, or on the laws of nature, or on the moral laws which govern the constant and universal though free action of man, *e. g.,* 'Things which are equal to the same thing are equal to each other'; 'if you put your hand into the fire you will feel pain'; 'Your mother is not praying that you may die a disgraceful death.'

NOTE (1).—Moral certitude, taken *strictly,* must exclude absolutely all fear of error. Very often, however, a thing is said to be morally certain when it is only *very probable;* but this is not the sense in which the words are taken here.

(2).—When we speak of various kinds or degres of certitude, we consider, not so much the connection between subject and predicate in the proposition we assent to, as the connection between the proposition itself and the motive accompanying it, which renders the contradictory (metaphysically, physically or morally) impossible in the given case.

Hence, when a judgment is metaphysically certain, its contradictory is *absolutely* impossible.

When a judgment is physically certain, the contradictory is *physically* impossible, i. e., unless God suspends the laws of nature in the given case.

When a judgment is morally certain, the contradictory is *morally* impossible, i. e., unless man belies his nature and acts contrary to its tendencies in the given case.

(b) *Direct* certitude is that which immediately accompanies the *direct* perception of a truth.

Reflex certitude is had when the mind, going back on its direct judgment, examines the motive distinctly and perceives that its direct certitude is justified and says, as it were, I am certain that I am certain.

(ii). *Existence of Certitude.*

89. **Scepticism**, as we have said, is, A state of doubt in regard to those things which are known with certainty by means of our natural faculties properly disposed and applied.

(a) *Objective* Scepticism admits that we can be certain of our existence, or, at least, of the existence of our thoughts as phenomena; but holds that we have no means of acquiring certain knowledge in regard to anything else, and hence, that we must doubt of all else.

(b) *Subjective* Scepticism denies, moreover, that we can be certain even of our own existence, or of our own thoughts (*universal* scepticism).

NOTE.—Some objective sceptics deny the veracity of *all* our faculties except consciousness; others deny only the veracity of the senses; others that of reason only, etc. (*partial* scepticism).

90. **Universal or perfect scepticism is absurd, whether it be regarded as an internal mental fact, or as a doctrinal system.**

Note.—As a *fact,* i. e., it is impossible for a man actually to doubt of all things.   As a *doctrinal system,* i. e., as a system attempting logical exposition and proof it contradicts itself.

Proof of First Part.—The man who affirms, either in thought or speech, that he doubts about all things, at the same time affirms that he does not doubt about all things, *e. g.,* 'his own existence and his present state of mind.' He affirms that he exists and that he doubts about all things. To say I doubt, is as much an affirmation as to say, I am certain.

Again, such a doubt would be a positive act of resistance to the tendency spontaneous, natural and necessary in all men, to accept many truths as certain and evident. But such an act against man's natural tendency requires either some reason inducing the mind to doubt, or some end soliciting the will to impel the mind to doubt, and hence, a certainty of something.

For the rest, our consciousness tells us clearly enough that it is absolutely impossible for any one to doubt of everything; and every action of man's daily life proves the same thing.

Proof of Second Part.—A doctrinal system which implies that two contradictories are simultaneously true is absurd. But scepticism as a doctrinal system implies, etc. For, according to doctrinal sceptics nothing is certain, and at the same time some things are certain, i. e., their doctrine and all that goes to declare and prove it. It is as if a man were to make a long speech to prove that he is dumb. The mind proves that it does not exist, and that it is essentially untrustworthy; that uncertainty is certainty.

91. **Partial scepticism logically leads to perfect or universal.**

Proof.—Partial scepticism teaches that some of our natural cognitive faculties, properly disposed and rightly applied are untrustworthy. But this leads to universal; for, if some of our natural cognitive faculties, properly disposed, etc., are untrustworthy, there is no reason why we should not distrust them all.

Further, our faculties are so connected that the higher to a great extent depend, at least extrinsically, on the lower.

Again, to argue from the common sense and daily life of sceptics themselves; they trust eyes, ears, taste, touch, smell and reason just as much as other men.

NOTE (1).—Hence, it is impossible, logically speaking, for a sceptic to argue, or to be argued with. "Every assertor of such a philosophy must be in the position of a man who saws across the branch of a tree on which he sits, at a point beween himself and the trunk." (St. George Mivart.) "Scepticism is a drug which purges out everything, itself included."

(2). Self evident as these propositions are, it is yet good that their truth be clearly brought home to us. The systems of philosophy prevalent in our day are more or less sceptical, and it is well to remember that any position which logically leads to perfect scepticism may be disproved by a *reductio ad absurdum*. Thus, Mivart refutes the Agnostic system which holds that all knowledge is merely relative and apparent. "Every philosophy starts with the assumption that something is really knowable and absolutely true. But if nothing we can assert has more than a relative value, this character must also appertain to the doctrine of the relativity of all our knowledge; therefore, either this system is absolutely and objectively true (and then all knowledge is not merely relative and apparent); or it is merely relative, and then it has no absolute value, and does not correspond with the objective reality. Such a system, then, refutes itself, and is necessarily suicidal."

92. **To require that every truth be demonstrated is scepticism.**

Proof.—Every demonstration is a deduction from certain premises, and these premises are either certain and self-evident in themselves or need to be demonstrated. If they need to be demonstrated, then they must be proved from other premises. These other premises, again, either require demonstration or they do not; and so on to infinity, unless it be admitted that some truths are self-evident and certain without demonstration. Hence, to deny that we can have certainty without demonstration is to deny the possibility of being certain of anything, i. e., it is scepticism.

NOTE.—Hence it would be absurd to expect a demonstration of the possibility of certitude in regard to self-evident truths. Nor do we assent blindly to such truths, but because of their self-evidence.

93. **These three self-evident truths are implied and necessarily admitted in every judgment,** viz.: the existence of the thinking subject, the principle of contradiction, the natural capacity of our reason to know the truth; i. e., the first fact, the first principle, the first condition of certain knowledge.

Proof.—If any of them be denied or doubted, there can be no certitude. For there can be no thought without an existing thinker. There can be no certitude if two contradictories can be simultaneously true. There can be no certitude, if the mind is incapable of certitude.

These three truths cannot be *demonstrated* without begging the question; for they are, and must be, assumed in every demonstration, since there can be no certain premise in which they are not implied and necessarily admitted.

NOTE (1).—Nor need they be demonstrated, for they are self-evident, and in their very denial are affirmed.

(2).—Hence the absurdity of Kant's criticism or examination of the reliability of reason in its perception of truth. In his examination he employs the very faculty of whose reliability he professes to doubt, and hence involves himself in the contradiction essential to all scepticism.

(3).—Hence, too, the absurdity of Descartes' "Methodical Doubt," as he calls it. He held that a philosopher should try to doubt about all things, until they are *demonstrated*. Finding he could not doubt of the existence of his own thought, he takes this as the one principle of all philosophy, and thence, argues, "I think, therefore I am." But this argument is good for nothing, unless the principle of contradiction and the infallibility of the reason, which perceives and affirms the fact of its own existence, be admitted as true. And even granting the premise, how is the conclusion certain if reason which deduces it be unreliable? Further, if all our other natural faculties are unreliable, why should not the faculty of consciousness, which tells me I think, be so too?

94. **The human mind spontaneously and naturally assents to many truths as objectively certain.**

Proof.—Spontaneously. It is *a fact* that men constantly, invincibly and universally, without reasoning or reflection, but merely from perceiving the objective necessity of uniting subject and predicate, hold many truths as objectively certain. But this fact proves the spontaneity of such assent.

Naturally. What men do constantly, universally and invincibly, must be attributed not to accidental circumstances (e. g., education, prejudice, etc.), but to their nature.

95. **This assent is certain in the true and proper sense of the word.**

Proof.—It is firm and without fear of error. For it is a fact that men so adhere to such truths as to be absolutely without doubt of fear of error.

It is from a sufficient objective motive. For, again, it is a fact that men in assenting to such truths are conscious of seeing that they are objectively true and could not be otherwise, *e. g.,* in the judgment, a triangle is not a square.

Hence many of our direct spontaneous judgments are, in the strict sense of the word, *certain* (metaphysically, physically, or morally, according to the subject-matter).

96. **In regard to its positive subjective element, certitude is proportionate, on the one hand, to the objective motive and the light in which it is presented to the mind; on the other, to the perfection of the thinking faculty.**

Proof.—Every effect is proportionate to its cause. But the firmness of assent is the effect of the motive, the light in which it is presented and the thinking subject. Therefore, etc.

NOTE (1).—Hence, the greater the objective necessity of uniting or separating subject and predicate, and the more perfectly this is seen, the closer and firmer is the mental adhesion to the truth. Hence, the intensity of adhesion varies in metaphysical, physical and moral certitude. Of course, in all certitude the mind perceives the objective necessity of uniting or separating subject and predicate. In metaphysical certitude, however, it is perceived that this necessity is absolute, and can never admit an exception. In physical and moral certitude, though we perceive that in the *given case* no exception is made, yet an exception is possible should God will to suspend in this instance the law of nature, or should man will to contradict the natural laws of his own moral nature.

(2).—If, in a given case, no reason can be assigned why we should admit that God has made an exception to the ordinary course of nature, or that man has contradicted his natural moral instincts, we can be certain that the universal constant law holds good. Such an exception must have a sufficient cause or reason, and this is wanting in the given case.

(3).—Hence, the superiority in the assent of Divine faith above all merely natural assents. For here, the motive is the infallible authority of God, while the assenting faculty is elevated immeasurably above and beyond itself by the illumination of the Holy Ghost. Hence, in cases where the material object to which we assent is the same, *e. g.,* the existence of God, the certitude of the assent of faith is far higher than that of unaided reason, even though the latter be based on the clearest metaphysical motives.

97. Objections.

(a) An error may present itself to the mind as truth. In that case the mind cannot help assenting with certainty. Therefore an erroneous judgment may be certain.

Answer.—D. maj.; as clearly and *evidently* true, n. maj.; as having much apparent truth, c. maj. D. min.; the intellect may be greatly attracted by the apparent truth, c. min.; can be necessitated by it, n. min.

NOTE.—There may be cases where error is *morally* unavoidable. It is never *physically* unavoidable.

(b) Exclusion of fear of error is requisite and sufficient for certitude. But a motive which shows the contradictory to be *improbable,* excludes the fear of error. Therefore, certitude does not require a motive which shows the contradictory to be *impossible.*

Answer.—D. maj.; perfect exclusion of reasonable fear of error, c. maj.; otherwise, n. maj. A motive which shows that the contradictory has *no* objective probability, c. min. (but this shows it to be impossible, as having no sufficient reason).

NOTE (1).—Moral and physical certitude may in some cases be *implicitly* metaphysical, i. e., when the relation between the motive and the contradictory is such that to assert their co-existence would *imply* a denial of some metaphysical principle, *e. g.,* of the Principle of Contradiction, or of the Principle of Sufficient Reason, or Causality, etc.

(2).—The basis or motive of physical certitude implies two elements, viz.: (a) the constancy of the laws of nature positively known to us; and (b) the absence of rational grounds for admitting that in a given case, these laws have been or will be suspended or interfered with by the Creator's omnipotent power.

(c) Scepticism teaches that all things are doubtful or merely probable. But this doctrine involves no contradiction.

Answer.—C. maj. N. min. The words have no meaning, unless the sceptic admits the three propositions mentioned in n. 93.

(d) The human mind is fallible, i. e., liable to err. Therefore, we cannot trust it.

Answer.—D. maj. fallible *per se,* i. e., in its purely intellectual acts motived by evidence, n. maj.; fallible *per accidens,* i. e., when it judges not on evidence, but under the influence of the will, c. maj.

D. concl. in the same way.

NOTE.—The *intellect* can never find its object, the *true,* in error; but the *will* may find some *good,* utility or pleasure in error. In that case the will can fix the eye of the mind only on the apparent truth in the error, and compel the mind to assent; "the *wish* is father of the thought."

ARTICLE IV.—OPINION.

98.   **Opinion,** as we have said, is a state of mind in regard to truth midway between doubt and certitude, i. e., the mind forms a judgment in regard to a certain matter and has a motive for doing so; yet this motive is not such as to exclude

all fear of error. As in *certitude,* the motive is the objective *necessity* of uniting or separating subject and predicate; so in opinion, the motive is the objective probability or likelihood of this union or separation being true.

NOTE (1).—Objective probability is *intrinsic* if it is based upon the nature of the object of which there is question; *extrinsic* if it is based upon the authority of prudent men.

(2). Probability admits of degrees and is greater or less according as it excludes more or less the danger of error, and more or less warrants firmness of assent. Hence, we have opinions which are slightly probable, solidly probable, more probable, most probable.

99. **Opinion, even when most probable, essentially differs from certitude.**

Proof.—Two things essentially differ when one includes, as an essential element, something which the other does not include. But certitude includes, as an essential element, the exclusion of all rational fear of error, which opinion, even when most probable, does not include. The motive of assent either excludes the fear of error, or it does not; there is no mean. If it does, we have *certitude;* if it does not, no matter how much it may really lessen the fear of error, we can only have *opinion.*

NOTE (1).—At times many distinct motives, each of which taken separately could only produce opinion, when taken together produce certainty. But in this case the certitude is the result, not of the mere sum of the separate probabilities, but of the *collection* of motives, taken as a whole, in which each motive gains from and gives to all the rest an entirely new force and value, *e. g.,* the case of several independent witnesses.

(2). A solidly probable opinion does not cease to be so,

because the contradictory opinion is more probable. For, a good motive does not lose its force by being compared with a better; therefore, the opinion founded on the one does not lose its value by being compared with that founded on the other, so long as this other does not give us certainty.

CHAPTER II.

The Trustworthiness of Our Faculties for the Attainment of Conceptional Truth.

100. **Our faculties of cognition are of two orders,** *sensitive* and *intellectual.* By the former we perceive individual concrete, material objects, facts and phenomena. The proper object of the latter are positively immaterial objects, and material objects abstracted from the *individual* and universalized.

101. As truth and certitude in the strict sense of the word, belong only to the *judgments* of the intellect, the simplest way to treat our present subject will be to group our judgments under three general heads according to the different classes of objects about which we judge. These are, (a) our own internal states, acts, feelings, (b) external individual material objects, (c) positively immaterial objects, and universalized material objects. Of the trustworthiness of our judgments in regard to these three different classes of objects, we shall speak in the three following articles on Consciousness, the External Senses, and the Intellect.

Article I.—Consciousness.

102. **By consciousness** we here mean the intellect *inasmuch* as it apprehends and judges of the *existence* of *pres-*

ent acts, feelings and other internal phenomena of *self* (i. e.,
the composite substantial self knowing, desiring, feeling pain
and pleasure. etc.).

NOTE (1).—The subjective phenomena are the *direct*
object of consciousness; the enduring substantial self to which
the phenomena are referred is the *indirect* object. That is, in
apprehending the phenomena we apprehend the *existence* of
the Self of which they are the phenomena.

(2).—We do not say that *all* internal acts and phenomena
are appended by consciousness; we speak only of those that
are apprehended.

103. **The man who would profess to deny, or to doubt
of the veracity of consciousness in regard to its proper
object would, in the denial, affirm its veracity.** For, in
affirming his mental doubt or denial, he would affirm the
veracity of the consciousness which perceives that he doubts
or denies.

Again, to say that *I* perceive myself to be internally
affirming or denying a given statement, to be deliberately consenting to a given suggestion, to be experiencing sensations
of pain or pleasure, to say that *I* clearly perceive these things
in *myself* and to deny that these things are in myself, is to say
that the same acts, feeling and phenomena can be in a given
subject and not in it at one and the same time.

NOTE (1).—Hence, the certitude of the clear, normal
judgments of consciousness in regard to its proper object is
metaphysical, being based immediately on the principle of contradiction. So, too, in our certitude of the existence of a
permanent Self in us.

(2).—We say, *clear, normal judgment in regard to its
proper objects* (i. e., present internal facts), in order to exclude the occasional error, which may arise from a diseased

or disturbed imagination, *e. g.,* a past experience of pain may be so vividly recalled, that if we are inattentive we may take it for actual present suffering. In this case, however, it is not the simple perception of consciousness that is at fault; it truly affirms the presence before the mind of that which is actually represented by the imagination. The error is in the judgment confounding the imaginary representation with an actual sensation of pain. A *sane* man can always safeguard himself against such erroneous judgments.

The occasion for error is the similarity that one mental state or act may bear to another, on account of which we may hastily judge of it, as if it were that other. But the error is not to be attributed to the intellect which of itself yields only to evidence, but to our more or less wilful inattention and hastiness.

(3).—When a man complains of a pain in an amputated arm, the pain is really felt in the corresponding branch of the nervous system, but confusedly. Imagination and custom may cause one to attribute it to the missing member.

(4).—Note the distinction between *consciousness* (the intellect judging of the *existence* of present mental facts), and *conscience* (the intellect judging of the *morality* of our acts).

Article II.—The External Senses.

104. **External sensation** implies three essential conditions, viz.: a living organ capable of perception, an individual material object capable of being perceived, and a certain *presence* of the latter in the former. How is this presence accomplished? The *action* of the object is received in the sensitive faculty and *perceived* by it as *objective,* and thus, the object itself in so far as it manifests itself by its action, is

perceived by us. This vital perception of the *acting object* may be accompanied by *subjective* feelings of pain, pleasure, etc. But in normal conditions we find no difficulty in distinguishing the *subjective* element from the *objective* element in our sensations.

That the direct object of our external sense-perception is not something merely subjective, but something objective, is clearly seen by considering the difference which consciousness distinctly recognizes between our external sensations and purely internal phenomena, *e. g.,* the former are clearly perceived to be determined from without; the latter, from within. Again, we clearly distinguish our direct sensations of objects from the representations of the same objects preserved and recalled by *memory;* the latter we can alter and group as we will, while the order, succession, etc., of the former are independent of our will.

105. Hence, in our external sensations, we perceive **external objects directly and immediately,** and not merely subjective affections or modifications; for, our own consciousness and the common sense of mankind tell us so. If one denies, in the case of the constant inevitable declaration of normal human nature, that we perceive, immediately and directly, extended resistant bodies distinct from ourselves, he must logically fall into absolute hopeless scepticism. For, if we cannot trust the necessary evident perceptions of our faculties in this, we have no ground for trusting them in anything.

NOTE.—*Idealism* denies that there is any objective reality which corresponds to our external sense-perceptions. *Subjective* idealism holds that our sensations are *merely subjective modifications,* the sole work of the subject in which they exist; and that what is supposed to be an external world, may be, for all we know, "a projection of the Ego on a background of nothingness." *Objective* idealism (Berkely) holds that it is God himself who immediately produces in our senses the impressions which we suppose to come from an external world. *Transfigured Realism* (H. Spencer) holds that there is an external world, which is the cause of our sense-perceptions; but that it in no way corresponds to our perceptions, but is, and must always be unknown and unknowable to us; "what we are conscious of, are but subjective affections produced by objective agencies which are unknown and unknowable."

All these views are based on the assumption that the object of all our knowledge is simply and wholly our own subjective states. The argument given above is a simple and conclusive 'Reductio ad Absurdum' of all forms of idealism. The consistent idealist must deny not only the existence of his fellow-men, and all experimental science, but even the testimony of consciousness and his own existence. In their normal conditions, either all our own natural faculties are valid, or none are.

106. **The external senses** are Sight, Hearing, Taste, Touch, Smell. These senses are really distinct from each other, for each has its own organ and perceives an object formally distinct from that of any other sense. The act of external sensation in each case, is produced, not immediately in the brain, but in the living organ proper to each sense. Our own consciousness declares that we do not see, or taste, or smell with our brains, nor is there any valid reason for saying that we do. And again, if all sensation is produced in the brain, no reason can be assigned for the marvelous diversity of structure manifest in the different sense-organs, and the adaptation of each to its peculiar functions.

107. That which is represented in an act of cognitive sensation is called **the object of the act.** We may distinguish

three classes of objects in regard to which the act of sensation may be exercised, viz.:

(a) The **proper** object of a sensitive faculty is that which belongs to the faculty in question alone, and can be perceived by no other, *e. g.*, 'colored extension' is the proper object of sight; 'sound,' of hearing, etc.

(b) A **common** object of sensation is that which can be perceived by several sensitive faculties, *e. g.*, 'extension,' 'shape,' 'rest,' 'motion,' etc., can be perceived both by sight and by touch.

(c) The **accidental** object of sense is that which accompanies or sustains those qualities which constitute the proper and common objects of sensations, *e. g.*, 'substance,' in *a* broad, indeterminate sense of the word, i. e., inasmuch as it is the subject of substratum of sensile qualities. For, our senses do not perceive color, extension, etc., in the abstract, but in the concrete, i. e., we perceive this or that particular colored, extended thing

108. In the following propositions on the validity of the testimony of our external senses it is supposed that all the necessary conditions for the natural action of the faculties in question are verified, viz.:

(a) The sense organ should be sound and in a neutral, normal condition; to the jaundiced eye all things are yellow.

(b) The object should be properly applied to the faculty, i. e., the *distance* at which the object acts, the *medium* through which it acts, and the *manner* in which it is presented should be such as to allow it to produce a sufficient impression on the sense. Thus, it could not be expected that one at a distance of half a mile could distinguish the colors green, blue and violet; or that one looking through green spectacales could perceive a pure white color as such; or that one standing still could distinguish accurately the various colors of a body in rapid motion.

109. **The testimony of our external senses in regard to their proper objects is reliable.**

Proof.—They are our *natural* means of perceiving these objects; for there is in all men an invincible tendency to accept without fear of error, and abide by the testimony of their senses in regard to such objects; and, a consciousness of perceiving a necessitating objective motive for doing so. But if they are the means which nature has given us to perceive those objects, they are, when normally disposed and properly applied, reliable; else, our normal nature would necessitate constant invincible error, and there would be nothing left for us but universal scepticism.

110. **The united testimony of the external senses concerned, in regard to the common objects of sensation, is reliable.**

Proof.—They are our *natural* means of perceiving such objects, and to doubt the validity of ther normal action is scepticism.

111. **The testimony of the external senses in regard to the accidental objects of sensation is never, indeed positively false; but it may easily give occasion to erroneous judgments.**

Proof of First Part.—*Never positively false;* for, the accidental object of sensation is, *e. g., the substance precisely as affected by the qualities* which are the proper or common objects of sensation, and *not the substance according to its intrinsic essential nature.* Of this the senses tell us nothing. In other words, the senses perceive that there is *something* colored hard, odorous, etc.; but they do not pretend to perceive or to inform us what that something is. But in this there is no positive falsity.

Proof of Second Part.—May easily give occasion to erroneous judgments; for, where the sensile qualities perceived by a given sense are the same, the sensile representation (at least in regard to these qualities) is the same. But the substances underlying those qualities may be altogether different, *e. g.,* 'in a living rose, an artificial rose, the image of a rose formed in front of a concave mirror.' In such cases, the sense-representation may readily give occasion to the false judgment that the artificial rose is really a living flower.

112. *Supplementary Notes.*

(a) Intellectual judgments *immediately* following upon *normal* sense-perception (in regard to the *proper* and *common* objects of sensation) can never be erroneous.

(b) As to the certitude of such judgments: (1) Our certitude of the existence of an external material world in general, is equivalently metaphysical; since the contradictory world involve the existence of an effect (our necessary perception of an external world) without a proportionate cause. (2) Our certitude of the existence of a particular material object of which we have constant and uniform perception, is also equivalently metaphysical, for the same reason. (3) Our certitude of the objective existence of a particular material object here and now represented by our sensation, is physical, inasmuch as God could directly determine such a sensation. However, even here, in most cases, the certitude may also be equivalently metaphysical for the reason given above.

(c) We can know that the conditions requisite for normal sense-perception (108) are verified, for defects in the organs of sense and in the proper presentation of their objects, are not natural, but occasional and accidental, and can be recognized by attention, and comparison with normal cases.

(d) When it is said that our sense-perception is *entitatively* subjective, *representatively* objective, the meaning is that the *act of perception* is in the sentient subject, *the thing perceived* is the determining object as acting on, and so far manifesting itself to, the perceptive sense. Hence, to say that we need to compare our normal perception with their objects before we can be sure of a correspondence between them, is the same as saying that we must compare an object with itself to be sure that it corresponds with itself.

(e) We do not affirm that bodies have in themselves the *sensations* of *e. g.*, 'extension,' 'harness,' etc.; but we do affirm that there are formally in the bodies which determine these sensations in us, qualities corresponding to the sensations produced. To deny this leads logically to universal scepticism. If you deny that a piece of coal is black, you have no right to affirm that it has extension or even existence.

(f) Our sight informs us that the oar in the water is broken, when it is not; but in the first place, the *shape* or *figure* of the oar is not the *proper* object of sight. Again, the *medium* through which the different parts of the oar affect the eye is not uniform.

(g) From what has been said above, we can readily answer the objection: That our senses deceive us in regard to magnitude, *e. g.*, 'of the sun'; or in regard to the apparent motions of bodies really at rest, *e. g.*, 'of houses,' 'trees,' etc., as they appear to one on board a fast train.

(b) In the Blessed Sacrament, the *quantity* of the bread and wine exists (miraculously, it is true) after the manner of a substance; therefore, when our senses tell us that something objective exists with the taste, color, weight, etc., of bread and wine, they do not deceive us; though to one ignorant of the mystery of the Eucharist, their testimony might in this case readily give rise to the erroneous judgment that the *substance* of bread and wine is present.

ARTICLE III.—THE INTELLECT.

113. **Consciousness and experience testify that there is in man a faculty that perceives and represents:** (a) Objects which in no way come within the sphere of sensitive cognition, *e. g.,* 'possibility,' 'necessity,' 'certitude,' 'doubt,' 'relation,' 'eternity,' 'virtue and vice,' 'rights and duties,' 'liberty and obligation,' 'spirit,' 'thought,' 'God and His attributes'; (b) Sensile objects, but in a manner transcending the representations of sensitive cognition, *e. g.,* 'material objects, abstracted from individuating notes, from all the concrete conditions of actual existence (shape, size, etc.) and even from the note of actual existence itself.' (c) Sensile objects which make no impression on the senses, *e. g.,* 'the effect, as yet unproduced, in the cause'; 'the cause, which has ceased to exist, in the effect'; (d) Itself and its own acts. Now, such a faculty is necessarily a faculty which elicits its acts independently of a material organ, i. e., a spiritual faculty. For immaterial or universalized objects cannot be represented in or perceived by a material, extended subject, nor can such a subject reflect upon itself and make itself the object of its own perception.

"Ideas are not sensible pictures. The least experience is sufficient to convince us that we have many ideas which can not be reduced to any sensible picture."—Lewes. "Neither sense-experiences, nor any modification of them."—Huxley.

NOTE.—The intellect is in its action, *intrinsically* independent of the material organism, i. e., it does not need the concurrence of a material organ to elicit its acts; hence, it is *said* to be *subjected* in the soul alone. The sensitive faculties, on the contrary, need the concurrence of a material organ in eliciting their acts; hence they are said to be *subjected,* not in the soul alone, nor in the body alone, but in the living *compound*. While the soul is united to the body, the intellect is dependent on the senses—not, indeed, intrinsically, i. e., in eliciting its acts, but *extrinsically*—i. e., the senses furnish the matter upon which the intellect *begins* its work.

114. The three primary functions of the intellect are simple apprehension, judgment and reasoning. It is one and the same faculty which performs all these various functions; but considered in relation to its acts of simple apprehension and immediate judgment, it may be called *intelligence* or *intellect;* in relation to its act of mediate judgment or reasoning it is called *reason.*

We shall therefore briefly consider the validity of each of the three primary acts of the intellect in three separate paragraphs:

(i)   *Ideas.*

115. We have already enumerated and defined the principal classes of ideas. It only remains here to answer the question, Have our ideas an objective value? i. e., are they merely subjective creations of our mind, to which nothing real and objective corresponds? or, on the contrary, do they represent and correspond with objective realities? For instance, when I mentally represent, 'The whole as greater than the part,' 'The sum of the angles of a triangle as equal to two right angles,' do these representations hold good in reality as well as in thought? Are they true in the world of actual and possible things, quite independently of my thoughts? Do they express laws of *being* as well as laws of *thinking?* This is what is meant by asking are our ideas valid.

116. Now, to deny or doubt the validity of ideas in general is absolute scepticism and involves an open contradiction. For, to deny or doubt the possibility of attaining truth is scepticism. But to deny or doubt the validity of our ideas is to deny or doubt the possibility of attaining truth (i. e., conformity of thought with objective reality).

Again, every judgment, affirmative or negative—even the
negation of the validity of our ideas—implies something objective corresponding to the terms, i. e., implies the conformity
of our thought with the reality of things. Hence, the validity
of ideas is affirmed in its negation.

For the rest, the idealist reasons about his own past mental states, about other men's opinions, etc., and thus practically
admits that his ideas represent objective realities different
from themselves.

NOTE.—Hence ideas or intellectual perceptions are like
sense-perceptions, *entitatively* subjective, *representatively* objective.

117. **A special difficulty is raised against the objectivity or validity of the universal idea** (11. b.) i. e., that which
represents a note univocally common to and predicable of
many objects *distributively*. A few words on the different
erroneous views—Nominalism, Conceptualism and Exaggerated Realism—before explaining the true theory—moderate
Realism.

(a) **Nominalism** admits *common names* for things, but
rejects any universality in ideas or in objects. But words have
no meaning except inasmuch as they are signs of ideas and of
things. Hence, when we intelligently apply a common name,
e. g., circle, to many distinct individual objects, there must be
something corresponding to the word in our thought, and in
each and all of the things to which the word is applied. Else
all speech is nonsense.

(b) **Conceptualists** admit universality in ideas, but
contend that such ideas are mere intellectual fictions to which
no objective reality corresponds; since, as they truly say, every
existing thing must be a definite individual. They admit,
however, that the universal concept is univocally predicable
of many distinct individual objects. But a concept is a repre-

sentation; and hence, a *common* or universal concept must represent something common to all the inferiors of its extension, i. e., something objective in things, else the concept would be universal and not universal at the same time.

(c) **Exaggerated Realism** holds that the *formal universal* exists as a real object, i. e., that there actually exists in nature an object corresponding to our universal idea, not only as to what is represented by the idea, but *also* as to the *manner* in which it is represented, viz., apart from individuation, e. g., an existing circle, horse, etc., which is no particular circle or horse, but circle or horse in general. This is clearly absurd. For, the universal man, for instance, would either exist in every individual man, or he would not. In the latter case, he would not be a universal man, but an individual, and no other object but himself could be truly called a man. In the former case, he would either be one and the same identical man, in each and all of the individuals called by that name; and then there would be but one man in all the world, and every so-called man would be his own son, grandfather, neighbors, etc.—one man multilocated in time and space; or he would be different men, multiplied as often as there are actual or possible men, and then he would be one and many at the same time.

118. But, leaving aside these self-contradictory views, let us explain the true view.—**Moderate Realism.**

A universal idea *represents one thing (one note or one sum of notes) as capable of belonging to many distinct objects and of being predicated of each and all of them univocally.* The *matter* of the idea is *that which* is represented by it: the *form* is the *manner* in which the matter is represented. The *matter* of the universal idea is derived from concrete individual objects; the *form* is due to abstraction, reflection and comparison on the part of the intellect.

Thus, as we said above (11. c, Note), seeing a single concrete circle described and seeing how it is done the mind by its power of abstraction (9. Note) can neglect the concrete characters of place, time, size, material, etc., which make the figure *this particular, individual* circle and attend only to what makes it a *circle.* What is represented in this abstract or prescinded idea, is merely the *nature* or *essence* of circle without any reference to the peculiarities or individuation of particular circles. This idea is called the *direct* universal idea. It represents *one* nature or essence, that of Circle. Its contents or Matter is real, and realized in the given circle we are considering, though not in the abstract Form or manner in which it is conceived.

The mind *reflecting* on this direct universal idea, which simply represents the abstract nature or essence of Circle and *comparing* it with the many individual objects and circumstances in which it *is* or *may be* realized, forms a new concept, of *one nature or sum of notes capable of being univocally realized in and predicated of any number of actual or possible individuals.* This is the *reflex* universal idea. It differs from the direct universal in this, that the latter represents one nature, *absolutely* and without any reference to predication; while the former represents that same one nature, as predicable of many individuals.

Hence, there are three ways in which we can consider any one nature as predicable: (1) as individuated in a concrete existing or possible being (represented by a *singular* idea), (2) absolutely and in itself without reference to individuation or Extension, (represented by a *direct* universal idea), (3) as multiplied or multipliable in many individuals, i. e., as having Extension, (represented by a *reflex* universal idea).

119.   Hence we say that:

(a)   Our *direct* universal idea is *objectively real,* i. e., the sum of its contents is realized and realizable in objects (though not in the *manner* in which it is conceived).

(b)   Our *reflex* universal idea is *logical,* i. e., the sum of its positive contents (*one* thing wholly and completely in each and all of *many* distinct things, i. e., one and manifold at the same time) is not realized or realizable in objects. Yet it is not without a solid foundation and justification in the *real* order of things.   For, though the distinct objects covered by the reflex universal idea have not one and the same numerically *identical* nature, yet they have absolutely *similar* natures, and this justifies the mind in embracing them all under a common concept.

NOTE (1).—The object represented by a direct universal idea, *e. g.,* the nature of a circle, is said to be *eternal* and *necessary,* because all circumstances of time, place, etc., are prescinded from in the concept, and because the sum of notes represented is always and everywhere requisite and sufficient to constitute the nature represented by the concept.

(2).   In a judgment, the Comprehension of the predicate as a *direct universal* is affirmed or denied of the subject.

(3).—Observe carefully the difference between the clear-cut, universal *idea, e. g.,* of a circle, and the vague, indefinite picture in the imagination, which accompanies it.   This latter is sometimes called a *common phantasm,* but in reality it is rather a confused, unsteady image of a *particular* circle, than a clear representation of that which is realized and realizable in each and every actual and possible circle.   Compare also the phantasms excited by the words 'mathematical point,' 'line,' 'a twenty-sided plane figure,' 'justice,' 'patriotism,' etc. (See Clarke, Logic, p. 110 seqq.: Maher, Psychology, p. 274, 279).

(ii)   *Judgments.*

120.   In the present article we shall only consider imme-

diate judgments. They are either *analytical* or *synthetical,*
i. e., they are either about abstract truths or concrete facts
(external or internal).

121. It is clear that so long as our senses and our consciousness do not deceive us, **our immediate synthetical
judgments, in regard to what they testify, cannot be
erroneous;** in other words, if my consciousness truly perceives me thinking, if my sense of sight truly perceives this
white paper, my judgments, *I am thinking; This paper is white,*
cannot be wrong.

122. **In immediate analytical judgments,** the predicate
is a note which necessarily belongs to the subject, and which
the mind, by merely comparing the terms, sees at once so to
belong to it, that to deny that the predicate in question belongs to the subject in question would be to deny the identity
of the subject with itself, *e. g.,* by merely considering the idea
of a *whole,* we are at once forced to attribute to it the predicate
greater than any of its parts. Such judgments are necessary
and universal. The mind cannot help pronouncing them, and
cannot attempt to think a possible case in which they are not
true. The certitude of such judgments is *metaphysical,* i. e.,
in no hypothesis can their contradictories be true.

NOTE (1).—Certain analytical judgments are of such universal application that they are called axioms, or first principles of all scientific knowledge. Such are, for instance, the
judgments—

(a) Every actual or possible being has, either in itself
or outside of itself, a sufficient reason for its existence or
possibility.

(b) Every new being, i. e., everything which begins to
be, or acquires an existence which it had not before (and,
therefore, every change, every phenomenon, etc.), supposes a

cause, i. e., an existing being, prior to itself, and necessary and sufficient to account for the existence of the new being.

(c) Similar *necessary* (as opposed to *free*) causes, in similar circumstances produce similar effects, unless the laws of nature be suspended.

(2).—*Synthetical* judgments, as they are concerned about matters of fact, of themselves, can never become scientific principles. It is only by menas of analytical principles that, after sufficiently numerous and varied experiments, we are enabled to form the universal judgment, *e. g.*, that *all fire will produce painful sensations in sensitive organs.* Synthetical judgments thus universalized are called *empirical* or experimental axioms or principles. They are of constant application in science and in practical life.

(3).—There is no *one* axiom in which all others are virtually contained, or from which they can be directly demonstrated. Yet there is one axiom which is implicitly contained in all others, whose denial involves the denial of all others, and to a denial of which we may reduce an adversary who denies any evidently true judgment. This is the *Principle of Contradiction:* "Nothing can be, and not be, at the same time."

(iii) *Reasoning.*

123. **Demonstrative reasoning is an infallible means of acquiring true and new knowledge.**

True knowledge. For if A and B are each identical with C, they must be identical with each other. If all A is contained under B, and all B under C, all A must be contained under C. In other words, the conclusion simply expresses explicitly what is expressed implicitly in the true and certain premises; therefore, it is true and certain.

New knowledge. It is new knowledge for me, if now I

know *explicitly* that a certain predicate belongs to a certain subject, which before I did not know belonged to it; or if I now learn for the first time *why* it belongs to it.   But this knowledge I acquire by demonstrative reasoning.

NOTE (1).—Of course, there are such things as erroneous conclusions, but they do not follow *legitimately* from *true* premises. Either we have *irrationally* admitted as *true,* premises which are not so, or we have *irrationally* violated one or other of the laws of reasoning.

(2).—*Memory* is the power of retaining, recalling and recognizing knowledge acquired by us in the past.   As the validity of our reasoning depends on the validity of the premises, and as we depend greatly on our *memory* for our premises, a word must be said here on the trustworthiness of memory.

Intellectual memory is not a distinct faculty; it is merely another name for the *intellect* considered in relation to a special *function*—that of reproducing and recognizing our past mental states. It is, therefore, in itself a matter of *simple apprehension—Before my mind is an idea or judgment which I have had before.* Hence, as in other acts of simple apprehension, we must admit that the object apprehended has the characters clearly and evidently apprehended in it, unless we are prepared to deny the capacity of the mind for perceiving truth.   We are as much necessitated to accept many of the judgments founded on memory as we are those founded on present consciousness; and if evidence can compel us to err in the one case, there is no ground for security in the other.

On the other hand, the man who would argue against the trustworthiness of memory, would, like every other sceptic, assert its trustworthiness in *his* argument against it. For, to go no farther than his argument itself, what happened the ten-billionth part of a second ago, is as truly past as what hap-

pened a billion centuries ago; hence, he can never state his
conclusion unless he trusts memory for the fact that he has
stated his premises—nay, he cannot be sure he existed when
the premises were stated. Hence all science, as well as all
practical and social life, is based on the trustworthiness of
memory.

Rule.—Assert only what memory *districtly* recognizes,
and *as* it recognizes it, and memory will never give occasion
to erroneous judgments.

124. In the present chapter we have considered the
various faculties which man possesses for the attainment of
true and certain knowledge, their proper objects, the conditions of their normal exercise and their general trustworthiness within their natural limits. It must be borne in mind
that this last point cannot be *demonstrated* directly without
'Begging the Question.' The validity of our faculties in their
normal exercise is a primary fact which must be accepted on
its own self-evidence under penalty of falling into absolute
scepticism. Hence, we can prove the validity of our faculties,
only *indirectly,* i. e., by showing that to deny their validity involves contradiction and all the absurdities of universal scepticism.

CHAPTER III.

The Objective Causes of Certitude.

We have so far considered the nature of Conceptual
Truth, the possibility of attaining it with certainty, and the
trustworthiness of our faculties, or the *subjective* causes of
our certain knowledge. In the present chapter we shall examine the objective causes or motives of certitude.

125. **The motive, or objective cause, or formal object,**
of a certain judgment is that which determines or compels
the mind to pronounce it. It is usually expressed in the answer one gives to the question, *Why do you hold such a prop-*

osition? If I am asked why do I hold with certainty that the whole is greater than any of its parts, I answer, *Because it is self-evident.* Thus, I assign, as the objective cause of my judgment, the *immediate intrinsic evidence* of the proposition. Again, if I am asked why do I hold that in a right-angled triangle the squares of the hypothenuse is equal to the sum of the square of the other two sides, I answer, *Because it follows, with evident consequence, from immediately evident principles.* Though not evident to me at first sight, or from the mere consideration of the subject and predicate, yet, by a process of legitimate reasoning from prior truths, I at length come to see the evident intrinsic necessity of uniting them; and I say that the objective cause of my assent is the *mediate intrinsic evidence* of the proposition. Again, if I am asked why I am certain that I am bored by this logic lecture, or that the sun is now shining, I answer, *Because they are facts, here and now evident; the one to my consciousness, the other to my senses,* i. e., here again, it is inexorable *objective evidence* of the truth that at once compels and justifies my assent. Lastly, if I am asked how I can be certain that the city of Tien-Tsin exists, since I have no intrinsic objective evidence of the fact, i. e., the existence of Tien-Tsin has never immediately manifested itself to me as a physical fact; nor from the mere consideration of the intrinsic nature of the terms can I gather either immediately, or by any process of reasoning, that *existing city* is a predicate objectively to be attributed to Tien-Tsin, I answer, *What you say is quite true. I have no intrinsic evidence of the truth of the proposition; but yet I am perfectly certain of it, for I have testimony which bears on its face intrinsic evidence of its truthworthiness, and this testimony assures me that Tien-Tsin exists.* That is to say, I have *extrinsic evidence* of the truth of the proposition.

These instances show us that the objective motives of certitude may be either *intrinsic* or *extrinsic* to the truth to which we assent; and they will serve to introduce us to our subject, which we will examine in the following articles, viz. :

1. The extrinsic motives of certitude.

2. The intrinsic motives of certitude.

3. The ultimate and fundamental motive or criterion of natural certitude.

ARTICLE 1.—THE EXTRINSIC MOTIVES OF CERTITUDE.

126. As we have said, the truth which we here and now mentally affirm is called the *material* object of our assent; while the motive or objective reason why we assent to it and hold to it with certainty is called the *formal* object. Now, we have seen that, while in some cases the formal object is something intrinsically connected with the material object, in other cases the formal object is something quite extrinsic to the material object. In the former case we *see* the necessity of uniting subject and predicate, and our knowledge is called *science* or *experience*, as the case may be; in the latter, we *believe* the necessity of joining subject and predicate, and our knowledge may be called by the general name of *faith*.

127. **Testimony** in general, is the act by which one communicates to others a fact or truth as known to himself. The one who gives the testimony is called a *witness; immediate,* if he has himself perceived the truth or experienced the fact; *mediate,* if he has received the truth or fact from others. The *authority* of the testimony is the force or weight which it has to win the rational assent of the hearer, i. e., the witness' *right* to credence. The act by which the hearer assents to the truth testified to is called *faith;* which is either *divine* or *human,* according as the witness is God or man. The natural inclination of the human mind to accept with certainty what is at-

tested by sufficient authority, is called *credulity,* or the instinct of *faith.*

In regard to the matter testified to, testimony is either *doctrinal* or *historical,* i. e., either to a scientific truth, or to a concrete individual fact of experience.

Human testimony is either *particular,* i. e., that of some who are in a position to know the fact or truth to which they bear witness; or *universal,* i. e., the spontaneous natural utterance of human nature in all times and places. In the latter case it is called the testimony of the Common Sense of mankind.

128. The principles on which we base our trust in human testimony are the *moral laws* which govern human action, i. e., certain constant and uniform modes of action which men, though free, spontaneously follow, from the very nature of the will as an innate tendency *towards* good, and *away from* evil. They may in truth be called *physical laws* of the free will. These laws, as far as they concern us here, are:

(a) Every man naturally desires to know the truth, especially in regard to matters of general importance, or which greatly affect his interests. "Omnis homo natura scire desiderat."

(b) A lie is, *of itself,* neither good, useful nor pleasurable to human nature, but repugnant to it. Hence, if in a particular case, it is apprehended as useful or desirable, this is not for its own sake, but for the sake of something else which the liar apprehends as good, useful or pleasurable. Hence the saying, "Nemo gratis mendax," "No one lies gratuitously;" and much less will one lie for the sake of bringing trouble and ruin on himself.

(i). *Particular Human Testimony.*

129. **In general, we may say it is not only a useful, but a necessary means of acquiring knowledge.** Man is born and

lives a social being, in communion with his fellow-man, and each is to be helped by, and to help the other. There are many things a child must know, which, if left to himself, it would take him his lifetime to discover. As he grows up, there are still a thousand truths, useful and necessary for him to know, which he has neither the time, nor the means, nor the ability, to verify for himself. It is only by testimony that we know the place of our birth, that the property we inherit is lawfully ours, that the laws we obey were really made by competent authority, etc. Testimony, again, is the only means we have of knowing the chief facts of history and geography. The physical sciences, too (physics, chemistry, astronomy, etc.), are, to a great extent, inductive, and therefore based upon multipiied observations and experiments beyond the power of any one man to verify. In a word, the greater part of our knowledge is motived by human testimony; and we may even say with St. Augustine, that "the whole practical life of man is founded on faith." This natural necessity, and the in-stinctive tendency of man to trust to the testimony of his fel-lowmen in many of the most important concerns of life, is sufficient proof that human testimony is, at least, a safe and prudent motive for assent; else, nature and nature's God would have placed us in such a condition that, from morning to night, we should be hopelessly and unavoidably deceived in regard to those matters which it most interests us to know Our own experience, too, shows us that as a rule, in our pru-dent assents motived by human testimony, we have not been deceived. But the question with which we are concerned here is, can human testimony ever be a sufficient motive of perfect certitude?

130. **In regard to mere matters of fact, particular hu-man testimony is in certain cases a sufficient motive of perfect certitude.**

NOTE (1).—We say *in regard to matters of fact;* for,

though the testimony of scientific men in regard to scientific conclusions may, in many cases, justify and even *demand* assent, yet it is comparatively rare that such testimony has all the conditions requisite for a motive of perfect certitude.

(2).—We say *in regard to mere matters of fact;* for, all theoretical speculations as to the nature, causes, consequences, purposes, etc., of the facts in question, are really scientific conclusions about the facts, and to be regarded as such. Hence, in regard to such *mere matters of fact,* the testimony of a simple, unlettered laborer is, *ceteris paribus,* as valuable as that of a learned lawyer or professor.

(3). We say *in certain cases, e. g.,* when the facts, actions, statements, phenomena, etc., are public, of general importance and easily perceptible to any one who has the normal use of his senses.

Proof.—If we can be certain of the *knowledge* and *veracity* of the witnesses, we can have in particular human testimony a sufficient motive for assenting, with perfect certitude, to that to which it testifies. But in regard to mere matters of fact, we can, *in certain cases,* be certain of the knowledge and veracity of the witnesses. Therefore, in regard to mere matters of fact, we can have at times in particular human testimony a sufficient motive of perfect certitude. The *major* is clear; for it is an immediate application of the principle of contradiction. Granting that men know the fact truly, and truly communicate their true knowledge to me, it is a contradiction in terms to say that what they communicate to me is false, or that I can err in assenting to it.

Proof of the Minor.

(a) We can be certain of our witnesses' *knowledge* of the fact; for it is a certain truth that men's faculties do not deceive them when properly disposed and duly applied. Now in certain circumstances, we can be certain that men's faculties are normally disposed and duly applied.

For a *normal disposition* of the senses is natural and general, the contrary is rare and accidental and should be proved before it can be reasonably assumed. Again, if the witnesses are *many,* it is clearly unreasonable to suppose that the senses of all are indisposed in the same way. Finally, there are many facts so obvious that no one can be mistaken about them, *e. g.,* 'a severe earthquake,' etc.

As to *due application* of the senses, this is sufficiently guaranteed by man's natural desire of true knowledge in regard to obvious facts which are of general importance and affect serious interests, also by the known prudence and cautiousness of the witnesses, etc.

(b) We can be certain of the *veracity* of our witnesses. For if the witnesses be *many* differing in conditions, pursuits, habits, aims and interests—such, in fact that they can have no common motive or purpose in deceiving us, we can be sure that when they all agree in affirming a fact, they are not deceiving us.

If the witnesses be but *few* or even *one,* a man's honesty and truthfulness may be so well known to us by experience, that it would be not only unreasonable, but even unjust, to doubt his veracity in a serious matter. Again, it may be clear from the circumstances, that our witness has absolutely nothing to gain, but, on the contrary, much to lose, by his testimony to the fact; in which case to suppose deception would be to suppose an effect without a cause.

NOTE.—At times we may have physical certainty on human testimony, *e. g.,* when it is absolutely clear that there is *no* motive in the given case to entice the witness to lie. In such a case a lie is *physically* impossible, as it is against the nature of the will to act without the attraction of at least some ap-

parent good. Nay, at times the certitude may be *metaphysical,*
e. g., if many independent witnesses of different interests, conditions, etc., where illusion and collusion are impossible, agree
in consistently narrating a certain fact as witnessed by each
and all—in such a case to doubt the veracity of their testimony would be to affirm the possibility of an effect without
a proportionate cause, and absolutely to deny the existence of
a moral order.

131. **Objections.**

(a) *Each one* of several independent witnesses can be
guilty of falsehood, therefore *all* can.

Answer.—Of different falsehoods, t. maj.; of one and the
same falsehood; sd.; if it can be apprehended by *all* as good,
useful or pleasurable, t.; if not, n.

(b) The stronger motive should commend our assent
rather than the weaker. The motive for admitting the occurrence of miraculous facts is *moral,* that for denying their occurrence is *physical* Therefore, the motive for denying their
occurrence being the stronger, it must command our assent.

Answer.—T. maj. As to min. 1st part, c. (and I observe,
that a moral motive may often give physical and even metaphysical certitude). As to min. 2d part, n. (and I observe,
that there is no physical motive for holding that miracles do
not occur, but simply for holding that the laws of nature are
constant *unless* God in a given case suspends or modifies them.
It is a metaphysical truth that God *can* so suspend or modify
the natural mode of action of His creatures, and that He *has*
done so in a given case may be proved with as much certainty
by legitimate testimony as any other matter of fact).

NOTE.—If the testimony for the occurrence of a given
miracle is not *certain,* but *solidly probable,* we may suspend
our judgment, and neither affirm positively that the miracle
has occurred, nor that the witness has erred or lied.

132 **Tradition** or *mediate* testimony. Competent immediate testimony can give us certainty as to the statements of others, and as to the number, character, etc., of those who made those statements themselves. In this way we can trace an important fact back to *immediate* trustworthy witnesses through a long series of *mediate* trustworthy witnesses. We can have certainty that each succeeding group of the series truly transmits what was learned from the original trustworthy witnesses. Hence, an unbroken public tradition coming down to us in many independent lines, and testifying to important facts, can give us perfect certitude just as truly as immediate witnesses can.

133. **History** or *written* testimony can give us perfect certitude if we have evidence of the authenticity and integrity of the work and of the knowledge and veracity of the writer.

A work is said to be *authentic* when it is really the work of the author to whom it is ascribed. This may be gathered from the style of the author, the character of the narrative, the agreement between the details of the narrative with what we know from *other* certain sources of the time and place in which the author lived, etc. These are called *internal* criteria. Of much more importance, however, are the *external* criteria, i. e., testimony of contemporaries to the authenticity of the work, continuous public tradition as to its authenticity, etc.

The same criteria serve to show the *integrity* of the work, i. e., that it has not been mutilated or interpolated in the course of its transmission to our time. If, moreover, the work was widely circulated among different people at its first publication, it is impossible that it should be altered in regard to any important matter without attention being called to the fact.

The knowledge and veracity of the writer may be determined as above (132).

NOTE.—Besides tradition and history, other sources of

knowledge of past facts are, historical *remains* (ruins, etc.), *monuments* (statues, medals, temples, inscriptions, etc.), *private* records, letters, etc. When all these various sources of information corroborate one another in attesting past facts, falsity in their common testimony is a *physical* impossibility.

134. The **New Criticism**, as it is called, pretends to determine on *a priori* rationalistic principles the value of historical and traditional testimony, especially in regard to *supernatural* facts.

(1).—It assumes, to start with, that the *supernatural* (revelation, inspiration, prophecy and miracle) is *incredible*. "The essence of criticism is the denial of the supernatural."— Renan.

(2).—It ignores or rejects *extrinsic* evidences of authenticity, integrity, veracity, etc., and trusts wholly or mainly to *internal* criteria based for the most part on arbitrary *a priori* principles (*e. g.*, the impossibility or incredibility of the supernatural, etc.).

(3).—History or tradition, therefore, which records facts contrary to these arbitrary principles is rejected as unauthoritative, no matter what abundance of testimony exists in its favor.

This method of treating early Christian history and tradition has been proposed under various forms, but its fundamental canons are the same in all. It is enough to observe that:

(a) External facts of the past are certified by legitimate *testimony,* not by *a priori theories;*

(b) The supernatural is neither impossible nor improbable; whether we consider the power and wisdom of God, the needs of man, or the general constancy of the laws of nature;

(c) The power to perceive and relate the *existence* of external important facts does not depend on scientific culture, though the *interpretation* and *explanation* of the facts may;

(d) In point of origin, contents, and recognition as authoritative by contemporary and succeeding generation, *Holy Scripture* cannot be placed on a common level with the Iliad, Odyssey, etc. (See Cath. Quarterly Review, July, 1894, p. 562.)

135. From what has been said, it is clear that though particular **human testimony may** be a sufficient motive for certain assent, yet it **can never be the ultimate motive of assent,** for I assent to a truth on testimony because I am certain of the knowledge and veracity of my informant. Now, I either *see* this knowledge and veracity myself, or I *believe* it on the testimony of others. In the former case the *ultimate* motive of assent is the *evidence* of the authority of my witnesses, because I *see* that they know what they tell me of, and that they are telling me the truth, as they know it. I assent to what they tell me. In the latter case the question recurs, on what grounds do I admit the authority of my informant in regard to the testimony of the witnesses? Either the authority of my informant is *immediately evident,* or it is *believed* on still prior testimony, etc.

(ii). *Universal Testimony.*

136. Reason is the distinctive attribute of man, and it is therefore no wonder that certain conclusions of reason, in regard especially to the most obvious and important interests of life, should be common to all men in all times. The investigations of succeeding ages have but confirmed the assertions of the ancient moralists that all nations have held and hold the existence of a personal God, the future life of man, and his accountability to an unseen Judge, the intrinsic goodness or malice of certain acts, etc. But we are not concerned here to prove the fact of the existence of such judgments, which would indeed be no hard task; but supposing the existence of universal, constant and uniform judgments in regard to certain

matters among all men, in all times and places, in this fact of itself a sufficient motive for our certain assent to the truths these judgments express?

137. **The universal constant uniform judgments of the common sense of mankind are an infallible motive of perfect certitude.**

NOTE.—*Universal* in existence, *constant* in duration, *uniform* in the *use* of subject and predicate.

Proof.—A constant, uniform, universal effect requires a corresponding cause. Therefore these universal, etc., judgments require a universal, etc., cause. But in men differing in every accidental circumstance of time, place, race, education, character, interests, etc., there is nothing common but their nature and their natural faculties. Therefore, the judgments of which we speak are the natural and spontaneous pronouncements of man's rational nature, and therefore cannot be false.

NOTE (1).—The universality required is, of course, not metaphysical, but moral

(2).—In regard to the objection that the judgment of the common sense of mankind has often erred (*e. g.*, in regard to Polytheism, etc.), we deny that such judgments have the notes of universality, etc.

(3).—The faculty which elicits such judgments is reason, and their motive, objective evidence. Their objects are important truths necessary for the conduct and preservation of human life and society—not, indeed, immediately evident, but requiring so very little of reflection and reasoning as to be, at least in regard to their substance, within easy reach of all who have the use of reason. Hence, their objects are rational truths, not matters of fact.

(4).—Of course we can also have, and we have universal, and therefore sufficient human testimony to facts of the highest importance and interest. Thus, when we examine the universal testimony, written and traditional, of all nations to certain primitive facts connected with the human race, we can find, by process of elimination, that as neither ignorance, nor prejudice, nor corruption of morals, nor superstition, nor education, nor self-interest, etc., can be a sufficient reason for the universality, constancy and steady uniformity of the testimony, our reason compels us to affirm that the testimony is originally based on the objective evidence of the fact, i. e., that the fact really happened, substantially at least, as it is recorded in the testimony.

(5).—Lastly, we can gather from what we have said of universal testimony that though it may be a sufficient motive for perfect certitude, yet it is not the ultimate or fundamental motive of our certitude in regard even to the truths it attests, and much less in regard to all truth. For, how do we know that all men at all times, and in all places, etc., have held such and such a proposition except by the *particular* testimony of historians, travelers, etc. Hence, when we assent to a proposition on the universal testimony of mankind, we do so because we believe the existence of the universal testimony on particular human testimony. Hence, if particular human testimony cannot be an ultimate motive of assent to the truths it attests, much less can universal testimony.

(iii). *Divine Testimony.*

138. God is essentially omniscient and all-holy, and therefore it is metaphysically impossible that He can be deceived or deceive us. His testimony, therefore, is the firmest of all motives of certitude.

139. It is not the province of Logic to determine at length the relations of reason to revealed truth. A word or two on the subject, however, will not be out of place here.

(a) Though no truth can be *against* reason, yet reason

itself shows that **there may be many truths above it,**
simply and absolutely exceeding its grasp. For, our natural
knowledge of God is not intuitive, but discursive, i. e., gathered
from effects in which His perfections are but faintly and analogically shadowed forth. But such knowledge, true though
it be, as far as it goes, is still very far from representing all
the perfections of its object. Hence, many truths must remain
to be known about the Nature, Attributes, and Free Action
of God, which lie forever beyond the reach of unaided human
reason.

NOTE.—A proposition *against* reason is one which involves
an evident contradiction. A proposition *above* reason is one in
regard to which unaided reason can find no *evident* motive
either for uniting or for separating subject and predicate.

(b) **Such superrational truths may be divinely revealed.** For, on the one hand, we can understand, with sufficient clearness for intellectual assent, the signification of subject and predicate, and, on the other, God, who has given man
so many ways of communicating his knowledge to his fellow-
man, cannot lack means of communicating to us His own
knowledge of the relation of subject and predicate in the given
case. Nor can this knowledge be said to be useless to man.
For (1) it perfects our knowledge of God and of our relations
to Him, which is, of all knowledge, the most useful and necessary for us; (2) it sobers and steadies the mind by giving it a
healthy sense of its very limited capacities; (3) it gives us an
occasion of exercising most noble worship of our Creator by
submitting and conforming our highest faculties to His; (4) it
gives us the firmest certitude in regard to the sublimest truths;
lastly (5) if, besides superrational truths, God should also reveal the principal truths in regard to man's origin, his place in
the universe, his final destiny and the means of attaining it,
his relations to his fellow-man and his Maker, his rights and

duties, etc.—truths, indeed, many of which, at least, are absolutely speaking, within the reach of cultivated human reason—such a revelation would be an incalculable benefit to the human race, as furnishing all men, lettered and ignorant, with a secure and easy means of acquiring perfect certitude in regard to the most important truths.

(c) Hence, supposing a revelation of such truths to have been made—which, as being a matter of fact, is to be proved by historical arguments just as any other fact—we should have **two orders of knowledge emanating from the same Eternal Source of Truth.** The one would be elaborated by reason, acting as its Maker fitted it to act in accordance with the laws of thought upon a basis of self-evident data; the other would consist of a body of truths divinely revealed, many of which at least, are supernatural (or super-rational). The latter would be in every way the higher and nobler order, and if entrusted for interpretation and exposition to an infallible teacher, would be as a pillar of light to guide the steps of reason, and save her from the many mazes of error.

(d) **The formal act of divine faith is,** as we have just said, intrinsically and wholly supernatural, i. e., it is **the assent of a supernaturally elevated mind to a certain truth, for a supernatural motive,** i. e., the supernatural revelation of God. We know, moreover, that it is a free act; for, it is a meritorious act. In the act of divine faith, then, *as such,* the intellect is not necessitated to assent by the objective evidence of the truth to which it assents; its assent is, therefore, determined by the free will. Again, the act of the will which *commands* the formal assent of faith is supernatural, i. e., elicited by the supernaturally elevated will. But this act of the will, to be a human, rational act, presupposes as *conditions* certain previous intellectual acts which in themselves, and absolutely, are within the reach of unaided reason, though, *de facto,* so far forth as they postitively dispose the mind for the formal act of faith, they are elicited by the help of supernatural grace.

Thus, the unaided mind can understand, at least obscurely, the terms of the proposition; it can see that the proposition is not in evident contradiction with the evident truths of reason; it can see that the truth in question is *evidently credible,* and that it is an *evident rational duty* to believe it.   Hence, **the assent of faith, far from being against reason, is such, that to refuse it is irrational.**   Hence, it is the Catholic doctrine that no adult can be received into the Church until he is certain that it is his duty, in prudence, to assent to Her teaching.

Nor can we, as rational beings, be indifferent as to whether God has given us a revelation or not.   Our reason will tell us that this is God's world, and that we are God's, absolutely and entirely at every moment of our lives, and that our first and essential duty is to use the natural means He has given us to find out what it is He would have us to do, and then to go and do it.   The man who denies this duty can, as the man who denies the facts of revelation, be proved to a demonstration to be acting irrationally.

(e)   But supposing the fact of supernatural revelation and our dutiful acceptance of the truths so proposed to us, **can these truths ever contradict the objectively evident knowledge which we acquire by the natural exercise of our reason?**   The question on the face of it is absurd; for it is asking, can God contradict Himself? can God lie? Of course, He cannot.   If He could, He would not be God.   Our faculties are from Him, and if their normal, rational use leads us to form certain judgments, He is accountable for those judgments. The objects around us, from the contemplation of which we derive our natural knowledge, have their being, and consequently their truth, from Him; and hence the knowledge we gather from them is ultimately derived from Him.   The truths of revelation come from Him immediately; hence, if there could be a contradiction between these rational and super-rational truths, as one of two contradictories must be false, it would follow that God had lied—that He was God and not God at the same time. When, then, we hear talk of the conflict between science and faith, all it shows is this, that the speaker is mistaken in his understanding either of the truths of revelation or of those of science. If he saw both orders of truth as they really are, he would see, not conflict, but harmony, as God intends.

(f) From what we have been saying, it follows that all **opinions, theories, hypotheses, etc.,** which in *themselves* or their *consequences* **contradict a revealed truth, or any of its necessary consequences,** are *ipso facto*, **proved false;** and that if there be an infallible custodian and exponent of revelation, he has the right and duty to pronounce upon them and condemn them. Nor can this be said to hinder the progress of science, any more than the pilot who keeps the ship off rocks and sand-banks can be said to hinder her progress into harbor.

140. **Supernatural revelation is not the ultimate motive of all perfect natural certitude;** for here, too, as in all other uses of testimony, before we can assert with certainty to what a witness attests, we must be certain, as a prior condition of our assent, that our witness exists, that he has spoken, that he is trustworthy, that we understand, at least obscurely, what he says, etc., for, either we *see* all these things ourselves or we *believe* them on others' testimony. In the former case, assent to testimony clearly implies, as a necessary condition, intrinsic evidence of certain truths; in the latter case, the same difficulty recurs, i. e., how do I know that this new witness exists, has spoken, is trustworthy? etc., *ad infinitum*.

Article II.—The Intrinsic Motive of Certitude.

We have already said that the intrinsic motive of certitude

is the intrinsic objective evidence, either mediate or immediate, of the truth of fact to which we give our perfectly
certain assent. Before going further, it will be well to explain
some of these terms.

141. We have already defined what is meant by a perfectly certain assent. We know, too, what a motive of assent
is, and what an intrinsic motive is. **Evidence** is, literally,
Visibility, Seeableness. Now, that an object may be visible
to me, two things are requisite, viz.: (1) That it be visible in
itself, i. e., an extended, colored, illuminated object; (2) That
this visibility manifest itself to my eyes. Again, if one is
asked what makes the object visible in itself, one can answer
that it is nothing really distinct from the colored, illuminated
object itself considered in relation to an actual or possible
faculty capable of perceiving it, i. e., the living eye.

But though the word *evidence* literally belongs only to
objects of sight, yet it is used of the objects of *all* our cognitive
faculties; and thus it may be broadly defined. The intrinsic
knowableness of an object clearly manifesting itself to a cognitive faculty.

Hence, it is clear that evidence, in the strict sense of the
word, is something *objective;* nay, is simply the object of our
knowledge manifesting or showing itself to our cognitive faculties—something quite independent of us and of our thoughts
of it, which would be just what it is whether we perceived it
or not.

What we mean, then, by **objective evidence** as a motive
of assent is this: The objective necessity of uniting or separating subject and predicate, manifesting itself to the mind,
and compelling the mind to judge accordingly; or, The objective identity or diversity of the two terms of judgment,
so manifesting itself to the mind as to necessitate assent or
dissent; or, again, The necessary objective relation between

subject and predicate manifesting itself to the mind, and necessitating assent to the clearly objective truth.

142. Now, as we have already said, the objective necessity of uniting or separating subject and predicate may be either *metaphysical* (i. e., when the contradictory is absolutely impossible), or *physical* (*i. e.,* when the contradictory is impossible, unless in the hypothesis that the ordinary laws of nature have been suspended or counteracted), or *moral* (*i. e.,* when the contradictory is impossible, unless on the hypothesis that man has contradicted the natural tendencies of his being). Accordingly, **evidence is either metaphysical, physical or moral.** In the first case, the objective truth or fact here and now clearly manifesting itself to my mind, *is,* and could not, on any supposition, *not be.* In the second case, though the truth or fact here and now manifesting itself to my mind, *is;* yet it *might not have been,* had God willed to suspend the laws of nature. In the third case, though the truth or fact actually manifesting itself to my mind, *is;* yet it *might not have been,* had men willed to contradict the natural tendencies of their being.

143. **Evidence is either immediate or mediate,** according as the objective necessity of uniting subject and predicate manifests itself to the mind, either immediately, or as a necessary logical consequence of immediately evident premises. In both cases we see that, at least here and now, the subject requires the union or separation (as the case may be) of the predicate.

144. In the assent of faith, as we have said, we do not *see* any intrinsic necessity of uniting subject and predicate, or that the subject, as it stands, requires the predicate; but we do *see* the *authority* of the witnesses or that the *subject,* These Witnesses, in the present circumstances, necessarily requires the predicate Cognizant and Truthful. Hence the truth of fact,

which we believe, with perfect certainty, is said to be **extrinsically evident,** i. e., the necessity of uniting subject and predicate is manifested to us, not by its own, but by a borrowed light. Again, such a truth or fact is said to be *evidently credible,* i. e., we have intrinsic evidence of the authority of the witnesses on whose testimony we assent to it.

145. **Intrinsic objective evidence is an infallible motive of perfect certitude.**

Proof.—Intrinsic objective evidence is the objective truth manifesting itself to the mind, as it actually is. But what actually is, cannot not be. Therefore, a judgment motived by intrinsic objective evidence is necessarily in conformity with its object—is, therefore, infallibly true.

NOTE.—As truth is the proper object of the mind, and as the mind is not a free faculty, it follows that when the mind is brought face to face with the evident objective truth, it cannot, unless its natural action be interfered with, help perceiving it, any more than our sight can help perceiving the colored extended object before it. We say *unless its natural action be interfered with!* for, as the will can close the eye, or turn it away from an object, so it can, in certain cases, turn the mind away from the evident truth. Thus:

(a) In regard to truths which are *immediately* evident all the will can do is to turn the mind away from their consideration; and even this is often impossible, *e. g.,* when they obtrude themselves upon us, so to say, in spite of ourselves, *e. g., s*uch truths as our own existence the principle of contradiction, etc. But in some cases it can really divert the intellect from the immediately evident truth and engage it upon the sophisms which are intended to establish its contradictory.

(b) In regard to truths that are *mediately* evident. If the will cannot hinder the mind from assenting to the premises, still it may divert the mind from comparing them together, and thus from assenting to the logical consequence from them. If the reasoning is complicated and abstruse, of course it is all the easier for the will to interfere.

Hence, there is a true sense in which we may say that all our mediate certitude is *free,* whether based on reasoning or on authority. The *intellect,* of course, is not free to give or withhold its assent in the presence of evident objective truth; but the *will* is free to turn attention *from* the *motives,* and fix it only *on* the *apparent reasons* which favor the contradictory.

145. **The comparative value of the different motives of certitude:**

(a) Other things being equal, intrinsic evidence is a higher motive than extrinsic, as giving greater satisfaction to the mind.

(b) Metaphysical evidence is a higher motive than physical, and physical than moral, for the same reason.

(c) The certitude of the assent of *divine truth* is strongest, because its subjective and objective causes are the highest and most perfect.

Article III.—The Ultimate or Fundamental Motive or Perfect Natural Certitude.

146. **By the ultimate or fundamental motive of certitude,** we mean that on which all other motives are based, to which they are ultimately reducible, and independently of which they have no force as rational motives, and which, moreover, is itself manifestly and necessarily connected with the truth.

Now, we have already seen that testimony cannot be this ultimate motive of natural certitude.

Nor can it be *verification by the senses;* for this is at best applicable only in the case of judgments concerning individual material objects, whereas the greater and nobler part of our knowledge regards the universal and spiritual, the scientific and philosophical; to make this, therefore, the ultimate motive of all certitude, is to deny all intellectual knowledge, and to reduce man to the level of the brute.

Nor can it be *consciousness;* for this merely informs me of the fact that *I am* certain, and does not (except in regard to internal facts) even assign the motive of my certitude, much less *constitute* the motive of it.

Nor can it be a *blind tendency to believe;* for this instead of giving a motive for rational certitude, would make all our knowledge unintelligent and motiveless.

Nor is it *clear and distinct ideas;* for these do not necessarily imply true *judgment.*

Nor is it a *consistency* or agreement with my other judgments; for a number of propositions may be quite consistent with one another, and yet the whole system very far from conformity with objective reality—a consistent novel is not necessarily true history.

Nor is it *the inconceivability of the opposite.* Some writers take *inconceivable* as synonymous with *unimaginable.* In this sense to say that what is *inconceivable* is impossible or untrue, is simply to deny all intellectual knowledge. Others mean by inconceivably the mere *inability* of the *human* mind to conceive a given union or separation of subject and predicate (*negative* inconceivability). But it does not follow that a thing is untrue or impossible because it is above and beyond my power of conception. Finally, a proposition is inconceivable in the strict and accurate sense of the word when it is clearly seen to be a contradiction in terms, self-destructive (*positive inconceivability*). The contradictory of such a proposition is indeed necessarily true, but even here our ultimate motive for assenting to it is the *objective evidence* either of its own truth, or of the positive inconceivability of the opposite.

We have, therefore, to look elsewhere for our ultimate motive. Now, suppose I put my hand on the stove when the fire is well lighted. I at once form the judgment, This is hot. Why do I form this judgment, and why is my judgment true? The stove is not hot because *I perceive* that it is hot; but because *it is hot* I perceive that it is so, and my judgment is true. It would be hot, and the judgment, This stove is hot, would be true if I were a thousand miles away. In a word, my judgment is not the cause of the objective truth, but the objective truth is the cause of my true judgment. In the same way, the judgment, Two and two are four, is not true because I perceive or feel that it is so; it would be true if I never existed   Hence, the ultimate motive of perfectly certain assent is somthing independent of us and our faculties—something objective.

153. **The ultimate motive of perfect natural certitude is intrinsic objective evidence.**

NOTE.—We speak here of *natural certitude,* and hence exclude the assent of *divine faith* in which the assent is supernatural, as proceeding from supernatural subjective and objective cases, and therefore firmer than any merely natural evidence could necessitate or justify.

Proof.—That is the ultimate motive of assent, which underlies all other motives, and on which their value as motives depends, and which is itself immediately perceived to be so necessarily connected with the objective truth that it necessarily compels the assent of the mind with absolute exclusion of all fear of error. But intrinsic objective evidence is such a motive.

(a) That *evidence* is the ultimate basis on which all

other motives rest, is clear from what we have already said of the extrinsic motives of certitude.

(b) That it is necessarily connected with the *objective* truth is also clear; for it is itself the objective truth clearly manifesting itself to the mind; and since the mind, while seeing that a thing *actually is,* cannot at the same time see or fear that it *is not,* it cannot help assenting without fear of error to the objective truth so manifesting itself.

Hence, as objective truth is the measure of subjective truth, objective evidence is the ultimate rule or standard or **criterion** by which subjective truth or the truth of our judgments, is to be measured.

NOTE.—The intrinsic evidence of certain axiomatic truths is so manifest to all who have the use of reason that they may be regarded as tests or standards by which we may determine the truth of other less obnoxious propositions. In this sense such axioms, especially the Principle of Contradiction, are called criteria of truth.

In the preceding pages we have considered the process of correct thinking, the nature of true thought, the possibility of attaining it, the faculties with which we are endowed for this purpose, and the motives which assure us of the possession of truth; and we have seen that as long as we are true to nature we are safe from error. "That we fall into error happens not from a defect in our nature, but from a defect in the employment of our faculties or in the use of our free will. . . . But if all our errors may be traced to the will it may seem strange that we should ever be deceived, since nobody wishes to be deceived. But it is one thing to wish *to be deceived,* another, to wish *to assent to something which involves error.* Truly no one wishes to be deceived, but there are few who do not sometimes wish to assent to what involves error."—Descartes.

METAPHYSICS.

ITS DEFINITION AND DIVISION.

I. Metaphysical means literally *beyond* the *physical*. If, then, we take the *physical,* as those who originally used the word seem to have done, as synonymous with the *material,* or that which is perceptible by the senses, Metaphysics will mean the Science of Immaterial Things. Now, things, real notes, may be either positively or negatively immaterial: *positively* immaterial if they cannot be realized in or predicated of matter, i. e., if they positively exclude matter; *negatively* immaterial if they neither include nor exclude matter, but can belong either to the material or immaterial. Hence the definition of **Metaphysics** will be The Science of Things which are either Positively or Negatively Immaterial.

II. Metaphysics may therefore be **divided** into General and Special Metaphysics.

General Metaphysics has for its object *negatively* immaterial real being. It is called General because it embraces all orders of beings, material or immaterial.

Special Metaphysics has for its object *positively* immaterial real being, and, strictly speaking, embraces two treatises: **Psychology,** or the science of the human soul; **Natural Theology,** or the science of God. Of late, however, as the *phenomena* of the material world have come to occupy almost exclusively the attention of physics, to the neglect of the nobler investigation of inner natures and ultimate ends, this latter aspect of material things has taken its place as a part of Special Metaphysics under the name of Rational Physics, or **Cos-**

mology. This branch of science has, at least, this much of title to a place in Metaphysics that its object is something suprasensible, i. e., those aspects of material things which lie beyond the limits of sense-perception.

III. We will begin with General Metaphysics as investigating real notes and supplying real principles which are common to all orders of beings. Then, proceeding according to the natural evolution of our knowledge, we shall take up successively Cosmology, Psychology, Natural Theology.

PART TWO.

GENERAL METAPHYSICS.

General Metaphysics, as we have said, is the science of negatively immaterial real being, i. e., the science of real being *as such*, and of those real notes or characters which are peculiar neither to spirit or matter, but may be common to both, *e. g.*, the notes of 'substance,' 'accident,' 'cause,' 'effect,' 'goodness,' 'truth,' etc. Hence the purpose of our present study is

(a) To examine and analyze those real notes which are common to all orders of being, and thus to set them clearly and distinctly before the mind;

(b) To set forth and defend the primary principles which flow from the analysis and comparison of such real notes.

Our subject may be divided into four chapters:

I.   Being and its Transcendental Attributes.
II. The Primary Division of Beings.
III. Causality.
IV. The Various Grades of Perfection of Being.

CHAPTER I.

REAL BEING AND ITS TRANSCENDENTAL ATTRIBUTES.

ARTICLE I.—REAL BEING.

5. Being is literally the participle of the verb to be. To be means primarily and strictly, *to exist*. Hence, Being means,

strictly, The Existing, that which actually exists. But, by our power of abstraction we can resolve the concept of existing things into two simpler concepts each of which represents an objective reality, viz.: the concept of *existence*, and *that which* has or is conceived to have existence; and to the objects of both concepts the same term being is applied.

Hence **Real Being** may signify either *existence*, or *that which* exists or is capable of existing. Now, considering that which exists or is capable of existence in relation to existence we may regard it either as positively *having* the act of existence, and then we have *actual* or existent being; or we may regard it as positively *without* the act of existence though capable of it, and in this case we have purely potential or *possible* being; or, finally, we may fix our thought only on itself and prescind from its actual existence or non-existence, and then we have *transcendental* being, the *Existible*, purely and precisely as such, without any regard to its *state* of existence or non-existence. It is in this last sense that Real Being and its synonyms, Thing, Entity, Reality, are taken in the present chapter.

NOTE (1).—As Being has two significations, so also, its opposite, **Nothing,** may be taken in two senses, viz.: either as opposed to *actually exsitent* being, or as opposed to *existible* being. In the former case we have *relative* nothing, *as,* 'when we say that the soul which God will create a year hence, is now nothing,' i. e., it is now non-existent though capable of receiving existence. In the latter case we have *absolute* nothing, *as,* 'when we say that a square circle is nothing,' i. e., it is not only non-existent, but incapable of ever receiving existence.

The *concept* of Nothing is formed by representing a reality *as wanting*.

(2) **Logical Being,** ens rationis, is that which is *incapable* of *extra-conceptual existence*, i. e., it can be *repre-*

sented in a concept, but the *contents* of that concept cannot be *realized* outside of the thinking mind, *e. g.,* 'the object represented by a reflex universal idea,' etc.

6. Real being, as above described, is:

(1). A *transcendental note,* i. e., it belongs to all that is not absolute nothing, whether existent or non-existent, whether substance or accident, whole or part, etc. Hence, it has the greatest possible *extension.*

(2).—It is a *most simple* note, incapable of resolution into other real notes, while all others can be resolved into it. Hence it has the least possible *comprehension.*

(3).—As predicated of its inferiors it is *not* an *equivocal* term; for they all agree, at least in this, that they are existible realities, not absolute nothings.

(4).—*Nor* is it a *generic* term; for the differential addition which contracts a genus neither includes nor is included in the notes of the genus it contracts, *e. g.,* 'we cannot say that rationality includes or is included in animality; while, on the contrary, of every conceivable real differential note, we can and must say it is an Entity, a Something.'

(5).—*Nor* yet is it a *univocal* term; for the infinite and finite, substances and accidents are not equally and independently beings.

(6).—Hence is is an *analogical* term of *intrinsic attribution, i. e.,* what it expresses is intrinsic in each of its inferiors, but not equally and independently in each.

(7).—Hence the objective concept of real being as such is contracted to its inferiors, not by the *addition* of notes which are not Being, but by conceiving and expressing in thought the special *modes* and determinations of that which was at first conceived merely as a Being, a Something. The former concept is *distinct;* the latter, *indistinct;* as if one looking at a room full of boys should first think of them confusedly as a large number and then distinctly as exactly sixty-five.

NOTE.—The **Infinite Being**, God, is, as we shall see, unthinkable as non-existent, while it would imply no contradiction of thought to conceive the whole universe of finite things as non-existent. Again, God possesses, or rather is eternally and independently, infinite pure perfection, without any limitation or admixture of imperfection; whereas, finite things are dependent and limited and lack more of perfection than they possess.

Hence, God is really the *primary analogate* to whom the title Real Being completely and independently belongs, and hence He is called in Holy Scripture, The Being; while finite beings, though our concept of being is first derived from them, are in reality but secondary analogates.

7. The **essence** of a being is given in the answer to the question, What is it? This answer may be given with various degrees of distinctness, *e. g.*, in answer to the question, What is a horse? it may be said, 'it is a substance,' 'a living, sentient substance,' etc., and all these answers, as far as they go, give us true *essential* characteristics. But in the strict sense of the word, in which we use it here, essence signifies the sum of real notes, which is *requisite* and *sufficient* to constitute a being the *specific* being, it is *e. g.*, 'a horse.'

Now it is clear that every being has an essence, which constitutes it the determinate specific being it is and that it cannot lose any of its essential notes without ceasing to be the being it is; and furthermore, that there is no thinkable point of space or time in which all these notes are not requisite and sufficient to constitute it the specific being it is.

But the further question arises, **Can we know what constitutes the specific essences of things?** Can we give complete essential definitions of things? Now to limit our question it must be admitted that in *moral* and *mathematical* science we can define with accuracy, 'humility,' 'patience,' 'theft,' 'murder,' etc.; as we can assign distinctly all that is necessary and sufficient to constitute 'a circle,' a 'triangle,' etc. The question then amounts to this, Can we know the intrinsic specific constituents of any of the *physical* things in the world around us?

Our answer is that we can and do attain to true, though imperfect, knowledge of the essences of many things in nature. For, by legitimate induction we can know properties of things which are independent of individual and accidental circumstances. Among these properties we can distinguish those which a given class of things, A, has *in common* with other classes of things, B. C. D, and those which are *peculiar to itself*. Finally, from the character of these constant common and peculiar properties, we can know the character of the *intrinsic principles* from which they flow, and thus we reach the generic and differential elements of the specific essence A.

This knowledge may well be called imperfect, as not being immediate and *intuitive*, but mediate and *discursive*, and only reached with difficulty after much patient study. It is no child's play to formulate essential definitions of things.

NOTE.—As the word **perfection** is often used as a synonym for entity, we may explain it briefly here. *Perfect,* etymologically, means *completely made;* but in common usage the word signifies that which has all it needs, to be complete in essence and action.

Hence the *perfections* of a thing are all of those elements, whether really distinct or not, which go to constitute its essence and render it capable of faultless action proportionate to its place in the hierarchy of beings. Each such element is called a *partial perfection*. All together constitute the *total perfection* of the thing.

A *pure* perfection is one whose objective concept does not imply the exclusion of any higher perfection, *e. g.,* 'intellect' as such. A *mixed* perfection, on the contrary, is one whose concept implies the exclusion of some higher perfection, *e. g.,* 'corporeal substance.' Hence the saying, "It has the defects of its perfections."

8. From the concept of Real Being flow three primary judgments or principles, which are as universal and objective as the concept from which they are derived.

(a) Comparing Being with itself, we have the **Principle of Identity,** Being is Being. It may be variously expressed, according to the sense in which the word Being is taken, *e. g.,* "the existible is existible," "what actually exists, actually exists," "a determinate essence is the determinate essence it is," etc. That this principle is not a mere tautology is evident from the way in which men use such expressions as, "Business is business," "A man's a man for a' that."

Applied to Logic, the principle gives us as a primary law of thought, that the mind must abide by its affirmations and negations.

(b) Comparing Being with its opposite, Not-being or Nothing, we have the **Principle of Contradiction,** Being is not Nothing. This again, may be variously formulated, e. g., 'the existible is not, under the same respect, non-existible,' 'the existent is not at the same time non-existent,' 'a given essence cannot at the same time be not that given essence,' etc.

Applied to Logic, it may be formulated thus, 'The mind must not, under the same respect, affirm and deny the same predicate of the same subject.'

(c) Lastly, again comparing Being with Not-Being, we get the **Principle of Excluded Middle.** It may be thus formulated, 'Every assignable combination of notes is either existible or non-existible,' 'every existible being is either actually existent or non-existent,' 'every real being either has a given real note, A, or it has not.'

In Logic we have the corresponding law that 'Every clearly defined subject, A, either admits a clearly defined predicate, B, or it does not.'

ARTICLE II.—UNITY.

9. The **transcendental attributes** of Being are so called because they are coextensive, identical in fact, with Being, and merely express aspects of every Real Being not explicitly conveyed in the word Being itself.

These transcendental attributes are Unity, Truth, Goodness. The first is called an *absolute* attribute, as being predicable of every real Being considered in itself. The others are called relative attributes, as belonging to every real Being considered in relation to *cognition* and *appetition* respectively.

10. **Unity** or Oneness means the absence of division, *indivision*. Now, as we have said in Logic (20, etc.), things may be divided into *constituent,* or into *subjective parts.* Hence we have four kinds of indivision or unity.

Indivision into *constituent* parts is called *formal* unity. Indivision into *subjective* parts is called *individual* or *numerical* unity.

(a) Unity of *simplicity,* when the Being is not composed of constituent parts, and is therefore not only *undivided,* but *indivisible.*

NOTE.—There is a simplicity of *imperfection,* i. e., when the object represented by an idea has *so little of reality* as to be *indivisible; e. g.,* 'the contents of the idea of transcendental Being,' 'a mathematical point,' etc. This may be called *negative* or *abstract* simplicity.

There is also a simplicity of *perfection,* i. e., when one indivisible Being possesses in its simple reality the *equivalence* of many perfections, *e. g.,* 'the human soul,' etc. This may be called *positive* or *real* simplicity; and it is more or less perfect, according as *all* composition, metaphysical and physical, or only *physical* composition is excluded.

(b) Unity of *composition,* when the Being, though *actually* undivided, yet consists of constituent parts into which it is *divisible.*

NOTE.—In a composite Being the indivision, and, consequently, the unity may be more or less perfect according to the character of the component parts and the manner of their union. Thus we have unity in the strict and *proper* sense of the word, *unum per se,* when either

(1) Some at least of the components are entitatively and intrinsically incomplete and imperfect in themselves and are destined to find their complete perfection only through their union with the other elements of the compound, *e. g.,* 'the human soul and body,' or

(2) When the parts into which the Being is divisible, but not divided, have identical extremities or common limits, *e. g.,* 'the parts of continuous extension.'

On the contrary the unity is only *improperly* so called, and *accidental, unum per accidens,* when the components are complete entities in themselves, and remain such, intrinsically unchanged in the compound, such, *e. g.,* is the unity of 'a watch' *artificial* unity, of 'a basket of eggs,' mere *aggregation.*

(c) Unity of *individuality* or *singularity,* when a Being is undivided and indivisible *into many such as itself,* i. e., into *subjectve* parts. This is often called *numerical* unity.

(d) Unity of *universality* when a Being is conceived as *divisible into many such as itself,* i. e., into *subjective* parts. This is called *logical* unity, and is exemplified in the object of a *reflex* universal idea.

11. **Every real Being as such is formally one.** For, either it is a *simple* Being, and then it is undivided and indivisible, or it is a *composite* Being; and then, though it is divisible, yet so long as it is a Being, even a heap of stones, it is undivided; else it would be, not Being, but Beings.

12. Every real Being is individually one, i. e., undivided and indivisible into many really distinct Beings, each of which is itself. For, if it were so divided it would, at the same time and under the same respect, be one Being and not one, *e. g.*, "If Λ were divided into a, b, c, each of which is A, then it would at the same time be one A and not one A, but three A's, i. e., it would be itself and not itself at the same time." Hence, though innumerable Beings, *like* A in all respects, can be produced, *this* Being, A, can never be *duplicated*.

Note (1).—It is not the same thing to say one and the same individual *nature* may belong to three distinct *persons*, or that one and the same individual Being may be *in many places* at the same time, as to say that one and the same individual Being may be at the same time, and under the same respect, one and many. The latter proposition is an evident contradiction in terms, which cannot be said or proved of the two former.

(2).—Without entering into any controversy on the subject, we may say in passing, that in a concrete individual Being, *e. g.*, 'a man,' there is no *real* distinction between his *specific* nature, that by which he is a *man*, and his individuality, that by which he is *this man*. His concrete nature and his Thisness are but one and the same real entity represented in thought by intrinsically different concepts.

One is often used in the sense of *unique*, i. e., that which has not got its *like or equal*, the sole, the only one of its *kind*, *e. g.*, one God, one true Church. If the Being *could* have its like, though as a matter of fact it has not, the uniqueness is *accidental;* if it *could not* have its like or equal, the uniqueness is *essential.*

13. Akin to Unity is **Identity** or *Sameness,* the oneness of Being with itself. It implies a comparison. If terms compared be really *one* Being, the identity is *real, e. g.,* 'This is the *same* (identical) pencil you gave me a year ago.' If the terms compared be not really one, but only *similar,* whether in nature or qualities, and therefore representable by one concept, the identity is *logical, e. g.,* 'My book is the same as yours.' Hence, in this last sense identity merely means likeness.

It is in this last sense that the axiom, "Two things which are identical with a third are identical with each other," is *usually* taken. Hence, for the validity of the axiom: (1) the two must be compared with *one* and *the same* third, (2) under exactly the *same respect,* and (3), the conclusion must be that they are alike precisely in that respect.

NOTE.—*Physical* identity is had when the terms compared are really and physically one: *e. g.,* "The substance of your soul is the same now as it was the day you were born." On the contrary, when the terms compared are not really and physically the same, but only according to the common estimate of men, the identity is *moral, e. g.,* 'The hand that signed the Declaration of Independence was the same that years before had cut down the cherry tree.'

14. Opposed to Unity is **Multitude** or *Plurality,* which may be described as Beings or Units divided off from each other, one of which is not the other.

Number is distinguished from mere Multitude in that it is Multitude as measurable by a common unit. Hence, for Number we need (1) plurality, (2) some sort of similarity in the several units, (3) a collecting or gathering together of the several units into a sort of unity under a common concept, on account of their similarity. Thus, if you have five men you cannot number them unless you prescind from individuation, and take as your common unit man as such; if you have five men, four horses, three stones and two thoughts, you must prescind from individual, specific and generic differences, and take as your common unit Thing, Being. Hence, *number,* as such, is beyond the reach of *sense-perception.*

15. The opposite of Identity is **Distinction** or 'Otherness.' Two things are distinct when one is not the other.

(a) If the Otherness is real, independently of our thoughts about it, the distinction is *real.* Thus between you and your neighbors, between your soul and your body, there is a real distinction.

When the distinct things are such that each exists, or can exist apart from the others, we have a *major* real distinction.

When the distinct things are such that either cannot exist apart from the other, we have a *minor* real distinction, *e. g.,* 'between our mind and its thoughts,' 'between a cannon ball and its velocity,' etc.

If we have no real Otherness, but only one and the same thing, as represented by various concepts of the mind, the distinction is called *mental, e. g.,* 'the distinction between six and half-a-dozen,' 'between Washington and the first President of the United States,' etc.

If the various concepts thus representing one and the same reality are *intrinsically identical* the distinction is said to be *purely logical, e. g.,* the distinction between man and rational animal.

But if these various concepts of one and the same thing are *intrinsically different,* i. e., different in contents or comprehension, the distinction is called *virtual,* or a mental distinction with a foundation in fact, inasmuch as one and the same object is capable of being represented in thought by intrinsically different concepts. Thus one and the same person may give ground for concepts of himself of such various comprehension as "society angel" and "domestic devil." In such cases each concept represents one and the same whole, but neither represents it *wholly.*

Lastly, if the intrinsically different concepts, representative of one and the same indivisible thing, are such that one neither formally nor implicitly expresses the notes represented in the other, we have an *adequate* or *complete virtual distinction;* and each concept gives what is called a metaphysical part of the whole. Thus, 'the human soul,' which is a *simple entity,* and therefore without real physical parts, may be considered as a *principle of vegetative life and as a principle of intellectual life,* neither of which concepts *implicitly* includes the contents of the other.

If, on the contrary, the concepts are such that one implicitly though not formally includes the notes of the other, we have an *inadequate virtual distinction.* Thus the concept of infinite self-existent power is not indeed, *formally* the concept of infinite wisdom or holiness, but essentially *implies* their contents.

Note.—The reason why our minds form intrinsically different concepts of one and the same simple object is to be found, *partly,* in the *perfection* of the object whose simple entity is virtually equivalent to several distinct entities, and *partly* in the *imperfection* of our *knowledge,* which cannot grasp this simple entity wholly by one act and express it in one adequate, distinct concept, but must represent it piecemeal, so to say, by many *true* but *inadequate* concepts.

ARTICLE III.—TRUTH.

16. As we speak of true thoughts so we speak of true things, *e. g.,* 'of true gold,' 'true friends,' 'true courage,' etc. And if we consider what is meant by the **truth of things,**

we shall find it is their *conforming to ideas, e. g.*, 'a true friend' is one who has all the characters comprehended in the idea of friend. This correspondence with an idea of itself is *actual,* if the Being is a term or object of actual thought, is actually known. It is *potential or aptitudinal,* if the Being is capable of being a term or object of true thought, is knowable, is capable of *determining* and *terminating* a true concept of itself.

17. **Can we say that every being is true,** conformed and conformable to a true idea of itself, known and knowable for what it is? To answer the question satisfactorily we must assume certain propositions which will be proved, independently of the present article, in other places.

God is an eternal, self-existent, infinitely perfect Being, possessing in His simple, infinite essence all pure perfection in an infinitely perfect way, so that every Being is a Being, only inasmuch as it is in its grade and measure a far-off, limited imitation of God. This infinite, "ocean of all-perfect Being" is the eternal object of the Divine Mind, which comprehends it and its imitability and all its possible imitations, and consequently all finite things, in eternal, infinitely perfect thought. Hence every *existible* being is an *actual object* of eternal, true thought, and is, therefore, true.

Furthermore, nothing exists, or has ever existed, or will ever exist, even a child's transient thought, which God has not foreknown and ordained or permitted and produced or co-operated to produce; so that there never can be an *existent* Being which does not depend for its existence on the divine thought, just as a work of art depends for its existence on the mind of the artist who conceived it. Hence, again, every *existent* being is an object of eternal, perfect thought, and is therefore true.

Lastly, among existent imitations of God there are finite intelligences very limited indeed in capacity, but still modeled after God's own mind and so capable of apprehending more or less perfectly the Divine Being and its imitations.   In regard to these, therefore, also every Being is true, i. e., capable of determining and terminating true knowledge of itself.

Creatures correspond to God's knowledge of them and are capable of making themselves known, and tend to make themselves known just for what they are to finite intellects made in the image and likeness of God.

All things, then, are true, *primarily,* in regard to the Divine Mind in which they are actually, perfectly and eternally represented, *secondarily,* in regard to finite minds in which they are capable of being more or less perfectly represented. Hence we might say that *things* are ultimately true because they correspond to the divine ideas; and that *our thoughts* are true because, being conformed to things, they thus correspond with the thought of God.

18.   Hence when things are spoken of as *false,* the epithet can only be applied to them by a metonymy, i. e., as *accidentally,* by their likeness to other things, *giving occasion* to the imperfect finite mind to judge them to be what they are not. But in regard to God, nothing can be called false; even the sinful act itself, though in discord with His law, is eternally before His mind in all its deformity.

ARTICLE IV.—GOODNESS.

19.   We have said that the perfections of a thing are those elements really or virtually distinct, which constitute its essence and render it capable of attaining and holding the place proportioned to its nature in the commonwealth of things.   Now, everything has, or may be conceived to have, an inclination, tendency, appetite for all that goes to fill up the measure of its adequate perfection; and that which is in any way capable of satisfying such inclination, tendency, etc., is said to be good for that Being.   Hence, **goodness** is usually defined, *entity as*

appetible. But as entity is appetible only inasmuch as it really or apparently, completely or partially, perfects that which desires it, the more radical definition of goodness would be, *entity as perfective,* or Being, as connoting some appetite, tendency or capacity which it is capable of satisfying.

20. That, then, which perfects a Being is good for it. Now, between that which perfects and that which is perfected, between the *perfective* and the *perfectible,* there may be only a mental distinction, *e. g.,* we may consider 'a beautiful flower as perfected by all that which makes it what it is, and we may even attribute to it a sort of metaphorical joy and gladness in the possession of itself.' In this case we have Being as self-perfective, good *for* itself, good *in* itself. This is called the **absolute goodness of a thing,** i. e., its goodness in and for itself, apart from all reference to other things really distinct from itself.

This absolute goodness is adequate, if the Being has all that is needed to constitute its essence, to perfect its activities, and completely to satisfy all its tendencies, capacities, etc., *else* it is only *partial* or *inadequate.*

If, on the contrary, we do not consider the Being as self-perfective, but as a perfective, meeting the demands, of something really other than itself, we have what is called its **relative goodness,** i. e., its goodness, a perfectiveness, in regard to another. The various ways in which a thing may be relatively good will give us the divisions of goodness in the next paragraph.

NOTE (1).—There is *another sense* in which a Being may be called absolutely good, i. e., if it has all pure perfection without lack, or limit, or dependence. In this sense, God alone is absolutely good.

(2).—Among absolutely good and adequately good things one may be better than another, i. e., if its nature requires and admits higher and greater perfections, *e. g.,* 'an adequately good man is a *better* Being than an adequately good humming-bird.'

21. That which is an object of desire or affection may be so, either for its own sake, or for the sake of something different *from itself*. In the latter case we have what is called the **useful good,** the goodness of *utility*. Such an object is really desirable, yet not in and for itself, but as a means, remote or proximate, for attaining something which is desirable in and for itself, i. e., its relative goodness consists in its *usefulness*.

Again, that which is desirable in and for itself, may be so, either for the sake of its *objective entity,* as perfective of the appetent subject, *e. g.,* 'wholesome food'; or merely for the *subjective* pleasure it affords, *e. g.,* 'a cigar.' The latter gives us the **pleasurable** or pleasure-giving good, i. e., an object in which a vital faculty, spiritual or sensual, finds rest and repose, whether it be an object really perfective of the appetent suoject or not.

Lastly, that which by its objective entity is perfective of another is called the **befitting good,** i. e., that which is fitted to perfect and is, therefore, a suitable object of appetition for a Being bent on acquiring its perfection.

Taken in a broad sense of the word, in which sense it is also called *natural* good, the *Befitting* Good is *that which by itself* is perfective of a complete nature or of any natural faculty, *e. g.,* 'food is a natural good of animal nature,' 'knowledge is a natural good of the mind.'

Taken in a stricter sense, however, the Befitting Good is that which perfects, and so is a fitting, congruous object of desire for a *rational Being* as such, i. e., for a Being endowed with the power of deliberate, responsible choice. In this sense it is also called *moral good.*

NOTE (1).—One and the same object may be at once use-fully, pleasurably, naturally, morally good for the same sub-ject. But as a moral good, it is desirable under one aspect, as a pleasurable good under another, etc., *e. g.*, '*study*,' '*play*,' '*prayer*,' etc.

(2).—*True* good is that which really perfects the appetent subjects as a simple or composite whole. *Apparent* good is that which, though desired, does not so perfect the subject. Where there are, as there are in every finite Being, many different appetites or tendencies, all other appetites should be subordi-nate to the *primary specific* tendency of the Being; what is unsuitable to it, though agreeing with a lower tendency, is not the true good of the Being.

(3).—*Supernatural* good, in the strict sense of the word, is that which perfects a being in a manner above the exigencies of its own, or of any finite nature, *e. g.*, '*sanctifying grace*,' the *beatific vision of God*,' etc.

22. Every Real Being, as such, is absolutely good. For it is good for itself, as constituting itself the Being that it is, as distinguished from mere nothing.

Every Being is relatively good, i. e., good for *something* else, not for *everything* else. The Infinite Being, God, is good for all finite Being, as their exemplar, efficient and final cause; and finite Beings, in their turn, may be said to be good for God, inasmuch as being imitations of Himself and the work of His hands they are objects of His complacence and loving care. Again, even among finite Beings, one is good for an-other. For the universe is a cosmos of relations and correla-tions, so that it is literally true that a leaf cannot fall from a tree without affecting the equilibrium of the whole. Each material element can enter into some sort of combination with some other. Substance is good for accident, accident for sub-stance, part for whole, or whole for part. Some Beings supply necessaries of life, some pleasure; all are sources of knowledge, and in their way, if properly used, can act a part in lifting up the mind and heart of man to God.

23.   A Real Being, which as such is good, may lack some of the perfections it ought to have, and inasmuch as it is so wanting in due perfection it is called bad *in itself*, or **absolutely bad**. Thus we speak of 'bad food,' 'bad thoughts,' 'a bad lawyer,' etc.

Again, a Real Being, whether quite perfect in itself or not, may be such that, if brought into relation with some other real Being, it destroys or hinders the perfection of the latter. Such a Being is said to be **relatively bad**, i. e., bad for that whose perfection it destroys or hinders.

24.   Hence, **evil** or badness, absolute or relative, is *no positive entity;* for every Being as such is good.

Nor is it a mere *negation;* for no one would say that, *e. g.,* 'ink is bad merely because it is not nutritious.'

But it is a *privation,* or cause of privation, of that which a thing ought to have for its well-being and proportionate action.

25.   A **privation** as such is *non-entity*, absence of entity, which ought to be present, in a given subject.   Hence, evil or badness supposes a *subject* which it informs, as it were, and this subject, as a Being, is good; hence "there is some soul of goodness in things evil"; so that a bad thing is simply a good thing affected by a privation of some perfection it ought to have.

26.   **Absolute evil, or privation of due perfection, is not, it is clear, natural to any Being,** else it could not be called a privation.   Hence, it must be the effect of some cause which hinders or destroys the perfection in question.   But every efficient cause is a real Being, and, as such, is good. Therefore, the efficient cause of evil is good.

But as non-entity, as such, cannot be for its own sake an object of desire, nor in itself a direct effect of positive action, it follows that evil, as such, can only be caused *indirectly* and *accidentally*, i. e., the efficient cause directly producing a positive entity, which, as such, is good, produces indirectly the defect or privation affecting or accompanying it, i. e., produces a *something* which involves a privation.

NOTE (1).—*Physical* evil is privation, or that which causes privation of some natural good in a Being.

Moral evil is privation, or that which causes privation, of due rectitude in the free act of the will. A *sin* is an act of the will freely and deliberately elicited with knowledge of its repugnance to right reason and the law of God. Its formal badness is the lack of due rectitude in the physical act, which, as a physical entity, is good, but is intrinsically and wholly spoiled and marred by privation of the rectitude it ought to have.

(2).—*Physical* evil may sometimes be an object of rational choice, i. e., as a means to attain a higher good, *e. g.*, our lower appetites may and must at times be deprived of what they might legitimately claim, if we wish to strengthen our will and gain control over ourselves. But *moral* evil can never be rationally eligible, for it is necessarily a privation of the highest good of life, and a marring of our noblest faculty.

CHAPTER II.

THE PRIMARY DIVISIONS OF BEING.

27. Every real Being is either

(1). Actually Existent, or merely Possible;

(2). Such that it can *subsist in itself,* without needing another being as a *subject* or sustainer in which to inhere, i. e., a *Substance;* Such that it *cannot* naturally subsist in itself, but needs another being in which it inheres as a subject or sustainer, i. e., an *Accident.*

These two classes of disjunctive attributes which divide all real Being, give us the primary divisions of Being which we are to consider in the present chapter, viz.: *Actual* Being and *Possible* Being, *Substantial* Being and *Accidental* Being. Hence the chapter may be divided into two sections.

SECTION I.—ACTUAL AND POTENTIAL BEING.

ARTICLE I.—ACT AND POTENTIALITY.

28. When we see a block of marble transformed into a statue, our attention is at once called to two kinds of **power or capacity,** viz.: the power or capacity of the marble to *receive* the figure and lineaments of the statue, and the power of the sculptor to *produce* the figure. The latter is called active power; the former, *passive* or receptive power.

The active power may be in a state of inactivity, i. e., not exercising the energies it possesses, *e. g.,* 'the sculptor sitting idly by the unhewn marble.' In the same way the passive power or receptivity may be without that which it is capable of receiving. In both cases the active and passive powers are said to be in a state of *potentiality* or *potency,* and they are perfected by doing and receiving that which they are capable of doing and receiving respectively.

29. **Potentiality** or Potency, therefore, signifies capacity to *receive* perfection, and at the same time connotes the *absence* of that perfection, here and now. In the present article the word is used to signify *passive* or receptive potentiality.

30. **Act** signifies perfection as actually and really, here and now, *present.*

31. To the capacity of an *existing* being to receive a new modification or perfection, corresponds as *Act* this modification or perfection as received by it. This capacity or *receptivity* in an *existing* being is called **subjective potency.** The new modification received may be either *accidental* or *substantial,* and will be called an *accidental* or *substantial act* accordingly.

32. To the capacity of a *non-existent essence* to receive existence, corresponds as *act,* its real existence. The capacity of the non-existent essence, is called **objective potency** or *pure possibility.*

33. The capacity of an existing being to receive new perfection, i. e., its *subjective* potentiality, may be considered in relation to the ordinary agencies at work in nature, and then it is called **natural potentiality;** or it may be considered in relation to the special supernatural power of God, in which case it is called **supernatural or obediential potentiality.**

34. A **Pure Act** is an existent being in which *essence* and *existence,* active *power* and action, are *really* and *ideally identified,* and which is incapable of any intrinsic modification. It is *unthinkable* as non-existent, or as undergoing any intrinsic modification, substantial or accidental. In other words, its essence cannot be conceived as an objective or subjective potentiality. It is therefore *unproduced* by an active power and *unreceived* in any passive power or potentiality. It is wholly independent and unalterable, it is *in* itself and *of* itself, *self-existent.*

35. From the foregoing explanations it is clear that every Being is either a *pure act,* or a *pure potentiality,* or a compound of act and potentiality, i. e., a *mixed act.*

36. **Some axioms** in regard to Act and Potency.

(a) A thing is *perfect* so far forth as it is *actual; imperfect,* so far forth as it is *potential.*

(b) A thing *acts* only inasmuch as it is actual, and *receives* perfection only inasmuch as it is potential.

(c) Potentiality, as such, cannot give itself actuality. Else it would give itself what it has not got. Therefore, no Potential Being can be, of itself alone, the adequate cause of any new perfection it acquires; though, under the influence of some actual agency, it may co-operate in the production of such perfection. Thus, the intellect cannot form any concept unless determined by some object; though, under the determining influence of the object, it reacts and co-operates with it in producing the vital act of knowledge.

(d) Everything susceptible of change is a *mixed act,* i. e., a compound of act and potency.

(e) Absolutely speaking, Act is prior to Potency. For nothing can act unless it exists, or give what it has not got. But if Act were not prior to Potency, this would be the case. For Potency, which, as such, has not actuality, would give actuality.

(f) The ultimate act of every entity is *existence.*

37. A First Cause, as being *first,* cannot have an efficient cause. Therefore, there can be no distinction, not even a virtual distinction, between its essence and its existence, i. e., its essence is inconceivable as a purely possible Being. For if its existence be conceived as something distinct from its essence, then its existence must be conceived, either (1) as communicated to its essence by some extrinsic agency, in which case it would not be a *First* Cause; or (2) its existence must be conceived as *emanating* from its essence, in which case its essence must be conceived as existing before it exists; for nothing can emanate from that which does not exist. Therefore, its existence, being neither received from another nor emanating from its essence, is identical, even in concept, with its essence; and, hence, the essence of the First Cause is actual,

existing Being, an *unreceived Act of Being,* without any admixture of potentiality.

38. Again, the **First Cause is inconceivable as finite or limited in Actual Being.** For limitation results either because the *giver* is unable or unwilling to give more, or because the *receiver* is unable to receive more, or because the *thing possessed,* of its nature, excludes some ulterior perfection. But in the present case, there is neither giver nor receiver; and Actual Being, which is the essence of the First Cause, excludes no pure perfection. Therefore, the essence of the First Cause is unlimited, or infinite actual Being. Hence, the First Cause is an infinite Act of existent Being.

39. A created Being is one which has received existence from a cause distinct from itself. Now, the question may be asked, **In the concrete, existing, created Being, is its essence really distinct from its existence?** St. Thomas, and some of the greatest of ancient and modern philosophers, answer in the affirmative. Their argument amounts to this In the adequate concept or definition of the individual essence of any created Being, existence is not comprehended; therefore, in every such Being existence and essence are two distinct realities. The individuated essence really exists, but in virtue of something really distinct from itself, its acts of existence. Such a being is therefore a *compound* of act and potency, an actuated subjective potentiality.

ARTICLE II.—POSSIBLE BEING.

40. **A thing is said to be possible,** when, though nonexistent, it is *capable* of receiving existence. This capacity to receive existence may be considered absolutely, i. e., in the Being itself, which is said to be possible. So considered it consists of the congruity or *non-contradiction* between the

constitutive notes of the Being. Considered, then, merely as exhibiting a combination of non-contradictory notes, a Being is said to be *intrinsically* or *absolutely* possible.

NOTE.—As our human intellects are so very limited in range, it is clear that it would be the extreme of rashness for us to venture to determine in every case what is intrinsically possible and what is not. We are safe in pronouncing a thing *impossible,* only when we manifestly, *evidently* perceive that its constituents are *contradictory* and mutually destructive, *e. g.,* 'a square circle,' 'a potential First Cause,' 'a thinking stone,' etc.

41. The aptitude of a Being intrinsically possible, to receive existence, may further be considered in regard to the *extrinsic causes* capable of conferring upon it the existence it does not possess. So considered a Being is said to be extrinsically or *relatively possible.* Now, though, in regard to finite created forces, many things intrinsically possible are not extrinsically so; in regard to an omnipotent First Cause, the extrinsic possibility of things is limited only by their intrinsic possibility, every sum of notes not intrinsically self-destructive can, absolutely speaking, be realized and actuated by Omnipotence. Hence, the impossible is no limit on the Divine Power; it is unrealizable, not from any lack of power in the First Cause, but simply because it is *absolutely nothing.*

NOTE (1).—There may be cases where things which, taken separately, present no intrinsic contradiction, yet, when taken together, or in conjunction with certain circumstances, may involve contradictions. These give us the class of *Incompossibles,* i. e., things possible separately, but not conjointly.

(2).—In regard to extrinsic possibility, a thing is said to be *Physically Possible* with respect to an efficient cause which has the power sufficient to produce it; and this even though the circumstances be such that it is *Morally Impossible* for the cause to overcome the difficulties involved in its production.

42. Possible Being, as such,

(a) Is *Relative Nothing,* for it has no existence in the actual order of things;

(b) Yet it is *not Absolute Nothing,* for it can actually exist; it is a positive, thinkable thing; it can be a final cause and a motive of action, etc.: things which cannot be said of absolute Nothing.

43. **The intrinsic possibility of things is ultimately founded:—**

(a) Not on their *actual existence,* for many things are possible which have never existed and will never exist, *e. g.,* 'things good and bad in our own past history which might have been.' Again, that which is mutable and transient cannot be the ultimate foundation of that which is immutable and eternal. But finite existences are mutable and transient, whereas the intrinsic possibility of things is immutable and eternal.

(b) Nor on the *human mind,* for consciousness testifies that our minds do not cause, but merely perceive, the congruity or contradiction of constituent notes. These are congruous or contradictory, quite independently of us and of our thoughts about them.

(c) But *in God,* for God as a necessarily-existing infinite Being contains in the most perfect manner all pure perfection expressed by the word Being. But if the First Cause be such, no real Being is conceivable which is not in some way an imitation of Him. For, if any such Being were conceived it would consist of a reality in no way either formally or eminently contained in the infinite Being, in which case the latter would not be infinite. Again, God to be omniscient, must know all possible things; to act with wisdom in His works, He must be guided by His knowledge of the object He is to produce. But if the intrinsic possibility of things were not ultimately dependent on Him, both His knowledge and His action would be conditioned by and dependent on something anterior to and independent of Himself. He would be obliged in creating to work according to a rule which had no origin in Himself and to which He would, therefore, be subject. But in this case He would not be an absolute, all-perfect, self-sufficient Being, and therefore would not be God.

(d) Yet not on the *Divine Free Will,* for if so, antecedently to the act of the Divine Will, nothing would be possible or impossible, and hence, if God so willed it, a four-sided triangle, a self-existent creature, etc., would be possible, i. e., absolute nothing would be Being and real Being would be absolute nothing: i. e., notes intrinsically contradictory and incompatible would at the same time be congruous and compatible.

(e) Nor on the *Divine Omnipotence,* for the intrinsic possibilities of things are not actually existing entities; but only existing entities are produced by power. Again, if a Being were said to be possible, simply because God could produce it, it would follow that a thing was impossible simply because God could not produce it; and hence either all combinations of notes would be possible, or the ultimate reason of the impossibilities of things would be the limitation of Divine Power, viz.: because God is unable to produce them.

(f) But *immediately* and *formally* in the *Divine Intellect,* for possible Being in regard to God, is like a work of art before its execution in regard to the artist. But in the latter case, whatever being the ideal work of art has, it has it in the mind of the artist, i. e., it is formally represented there. Again, the divine intellect, being infinite in its grasp, must know distinctly all the ways in which the Divine Essence is capable of being imitated, and hence all the possibles must be formally and distinctly represented in the mind of God.

(g) *Ultimately* and *radically* in the *Divine Essence,* for on the one hand, the intellect, as such, does not make but perceives its object. That a mind may know, there must be an object to be known. On the other hand, the Divine Mind cannot be dependent for its knowledge on anything outside of God Himself. Hence the Divine Mind in perceiving and representing the Divine Essence perceives and represents the possibles.

But how? God, as we shall prove in the proper place, is an infinitely perfect Being, and therefore contains in Himself, in an infinitely perfect way, every conceivable perfection. The Divine Mind, eternally contemplating this infinite, self-existent essence, represents It and all its imitations in distinct, infinitely perfect thought. The *imitations* of the Divine Essence, formally represented in that Divine thought are the possibles.

NOTE (1).—Possible beings are not contained in the Divine Essence, either *entitatively* or *representatively;* yet the Divine Essence is that, through the comprehension of which the Divine Mind *knows* all possible beings.

(2)—The Divine Mind contains the possibles *not entitatively,* but *representatively.* Hence, the possibles are not the Divine Ideas, but those objects, non-existent, which are represented in the Divine Ideas.

SECTION II.—SUBSTANCE AND ACCIDENT.

ARTICLE I.—SUBSTANCE.

44. Etymologically, the word **Substance, sub-stare,** means that which underlies, supports something else. Hence it signifies the ultimate substratum which underlies, is affected by, sustains the various non-essential modifications, qualities, activities, phenomena of things. But to be the ultimate sustainer or subject, it must not be itself *subjected* in another.

Hence, it must not need a subject in which to inhere, but must be capable of subsisting in and by itself. Hence, a Substance is that which can subsist in and by itself, that to whose essence it belongs not to subsist in another, as in a subject of inhesion; whereas an **Accident** is that which cannot naturally subsist in itself, that to whose essence it belongs to subsist in another, as in a subject of inhesion.

The best way to realize the difference between substance and accident is to turn our thoughts in upon ourselves, and to consider the multitude, variety and succession of transient thoughts, volitions, movements, etc., which affect and modify the one, same permanently enduring subject, *self*. Hence, two notes go to constitute the essential concept of substance, viz. : Real Being and Independence of a Subject of Inhesion. But to be a subject of inhesion or a sustainer of accidents is not essential to the idea of substance.

NOTE.—When it is said that a substance is a Being which subsists or exists in itself, by itself, etc., all that is meant is, that it does not need a *subject in which to inhere,* in order to exist; not that it does not need the creative and conservative influence of a supreme cause in order to exist. Briefly, we might say that *Perseity,* In-itself-ness, is the essential characteristic of substance as such, *Inaliety,* In-another-ness, is the essential note of accident; while *Aseity,* Of-itself-ness, is the peculiar incommunicable attribute of that self-existent Substance which is the uncaused Cause of existence in all finite Beings.

45. **Our concept of substance as above described represents an objective reality.**

For, every Being that exists, either exists *in itself,* or *in another,* as the subject of inhesion. In the first case we have substance; in the second, accident. If the existence of the first is denied, then we ask what is that in which the second exists?

Either a substance or an accident; if a substance, then we have what we claim; if an accident, then the same question recurs; and so on to infinity, which is absurd, viz.: a multitude of entities sustained without a sustainer.

Again, our consciousness clearly testifies that beneath the ever-varying succession of thoughts, desires, feelings, etc., which fill up our life, there is an enduring, substantial Ego, a *self,* which is the ultimate source of their existence, and the ultimate subject of our varying modifications.

Our external experience, too, enables us to judge with certainty that the men and beasts and plants and minerals around us are not mere accidents, but substantial principles, each an independent unit subsisting in itself. Lastly, to the concurrent testimony of the common sense of mankind, we can add that of our adversaries themselves, who, in soberer moments when the rational nature in them is allowed to speak out, confess with Locke, that "Sensation convinces us that there are thinking ones;" or with Hume, that "'Tis vain to ask whether there be body or not, that is a point which we must take for granted in all our reasonings;" or with Spencer, that "We are compelled to think of a substance *affected* before we think of its *affections.*"

NOTE.—A Real Being, then, is called a Substance, inasmuch as it subsists in itself; it is called a Nature, inasmuch as it is an ultimate intrinsic principle of action; it is called an *Essence,* inasmuch as it possesses all the elements, really or virtually distinct, which are necessary to constitute it a Being complete in its kind or species.

46. An *Incomplete Substance* is one which by its nature is destined to be a *part,* essential or integral, of a physical compound, so that in composition with other incomplete, substantial elements it goes to constitute one complete nature, or first principle of action, *e. g.,* 'the human soul cannot exercise the

functions of sensitive or vegetable life unless it be united in substantial composition with matter, and much less can matter do so unless it be informed by a substantial vital principle.' But when soul and matter are substantially united, we have a New Being, a substantial source of new activities wholly unlike those of either component taken separately.

47. A *Compound Substance* is one which is composed of and can be resolved into, *physical* parts.

A *Simple Substance,* on the contrary, is one that is not composed of or resolvable into, physical parts.

A *Spiritual Substance* is a *simple* substance, whose action and *existence* are *intrinsically* independent of matter.

48. An *Individual Substance,* i. e., one undivided in itself, and divided off from every other, *complete* in itself as a nature, and *self-possessed,* i. e., not actually a part of a physical whole, nor destined by nature to be such a part, is called a **Suppositum,** or **Hypostasis,** as being the ultimate principle of attribution to which are ascribed all the actions, properties, passions, etc., of a Being. Thus the motion of your feet, the knowledge you have acquired, the headache you suffer, your good and evil actions, your faculties, your whole human nature, all are referred to and belong to the whole substantial self-possessed, You. *Self-possession,* For-itself-ness, then, is the special characteristic of a hypostasis; and the more perfectly a subject possesses itself, and its activities, the more perfect it is a hypostasis.

Hence, as an *intellectual* hypostasis possesses itself and controls its actions more perfectly than any other, it is called by a special name, **Person.** *Personality,* then, implies three elements, viz.: (1) an individual intellectual nature, (2) complete as a nature, (3) forming a whole by itself, or self-possessed.

Hence, the Sacred Humanity of Our Lord, though an individual intellectual nature perfect in every human endowment, yet as being possessed, owned as His own, in a way quite mysterious to us, by the Second Person of the Blessed Trinity, has not a human personality; it is the human nature of a Divine Person, and all its gifts and faculties, all its actions and sufferings, are His, and are ultimately attributed to Him, and have all the infinite worth of actions, etc., of a Divine Person.

And as the worth of actions depends on the dignity of the personal agent from whom they ultimately proceed, so, too, the gravity of an offense is chiefly measured by the dignity of the person offended. This is the reason why the personal character of the wrong done by sin should be chiefly insisted upon. The sinful act is inordinate in itself, it is true, but its full deformity is not perceived until we consider who is the *Person* offended.

ARTICLE II.—ACCIDENT.

49. We have said that an *accident* is a Being which cannot, naturally, subsist in and by itself, but needs another Being as a subject of inhesion in which to exist. But we must determine more precisely the special kind of **Inexistence** which is peculiar to accidental Being.

One thing can be said to be in another, either (1) as contained in container, *e. g.*, 'money in a safe,' or (2) as a constitutive part in a substantial whole, *e. g.*, 'the soul in the man,' or (3) as the specific nature in an individual, *e. g.*, 'human nature in Brown,' or (4) as a modification or affection in the thing modified, *e. g.*, 'learning,' 'desires,' 'feeding' in a man; 'heat,' 'color,' 'shape,' 'velocity' in a cannon-ball.

It is in this last sense that accidents are said to exist in a substance as in a subject of inhesion. They are Forms, which affect or modify the subject they inhere in and give it a title to various denominations which do not belong to it considered merely as a substance. *Thus,* 'a man is denominated learned;'

'stove, hot'; 'a piece of marble, a statue,' etc., not on account of their *substance,* but on account of accidental *modifications* which affect their substance without altering it as a substance.

50. According to Aristotelian and Scholastic philosophers, there are **nine ways in which a finite substance remaining unaltered as a substance** may be conceived as modified, and so acquire new denominations, viz.: in regard to its quantity, its action, passion, relation, ubication or position in space, quandocation or position in time, posture and habit.

Or, in other words, we may say that a substance can receive a new denomination:

(1) On account of something wholly *extrinsic* to itself, *e. g.,* 'a man is called well-dressed on account of his clothes'; here, the new name implies no new reality in the denominated subject; the man would be what he is if he were clad in rags.

(2) On account of something *intrinsic in* itself considered *with reference to an extrinsic term, e. g.,* 'the height of A considered in reference to the height of B, entitled A to the denomination, *Taller than B;* here, the height of A as considered with reference to the height of B is called a Referent or Relative accident.

(3) On account of something *intrinsic* in the subject considered *without any reference* to anything else, *thus,* a man may be called 'learned, 'tall,' 'clever,' 'virtuous,' etc., apart from any reference to other Beings, on account of certain physical realities in him over and above the substantial constitutives of his individual manhood. Such realities really inherent in a substance, really distinct from that substance, yet depending upon it for their existence, are called *Absolute* accidents. It is of this last class of accidents we speak in the present article.

To our concept of absolute accident there corresponds an objective reality.

(1) It cannot be denied that thought, volition, figure, velocity, etc., are real physical entities, real modifications which can come and go without any *substantial* alteration of the subjects in which they inhere.

(2) Real changes take place from hour to hour in ourselves, and many of the substances around us. Now, every real change implies the acquisition or loss of some "form," some reality, by the subject which is said to be changed. That which has neither gained nor lost anything cannot be truly said to be changed. But, on the other hand, it is equally clear that not every change in a substantial Being is a *substantial* change, *e. g.*, a man does not become a different *substance* because he acquires knowledge of a subject of which he was previously ignorant; nor does the wax change its substance when from a shapeless mass it is molded into the form of a beautiful flower; nor does the acquisition of its destructive velocity alter the *substance* of the cannon ball.

Hence, we have *real entities* which are not substances, but which inhere in substances and modify and *perfect* substances; which are products of real physical action; and which makes all the difference that exists between the scholar and the unlettered man, between the cannon-ball at rest and the cannon-ball in motion, etc. But such entities are what we call "absolute accidents," and hence, our concept of absolute accident represents an objective reality.

51. Furthermore, though these accidents intrinsically modify the substances they inhere in and are naturally dependent upon them, as upon subjects of inhesion, for their existence, yet it cannot be doubted that they are *really distinct* from them.

(1) That Being which really and intrinsically modifies

and perfects another is really distinct from that other.   But accidents, *e. g.,* knowledge, motion, heat, color, etc., really and intrinsically modify and perfect the substances in which they inhere.   Therefore, they are really distinct from them.

(2)   Things which are really separable from one another are really distinct.   But a man may lose his knowledge, desires, etc., a cannon-ball may lose its velocity, etc.

52. Of the absolute accidents of which we have been speaking some are such that they cannot, without a contradiction in thought, be conceived as existing, even miraculously, apart from a subject in which they actually inhere.   Such are, for example, motion, figure, etc.; also vital acts, such as thought, volition, etc.   Such accidents are often called purely *modal* or purely modifying accidents, i. e., "actual" inhesion in a subject is an essential character of their existence.

But must this be said of all accidents?   Can it be shown to evidence to be an impossibility, even for the Almighty Power of God to sustain in existence certain accidents or certain collections of accidents, apart from the subjects in which they should *connaturally* inhere?

To this question we answer in the *negative,* that it cannot be shown to be impossible that God should sustain in existence some accidents apart from their connatural subject of adhesion. For such accidents are real entities, really distinct from the substance they inhere in, and though, according to the ordinary course of nature, actual adhesion in substance is a characteristic of their existence, yet it cannot be *demonstrated* that actual inhesion in a subject is "essential" to their existence in such a way, that God has not within the resources of His omnipotence a means of miraculously supplying for the sustaining influence of the created subject in which they would connaturally inhere.

We do not mean to say that reason can prove the possibility of accidents so existing; but we say that if reason is powerless to affirm such a possibility, it is equally powerless to deny it, and that if a competent authority should declare that certain accidents do, as a matter of fact, so exist, reason would have nothing evident to urge against it; nor would such accidents lose their true character of accidents—they would always imply a natural need of a subject of inhesion to sustain them, and could exist apart from it only because its sustaining influence was replaced by a miraculous exercise of Divine Power.

ARTICLE III.— RELATION.

Of the nine Aristotelian categories of accidents, only *Relation* will be treated of here. The others, as far as they concern us, will be more conveniently examined in connection with the matter of other treatises. Thus, Action and Passion belong to the chapter on Causality. Quantity, Space and Time will find their place in the treatises on Cosmology.

53. Every real Being has its own proper entity, truth and goodness, and hence, may be considered in itself and on its own account. Such a Being, so considered, may be called "absolute." But such absolute Beings may be like or unlike one another; may be dependent in origin, one upon another, etc., and thus involve a reference of one to the other. Considered as thus referred one to another, they are called "related" Beings, and the reference or respect they bear towards each other is called a "relation."

54. A relation, then, implies three elements, viz.:

(1) A "subject," which is referred to another, as like or unlike that other, equal or unequal to it, its cause or its effect, etc.

(2) A *"term,"* to which the subject is referred, or correlative.

(3) A "foundation" or basis in the subject or term, or in both, on account of which one is referred to the other.

55. In order that a "relation" be *real,* both *subject* and *term* must be *real* Beings, *really distinct* from each other; and further, there must be a *real foundation* in either or in both on account of which one is referred to the other, independently of any operation of the mind. Hence, the mind does not make real relations, but perceives them.

56. A real relation is called *"mutual,"* if both subject and term are really referred to each other, on account of a real foundation in both, *e. g.,* A and B may be mutually referred to each other on account of a similarity of features, character, etc., in both; teacher and pupil are mutually related on account of a continuous new exercise and activity on both sides in communicating and receiving knowledge.

A real relation is *non-mutual,* if the basis or the foundation of the reference is found only in one of the extremes. Such is the relation between the Creator and the creature. The creature has a real relation to God, founded in its complete dependence on Him for all that it has. God, on the contrary, is not really referred to the creature, for the creature's existence implies no new reality in God which could be the basis of a real relation on His part.

57. A relation is merely *"mental"* or *"logical,"* when either the extremes are not real Beings, or are not really distinct, or when the foundation for referring one to the other is unreal, or a mere creation of the mind. Thus, the relation between "Washington" and the "first President of the United States," between six and half-a-dozen, is merely mental; and such, too, is the relation by which we can conceive God to be referred to His creatures.

58. That there exist *real* relations between the things around us is clear; for quite independently of our thoughts about them many things are similar to each other, in essence, in qualities, in quantity, etc.

But it may be further asked, is the real relation which one Being bears to another an entity *really distinct* from that which is the foundation, or reason why the subject is referred to the term; *e. g.,* when the wall A is said to be like the wall B, on account of its whiteness, is the likeness of A to B an entity *really distinct* from its whiteness? The answer is obviously negative. A white wall in San Francisco, which has been in existence for the past five years, may, without any change or newness of any kind in itself, acquire a real relation of likeness, by simply building another white wall in London. Of course there is a mental distinction between the San Francisco wall, considered absolutely in itself, and considered in reference to the London wall, inasmuch as the contents of both concepts are different; but in reality, the former is *ipso facto* referred to the latter as *like* it, by its whiteness, without the addition of a new entity to constitute the relation.

CHAPTER III.

CAUSALITY.

60. A **Principle** is that from which anything in any way proceeds. That which so proceeds is called a **Principiate.** The connection between the two may be *merely extrinsic,* i. e., a mere matter of precedence and sequence in time or space; but with such Principles and Principiates we are not concerned here. Or the connection between the two may be *intrinsic,* i. e., when the principiate really derives from the principle its truth, its entity, etc. Here we speak only of *Real* Principles, i. e. principles of entity.

But once more a Being may be a Real Principle in two ways, viz.: Either,

(1) By simply communicating the same numerically identical nature and perfection which itself possesses, as Revelation teaches us is the case in the Blessed Trinity; or

(2) By producing some perfection at least numerically different from its own. In this latter case we have what is called a *cause* and an *effect*.

In every case, however, there is always a real distinction between a Real Principle and its Principiate, as such, and a real relation between them, i. e., the relation between **giver** and receiver.

ARTICLE I.—CAUSES IN GENERAL.

61. A **cause** is a principle which, by its *positive influence,* determines the *existence* of a *new Being,* substantial or accidental, but other than itself. The new Being is called an **effect.**

Hence, a cause implies (1) a Real Being, (2) whose positive influence in the given case, is *necessary,* and at least partially *sufficient,* for the existence of a new Being, (3) really distinct from itself.

Now, there are five ways in which a Being may be thus requisite, and at least partially sufficient, for the existence of a new Being really distinct from itself, viz.:

(1) As the *Material* out of which it is made, *e. g.,* 'the marble of which a statue is made.'

(2) As the *Form* which determines the material, indeterminate and indifferent of itself, to be the particular thing it is, *e. g.,* 'a statue of Washington.'

(3) As the *Agent* by the exercise of whose energies the form is educed in, or introduced into, the material.

(4) As the *End* which efficaciously moves the agent to exercise his energies,

(5) Finally, as the *Exemplar* or type which guides the agent's energies in the execution of the work.

Whatever then contributes in any of these five ways to the existence of a new Being, fulfills the conditions of a cause in regard to it, and accordingly is called its *material, formal, efficient, final,* or *exemplary, cause,* as the case may be. In the following articles, we shall explain the nature, the chief divisions, and the character of the causality of each of these five classes of causes.

NOTE. (1). Hence, though every Cause is a Principle, not every Principle is a Cause; for a cause implies "entitative" *otherness,* and *dependence in its* principiate, which a Principle as such does not.

(2) Material and Formal causes, as being *constitutive* parts of the compound Being, resulting from their union, are called *intrinsic causes;* Efficient, Final and Exemplary causes are called *extrinsic causes.*

(3) A **Condition** differs from a cause in this, that though it is necessary, yet it in no way *suffices* to account for the existence of the effect, i. e., it exercises no *direct* positive influence upon its existence, *e. g.,* 'light is a condition for writing a letter.' A condition may be *requisite* for the existence of an effect inasmuch as it may be requisite to prepare, dispose or apply the true cause, or at least to remove what would otherwise hinder causation.

A **Condition sine qua non** is one whose place cannot be supplied by any other.

An **occasion** is neither necessary nor sufficient for the existence of the effect; yet by its presence it facilitates its production, so that, as a matter of fact, the effect is produced when otherwise it would not be produced.

ARTICLE II.—MATERIAL AND FORMAL CAUSES.

62. The **Material Cause** of the statue spoken of above, i. e., the marble out of which it is made, is of itself *passive, indifferent, potential,* as to being a statue or a mile-stone, and it will remain the same marble as it is, though it should be successively both.

The **Formal Cause,** by its union with the Material, *determines* its indeterminateness, *actuates* its potentiality, makes it actually be one particular thing of the many it is capable of becoming, *e. g.,* a statue, and finally, will pass away, to give place to other formal causes, as the same marble becomes successively mile-stone, door-step and mantel-piece.

Hence wherever we have a Being made up of two elements really distinct and separable, one of which is in itself indeterminate, potential and constant, while the other is determinant, actuating and variable, we have a material and formal cause, **Matter** and **Form,** in the broad sense of the word. In strictness, however, only corporeal Beings are said to consist of Matter and Form.

63. The constant element in the various *Substantial* changes which are continually taking place around us, is called Primordial Matter. It is the source of the passivity, inertia, divisibility, etc., which are common to all corporeal substances.

That which determines the same primordial matter to be, at different times, clay, or grass, or the flesh of an ox, or the brain of a man, is called a Substantial Form. It is the source of unity and of the various properties, activities, etc., by which one corporeal substance is specifically distinguished from another.

The constant element in the *Accidental* changes which corporeal substances undergo is called Secondary Matter, and the various forms which actuate its potency are called Accidental Forms, i. e., the absolute accidents spoken of above.

64. **That Matter primordial or secondary and Form substantial or accidental are true causes, cannot be doubted;** for surely the constituents of a thing exercise a direct positive influence on its existence. They contribute to the production of the new Being, the compound, not by any *efficiency,* i. e., by any exercise of their energies; but by their *entity,* as its constituents, i. e., their causality consists in their mutual self-communication and *intrinsic union.*

NOTE.—Hence, with more or less of metaphor, that which can in any way be conceived as affecting or determining a Being, whether it be a perfection, or a privation, or a mere extrinsic denomination, *e. g.,* 'being well known,' 'loved,' etc., can be called a *Form;* while that which is conceived, as determined, or affected by such a form, may be called *Matter.* Thus, the *matter* of a sin is the physical act of the will; the *form,* the deliberate privation of rectitude in it. So, too, we speak of the *matter* and *form of a poem,* a judgment, a society, etc. Indeed, in every proposition, that which is expressed by the predicate may be conceived as a Form of the subject considered as the Matter.

ARTICLE III.—EFFICIENT CAUSES.

65. **An Efficient Cause** is defined by Aristotle, "A principle of change in another." It may also be defined, A Being, which, by the exercise of its energies, makes something else to be which was not before, i. e., transfers something from non-existence to existence.

Action in general may be described as any exercise of energies. Now, as the term Principle has a greater extension than Cause, so Action has a greater extension than efficient or Causal Action. For *causal* action it is requisite that the term of the action, that which results from it, be some entity or perfection at least numerically *distinct* from the agent; while the concept of action, as such, is fully verified, even if the principiate is numerically identical in entity and perfection with the principle.

On the other hand, as we have seen, material and formal causes are truly causes, not by reason of any action or exercise of energies, on their part, but simply by their mutual intrinsic union.   Hence, not all causality is action, nor is all action causality.

Causal action, or efficient causality, amounts to this, that a Being, by the exercise of its energies, not by its mere entity as a constituent part, brings into existence something which did not previously exist, something that has not in itself the sufficient reason of its existence.

Now, this may be done in two ways, either by producing a *new form,* substantial or accidental, in a previously existing subject, or by producing the *whole* substantial Being independently of any pre-existing subject, i. e., *out of nothing.* The latter is called **creative action** or Creation; the **former** may be called Eductive or **transformative** action.

If the term of the causal action is produced *within* the agent the action is called **immanent,** as by it the agent modifies itself.   If, on the contrary, the term of the action is something produced outside the agent, the action is called **transitive,** as by it the agent modifies a Being really distinct from itself.   Lastly, if it be possible for an agent to produce a new Being outside of itself by merely willing it, without the exercise of any other energy, such an action may be called **formally immanent,** but **virtually transitive.**

A cause is said to be in **second act** when it is actually influencing the existence of the effect.   It is said to be in **proximate first act,** when, though not exactly producing the effect, yet none of the conditions for its doing so are wanting.

If all or some of the conditions are wanting, it is said to be in remote first act.

66. As to the various classes of efficient causes much might be said, but it will suffice for our purpose brieflly to enumerate the principal heads under which they may be classed.

The **First Cause** is that which uncaused itself and absolutely independent in its entity and action causes and preserves in existence and co-operates in each and every action of all other Beings. These latter, inasmuch as they are efficient causes, are called **secondary causes.**

A **universal** cause is one whose positive causal influence concurs immediately in the production of every effect, i. e., without whose concurrent efficiency no effect can be produced.

A **particular** cause is one whose causal influence extends only to a certain class or certain classes of effects.

NOTE.—Hence, *a free* universal cause would efficaciously control all causation, since no effect could be produced without its immediate concurrence.

When two causes so occur in the production of an effect that one acts by its *own proper energies,* while the other acts only as *moved* and directed by the former, *e. g.,* the sculptor and the chisel in the formation of a statue, the former is called a **principle** cause; the latter, an **instrumental** cause. The main characteristic perfections of the effect are due to the influence of the principal cause, yet the instrumental cause, while transmitting the influence of the principal, and moved and directed by it, still contributes some efficiency of its own, and thus manifests its own perfections, though only in a secondary degree, in the effect. The *total effect* is attributed to each, *primarily* to the principal cause, *secondarily* to the instrumental cause, though not *totally* to either, *e. g.,* we can speak of 'the pen that wrote the Declaration of Independence.'

A **free cause** is one which, though in First Proximate Act, i. e., all requisites for action being present, has still such dominion over its action that it can act or not act, act in this way or that, according to its own choice.

A **necessary** cause, on the contrary, is one which cannot but act, and in one determinate way when all requisites for its action are present, e. g., 'a machine.'

A **physical** cause is one which produces an effect directly, by the exercise of its own energies.

A **moral** cause is one which entices (by counsel, promises, threats, etc.) a physical cause to action; or does not hinder its action, when in a position, and under an obligation to do so.

A **direct cause,** *causa per se,* is one which produces an effect determined by the *nature* or by the *free choice* of the agent. An **indirect cause,** *causa per accidens,* is one which produces an effect not *intended* by the nature, or by the free choice of the agent, e. g., 'if a man should start to dig a grave and turn up a pot of gold.'

A cause is **univocal** when it *produces* an effect of the same *species* as itself; **analogical** when it produces an effect of a different kind or species from itself.

67. (a) **The Principle of Causality is analytical.** For every Being has, either in itself or in another, a *sufficient reason* why it exists, why it is as it is, and not otherwise. Now, no New Being, i. e., one that begins to exist, one that passes from non-existence to existence, has in itself the sufficient reason of its existence, of its transition from non-existence to existence; else a pure potentiality would give itself what it has not, i. e., actuality. Hence, the sufficient reason for the existence of such a Being must be sought for, in some actually existing Being really distinct from it.

But again the mere existence of this latter Being is not enough to account for the existence of the former; some influence must be exercised, in order to effect a transition from non-existence to existence. This influence is what is meant by efficient causality.

Hence, the Principle of Causality, "every new Being requires an efficient cause," is *analytical*. In other words, the concept of a New Being, involves the concept of another Being, which actually exists, and exercises the influence, necessary and sufficient, to give it the existence, it has not of itself.

NOTE.—The word *Chance* may mean, (1) the absence of all efficient causality; and in this sense, to say that anything happens or is produced by chance, is a contradiction in terms; or it may mean, (2) that owing to unperceived circumstances, the efficient causality exercised, results in an effect neither foreseen nor intended by the agent, i. e., an effect unforeseen and unintended resulting from an accidental concurrence of causes. In this sense, many things may be said to happen by chance in regard *to us,* but not in regard to an *All-wise Omnipotent Providence.*

(b) **To our concept of efficient cause there corresponds an objective reality,** i. e., efficient causality is actually exercised both within and around us. Wherever new Beings come into existence, there efficient causality is exercised. But new Beings come into existence, within and around us, as our internal and external experience abundantly testifies. Therefore, etc.

(c) Though it must be admitted, as we shall see later on, that the Divine Concurrence is absolutely necessary for each and every action of the creature, yet, **finite Beings are true efficient causes** really and truly acting on one another and producing things that are new. For our internal experience testifies that we exercise true efficient causality in our thoughts and resolutions, in many of the movements of our body, etc., i. e., we have immediate consciousness of our own efficient action.

As to corporeal substances distinct from ourselves, the

common sense of mankind is unanimous in asserting that the horses produce motion in the carriage, that fire burns, that food nourishes, that plants produce flowers, fruit, etc.

Again, if corporeal substances have no activity of their own, they can make no impression on our faculties, and as it is only by their action on our faculties that we come to know their nature, and even their very existence, it would follow that we have no certitude of their very existence, much less any knowledge of their nature. In a word, all impressions made by material things upon us, and upon everything else, would be simply Divine effects, and all corporeal Beings would be idle superfluities without purpose or function in the universe, incapable alike of manifesting themselves or their Creator.

NOTE (1).—It is one thing to know that a *thing is,* and quite another to know distinctly *what it is.* We readily admit that, while we know with certainty *that* efficient causality *is exercised* even by finite Beings in the universe around us, and have a sufficiently clear concept of it to distinguish it from a mere relation of invariable antecedence and sequence, yet our concept of *what* it precisely consists in, is far from being adequate or distinct.

(2).—God does not confer existence on things because He is incapable of accomplishing all He wishes by Himself alone. Existence and activities alike, are gifts of an omnipotent, self-sufficient Creator, who wishes His creatures to manifest, and participate in their measure, in His own Divine perfections.

(3).—As we shall see later on, God gives existence to His creatures and their faculties, and by a continuous positive free exercise of His Power preserves them in existence, and furthermore, co-operates with them in the immediate production of their effects, inasmuch as these latter are entities. Hence, to attribute true efficient causality to creatures, in no way dero-gates from God's absolute dominion over every created thing.

(d) An effect *as such* cannot surpass the actual perfec-tion of its efficient cause. For, the effect or new Being pro-duced has all that it has from its cause, as resulting from the exercise of its energies. But nothing can give what it has not actually got; the less cannot give the greater. Therefore, etc.

NOTE. (1).—In regard to *transitive* action, we must care-fully distinguish what is produced by the action of the *external* cause, and what results from the *reaction* of the *object* on which the external cause acts. In regard to the latter the ex-ternal agent is called an *equivocal cause,* though in reality it is rather a condition or an occasion.

(2).—The effect, it is clear, does not pre-exist in the cause *Entitatively,* i. e., the same, *numerically identical,* per-fection which is produced, did not previously exist in the cause; else we should have no New Being, no effect, but sim-ply a transference, so to say, of an existing entity from one Being to another. Hence, the effect is said to pre-exist in the cause *Virtually,* inasmuch as the latter has the power to pro-duce it; and, moreover, *Formally,* if the cause possesses *specifi-cally* the same perfection which it produces in the effect; *Emi-nently,* if the cause possesses not the specific perfection of the effect, but a higher perfection, which embraces and surpasses all the pure perfection of the effect, as, for instance, 'from a merely financial point of view, a ten-dollar gold piece em-braces and surpasses all the perfection of a silver dollar.'

ARTICLE IV.—FINAL CAUSES.

68. A **Final Cause**, or **End**, is that *on account of which,* or *for the sake of which,* an efficient cause exercises its ener-gies, acts, produces something. Hence, as positively influ-encing the action of the efficient cause, it exercises a positive influence upon the existence of the effect, and so is a true

cause. The final cause, however, influences the existence of the effect, not by its immediate physical action, but only inasmuch as itself is an object of appetition to the efficient cause, moving the latter to action. It may be something non-existent which the agent seeks *to produce,* or something really existing which the agent seeks *to get possession of,* or finally, something actually possessed which the agent *enjoys.*

The *effects* of the final cause are all those things which the efficient cause does for its sake, i. e., in producing it, in getting possession of it, in enjoying it. These things, inasmuch as they are selected and executed because they lead to the production, possession, or fruition of the end, are called **means.** Hence, the End is loved, sought, aimed at, for its own sake; the *means,* as such, only for the sake of the end.

A Being, then, which is, for its own sake, an object of appetition to another, and which by its true or apparent goodness, moves that other to action, is **a final cause** of those actions. It is the *goal,* the actions are the *means* to reach it; it is *first* in the Order of Intention, i. e., it is in this order, a Causal Principle of the actions necessary to produce, possess, or enjoy it, *last* in the Order of Achievement, i. e., in this order, it is the Term of the actions actually done in order to attain it.

The **effects** which the Final Cause produces are in detail:

   (1) *Complacence* or love for itself, in the efficient cause,

   (2) *Intention* or efficacious purpose to attain it,

   (3) Serious *consultation* about the means necessary to attain it,

   (4) *Election* or choice of determinate means to attain it,

   (5) *Execution* or actual employment of the means chosen,

   (6) *Attainment* of the end,

   (7) *Fruition* or enjoyment of the end possessed.

The first four regard what is called the Order of Intention; the rest the Order of Execution or achievement.

From what has been said, it follows that **an End exercises its causality** not precisely, inasmuch as it is something *really existing* in the physical order of things, but rather inasmuch as it is *represented in thought,* and perceived to be good for the agent, and attainable by it. Hence, in strictness only those Beings can be said to act *on account of an end, for the sake of an end,* which are capable of representing the end in thought, and of determining and choosing the means to attain it.

Of course **unintelligent Beings can be said to act for the sake of an End,** but they do so only inasmuch as their end is determined by an intelligent Being, which fits them to attain it, and thus directs them towards it. *Thus,* 'a steam-engine can be said to act for a certain end, but only because the end influences the conscious mind which constructed and controls it.'

69. A thing is strictly a Final Cause only so far forth as it is desired and aimed at for its own sake; it is a Means inasmuch as it is desired and sought after for the sake of something else. Now, as there are many ways in which a thing may be aimed at or intended for its own sake, these will give us the divisions of final causes. It will suffice for our purpose here, however, to call attention to a few of the principal ones.

An end is said to be **ultimate** or **final** when, while aimed at for its own sake, it is referred to no other ulterior end; and all other ends aimed at by the agent, are, in one way or another, referred to it, *e. g.,* God's glory in our eternal happiness. On the contrary, when, though desired for its own sake, it is referred and subordinated to an ulterior end, it may be called an **intermediate** or **proximate end,** *e. g.,* 'one may love play, or study, or prayer, for their own sake, without making them ultimate ends.'

Two things may be so connected that both may be achieved by the same action, and both may be desirable for their own sake and intended by the agent; yet one may be such that, for its sake, even if it were alone, the action would be performed, while the other, apart from it, would not, though very desirable, be sufficient to move the agent to action. In this case the former would be a **primary** or **total final cause,** the latter a **secondary** or **partial** one.

Again, we may consider the **end of the action** or **work produced,** and **the end of the agent** in producing it. The former is that which the action exercised by the efficient cause is of its nature destined and able to achieve. The latter is that which the agent intends to attain by his work. The latter may be called the *extrinsic* end of the effect; the former, its *intrinsic* end. The two may be identical or different. Thus, the end of the physician's action and of himself may be simply the restoration of the patient's health; or it may be that, while the treatment is of its nature directed to the cure of the patient, the doctor himself is mainly influenced by the prospect of fame or a fat fee, etc., for the attainment of which he regards his patient's cure merely as a means.

Lastly, we may consider the thing intended, the person for whom it is intended, and the possession or enjoyment of the former by the latter. Thus, a good teacher will aim at (1) accurate knowledge, (2) thoroughly possessed, (3) by his class for their advantage. These are not really distinct ends, but rather three elements of every final cause. For we are moved to action by a final cause, only inasmuch as it is (1) a good, (2) capable of being possessed, (3) by some one, whether by ourselves or by another it does not matter.

70. To our concept of final cause there corresponds an **objective reality.** For our consciousness places it beyond doubt that we are moved by ends which propose themselves to us as desirable, to carry out even long series of works to

achieve them. They are clearly causes in our regard, because they solicit and call forth into action our energies, which, without their influence, would remain inactive. They truly cause our action, not compelling indeed, or necessitating it, yet exercising upon its existence that positive influence without which none of our deliberate actions would exist. Hence, the existence of final causality as a fact in the world is absolutely certain from the simplest analysis of our own deliberate conduct.

But a much broader question may be asked, **Does every efficient agent act for an end?** As we have already said, in order that a Being can be said to act for an end, it must either be intelligent itself or be adapted for action, by an intelligent Being. Now, is there ground in reason for maintaining that the actions of the non-intelligent Beings in the world around us are the result of adaptation by intelligence?

But the question must be still more restricted. We can prove the existence of an infinitely intelligent First Cause, from the existence of any New Being, even a thought, and then we can show that such a First Cause must efficaciously control and *direct* for *wise* ends every action of every creature. Hence, the question we would briefly discuss here is this, Merely considering the natural mode of action of the *non-intelligent Beings* around us, are we forced to admit that they act for an end under the adaptation and direction of an intelligence not their own?

The argument for an affirmative answer is absolutely convincing for every unprejudiced mind. The argument may be briefly stated *thus,* 'Wherever we find a *constant uniform* fitness and tendency in a Being to produce a certain determinate effect, and this fitness and tendency has not its adequate sufficient reason in the material constituents of the Being, we must conclude that this fitness and tendency, this *directive* principle, has been caused in the Being for the sake of producing said effect. But in the non-intelligent Beings around us, minerals, plants and animals, there is a constant uniform fitness and tendency to produce determinate effects, and this tendency and fitness, this directive principle, has not its sufficient reason in their material constituent elements. Therefore, etc.

The *major* is simply the Principle of Sufficient Reason applied to our case. For, the constant uniform aptitude and tendency we speak of either comes from the material constituent elements of the Beings or from some directive principle distinct from those elements, and introduced into them in order to control and adapt them for the attainment of fixed, determinate ends.

As to the *minor,* it is a matter of evident experience that each of the material things around us has a uniform, constant aptitude and tendency to produce certain determinate effects. Nor is it less evident that this aptitude and tendency has not its sufficient reason in the material elements of which these Beings are composed. For, not to go farther back than the chemical ultimates recognized by science, these of themselves are simply indifferent to any one of innumerable combinations and modes of action and motion. Hence, the sufficient reason why they are combined as they are, to form Beings capable of producing fixed, determinate effects beneficial to themselves and to the universe at large must be sought in some ultimate cause outside of themselves which so originally combined them and introduced into them fixed directive principles, with a view and purpose of attaining such determinate results.

Hence, each and all of the unintelligent Beings around us act for the attainment of fixed ends, under the influence and determination of an intelligent cause distinct from themselves.

Article V.—Exemplary Causes.

72. An **exemplary** cause is a representation of a thing to be produced, existing in the mind of the efficient cause,

which guides and directs his energies in the execution of his work. This *practical* idea is a true cause inasmuch as it determines the work of the efficient cause, and guides his hand in its execution. Indeed, the effect is nothing but the more or less perfect realization, the transference, as it were, from the mind to the actual physical order, of the ideal in the mind of the agent.

The **causality of the exemplar** consists in directing the efficient cause in the accomplishment of his work; and as the effect of the final cause is simply the action of the efficient cause, so far forth as the latter is exercised *for the sake* of an end; so the effect of the exemplary cause is the same action of the efficient cause, inasmuch as the latter is *directed* to the realization of an idea. That such causality is really exercised in daily life is sufficiently evident from experience.

CHAPTER IV.

GRADES OF PERFECTION OF BEING.

73. We have already explained (8) the sense in which we use the word *perfection*. We have also said (21, note 2) that among good and perfect things of different orders one may be *better,* more perfect, than another. It is of this comparative perfection we shall treat in the present chapter. Perfection may regard the *essence* of a Being, or its *mode* of *existence,* or the *relations* which exist between many distinct Beings, or between the *parts* of one composite Being.

ARTICLE I.—PERFECTION IN REGARD TO ESSENCE.

(i) *Simple and Composite Beings.*

74. A **Simple** Being is one which is not composed of distinct components or parts, and is therefore incapable of being resolved into component parts.

A **Compound** Being, on the contrary, is one which is made up of distinct constituent parts, and is therefore capable of being resolved into its component parts.

75. A **physical compound** is composed of parts which are *really* distinct from one another. This may be again, *essential,* if the parts are essential constituents; *quantitative,* if the parts are quantitative; *accidental,* i. e., the physical compound resulting from a substance and its absolute accidents; such a Being, however, is a physical compound only in a *loose* analogical sense of the word.

A Being is **physically simple** when it consists neither of essential nor of quantitative parts.

NOTE.—A *metaphysical* compound is a physically simple Being, between whose various perfections there is a *complete virtual* distinction (16, c). Where, on the contrary, the virtual distinction between the perfections of the Being is only *incomplete,* the Being is said to be *metaphysically* simple.

76. **Composition is a mixed perfection,** i. e., it essentially involves *imperfection, e. g.,* 'limitation of parts,' 'dependence of the parts on each other, and of the whole on the parts,' 'divisibility' or 'dissolubility.'

Simplicity, on the contrary, is a pure perfection, i. e., it excludes no perfection, but only the imperfections of composition.

NOTE.—Hence, no *composite* Being can be a First Being, an All-Perfect Being, a Pure Act of Being.

(ii)   *Finite and Infinite Being.*

77. A **finite Being** is one that is *limited* in perfection or entity; i. e., it has so *much* perfection, but no *more.* The idea of the finite, therefore, is partly *positive,* partly *negative.*

An Infinite Being is one that is *unlimited* in perfection, in real entity.

NOTE.—The idea we can form of the Infinite is a perfectly *clear* one, though not as *distinct* or *direct* as the mind craves for. The idea is formed by combining the note of Real Being or Pure Perfection with the note absolutely unlimited, or absolutely excluding all lack or limit or imperfection. There is therefore no need of any roundabout theory to account for the origin of this idea. It is not *innate,* nor is it formed by adding together a vast *sum* of finite entities; we know what *Being* is, what a *limit* is, and what a *negation* is, and we have the power of combining those characters so as to form one complex concept expressing Being or perfection without any limit.

78. It is obvious that an infinitely perfect Being cannot be a *produced* or dependent Being, a *composite* Being, or a *mixed* Act. It is necessarily a First or uncaused Being, or a simple Being, a Pure Act of Being.

NOTE.—In the preceding paragraphs we have spoken of the *absolute* Infinite, the infinite in Being or pure perfection. We do not intend to enter into the question of the conceivability or possibility of an actually infinite *number* or *multitude,* relative infinity. We may content ourselves with saying with Fr. Rickaby that it will be time enough to answer the question when it can be intelligibly proposed.

ARTICLE II.—PERFECTION IN REGARD TO EXISTENCE.

79. **A self-existing Being** is one which has the sufficient reason of its existence *in itself,* in its own *essence,* one whose essence and existence are, even in concept, *identified.* **A caused Being,** on the contrary, has the sufficient reason of its existence not in itself, but in another Being distinct from itself.

80. **A necessary Being** is one whose *non-existence* is absolutely impossible, i. e., whose essence is positively inconceivable as non-existent, whose *essence* or nature involves, or rather *is, actual existence.*

A contingent Being is one whose *non-existence* is possible, i. e., whose essence is adequately conceivable as nonexistent—whose *adequate essence* does not include or imply actual existence.

81. Hence, (1) A *necessary* Being is a *self-existent* Being: whereas a *contingent* Being is a *caused* Being.

(2) A necessary Being is an infinitely perfect Being (39).

(3) A necessary Being is absolutely *immutable,* unbeginning, unending, unchangeable.

ARTICLE III.—PERFECTION ARISING FROM RELATIONS.

82. **Order** may be defined, An arrangement of distinct things, according to some *relation* which they bear to one another, for the attainment of a definite result. The things arranged are the *material cause* of the order, the arrangement or grouping, the *formal cause,* while the result achieved may be called the *end* or *final cause.* The relation attended to, in grouping, is called the *principle* of order.

83. If things are arranged according to their active properties or forces, we have *Dynamic Order;* if according to their substance, or more or less inactive properties, we have *Static order. Quantative* relations give us the basis for *Symmetry, qualitative* for *Harmony.* The relation of means to end gives us *final* order. Relations arising from rights and duties are the foundation of *Moral* and *Social Order,* etc.

If but *one* kind of relation is attended to in the grouping of the *material,* the order is said to be *Simple;* if the relations regarded in the arrangement are *manifold,* the order is *Complex.*

84. **Only intelligent Beings can perceive order as such,** for to do so, one must apprehend the relation or relations according to which the various ordered elements are grouped, and for this the power of intellectual abstraction and universalization is needed.

A fortiori **intelligence is needed to plan and produce order** as surely as this implies apprehension of the end to be attained, and of the various relations existing between the elements to be co-ordinated or subordinated in order to attain it.

Hence, a *constant ordered* arrangement of many distinct elements, *of themselves* unintelligent, and indifferent to this arrangement or another, requires intelligence as its proportionate efficient cause. This is a simple metaphysical principle universally recognized by the common sense of mankind. It is, in fact, an immediate application of the Principle of Causality.

SUPPLEMENTARY ARTICLE.—BEAUTY.

85. **Beauty** is that property or perfection in things, on account of which their *mere perception,* apart from *use, possession* or other advantages, *pleases;* "perfection giving pleasure to the *beholder."*

That an object be beautiful, therefore, it must be (1) perfect in entity and action; (2) all its elements, really or virtually distinct must be duly proportioned and harmoniously related to each other; (3) this perfection and harmony of parts must clearly manifest itself to the beholder.

Wherever, therefore, these three elements are found in any object, whether of the spiritual or material order, there we have beauty, the "splendide perfectum."

86.   As only intelligence can apprehend *completeness* and *harmony* of elements, it follows that the **intellect is strictly the aesthetic faculty;** as our power of reasoning may be cultivated and perfected, so our *taste* or power of apprehending and enjoying beauty may be perfected by culture.

PART THREE.

COSMOLOGY.

1. **Cosmology** is, The science of the material universe. Its material object is corporeal substance and its properties. Its formal objects are the ultimate supra-sensible causes of the same. As the ultimate *efficient, final* and *exemplary* Cause of all finite Beings is the subject-matter of Natural Theology, we shall confine ourselves here mainly to the investigation of the ultimate *material* and *formal* causes of corporeal substances, their properties and phenomena.

We start with the data of observation and experiment, and applying rational principles to these we shall deduce a systematic body of ultimate truth in regard to the nature and properties of corporeal substance in general and of the three highest genera into which it is divided, viz.: the mineral, vegetable and animal kingdoms of nature.

We may conveniently divide our subject into three Chapters:—

I.—The General Properties of Corporeal Substance.

II.—The Intrinsic Constituents of Corporeal Substance.

III.—Organic Life.

CHAPTER I.

GENERAL PROPERTIES OF CORPOREAL SUBSTANCE.

We may group what we have to say on this subject under two heads, viz.: I, QUANTITY; II, MOTION.

Article I.—Quantity.

2.   **Quantity.**—The most obviously manifested property of bodies is *quantity,* i. e., that property in virtue of which they are extended, have parts outside parts, are divisible and occupy space; so that different parts of the occupying body correspond to different parts of the occupied space.

Omitting other senses in which the word quantity may be used, we speak here only of **continuous quantity.** This is had when the extraposited parts are bounded by common limits, that is to say, the parts into which the extended substance is *divisible,* but *not* divided have, antecedently to division, no extremities of their own distinct from those of the whole. We have in reality but *one* thing, though that one thing is *divisible* into many parts, i. e., it is *actually* one; *potentially* many.

3.   That we have the concept of such continuous quantity is undisputed: the whole science of geometry is based upon it. Let us briefly analyze its contents. Take, for instance, a cubic foot of continuous extension, prescinding from the particular substance to which it belongs.   Extension thus conceived is *mathematical* quantity. It has three dimensions: length, breadth, and depth, or thickness.   The *solid* is bounded or terminated by *surfaces;* the surface, by *lines;* the line, by *points.*   A point has no extension; a line, neither breadth nor depth; a surface, no depth.   Points, lines and surfaces, then, are but the *limits* or extremities of linear, superficial and solid extension, respectively, and have no positive entity of their own apart from that of the extension they terminate.

Note.—All actual extension, therefore, is represented by lines, surfaces, or solids, i. e., extension of one, two or three dimensions.   This may be expressed algebraically by the symbols x, x^2, x^3, *e. g.*, 'an inch long,' 'an inch square,' 'a cubic inch.' But if we go on, in the same sense of the terms, to write $x^4 \ldots \ldots x^n$, it becomes impossible to realize or to conceive a *geometric* figure which such a symbol might represent. Hence, the *N-dimensional* extension of the non-Euclidean geometry becomes when applied to continuous quantity a mere *algebraic illusion*.

4. Continuous extension of whatever kind is necessarily *divisible*. **But how far is it divisible?** Take a line an inch long, for instance, halve it, take half of that half again, and so on, as often as you please. Shall you ever reach a part which is incapable of further division, that is to say, unextended? Clearly no; for, if you could divide the line into unextended points, then the sum of these points should give you the line, and you should have O, O, O, etc., equals 1 inch. In the same way, it is obvious that a surface cannot be divided into a sum of lines; or a solid into a sum of surfaces. Hence, continuous extension is divisible into parts which are themselves extended and, therefore, *indefinitely* divisible.

NOTE.—In the preceding paragraph we have been speaking of the divisibility of continuous quantity *as such*, i. e., considered in itself and without regard to the *substance* to which it belongs. If we consider, however, the *quantified* corporeal *substance*, then we admit that there is a *minimum* beyond which division cannot go, **atoms** in the literal sense of the word. Thus, there is a *minimum quantity* of material substance required for the smallest existible portion of O., C., H., etc. But in all these cases the indivisibility is due, not to the *quantity* as such, but to the *nature* of the *substance*. "Corpus *mathematice* acceptum divisible in infinitum; corpus *naturale* non est divisible in infinitum * * * sed requirit determinatam quantitatem."

5. But, again, we may ask: **In what sense are the parts into which it is divisible contained in the undivided con-**

tinuous whole? A quantitative part implies two things, viz.: (1) a positive extended reality, (2) with limits or extremities of its own so that it is impossible to conceive a part without conceiving it as terminated by limits of its own independent of those of the whole of which it is part. Now, in continuous extension we have the *positive reality,* but not the independent boundaries; consequently, we have no *actual* parts; we have *actual* unity and only *potential* plurality. Hence, if we are asked how many parts are there in a given continuous line, we answer there *are no* parts; there *may be* more than you can think.

6. But now we go on to ask, **Is continuous extension a real property of bodies in the world around us** (*physical* quantity) ? or are the bodies we see and touch made up of a multitude of unextended mathematical points? The question is general; nor do we care for the moment to inquire whether the larger tangible masses around us are themselves continuously extended, or merely composed of contiguous smaller masses which are so continuously extended. We are satisfied here, if it be admitted that there is in nature an objective reality corresponding to our concept of continuous quantity. Now, we say it is absurd to maintain that the extension and the extended resistance which our senses perceive in the material world can arise from a multitude of unextended points. For, either these points are contiguous, and then, as they have no extension either of length, breadth or solidity, any number of them touching each other will give us, as far as extension is concerned, only O, O, O, etc.=O; or they are not contiguous, but separated from each other by an interval, and then, as unextended points do not occupy space, the visible tangible universe becomes in reality an unoccupied vacuum; and extension a subjective illusion projected upon a background of nothingness. Nor will it help to say that it is the motion of these points in space which furnishes the basis of our perception of continuous extension. For, to perceive the motion of

an object is simply to perceive the object itself as it moves from place to place; but here the object is imperceptible, and, consequently, its motion and the path in which it moves are imperceptible. We conclude, therefore, that our concept of continuous extension is verified in the corporeal substances around us, i. e., that bodies have continuous extension of dimensions.

NOTE.—Some have supposed that the continuous extension we perceive can be accounted for by supposing that bodies are made up of unextended points of *force* separated off from one another and acting across the interval which divides them.

In this supposition, we ask what sort of a being is it that bridges over the vacuum between unextended force centers and gives us the continuity we perceive in our own bodies and in the material world around us? *A substance?* Then we have real extension. An *accident?* Then we have an accident self-supporting, an accident which is not an accident but a substance and extended so as to fill the interval. *Nothing?* Then the continuous extension which our senses, whether alone or when aided by the most powerful physical instruments, cannot help perceiving is merely an inevitable *illusion,* and idealism and scepticism are the necessary logical consequence.

It is true that science reveals that many bodies which seem to be continuous to the unaided senses are in reality *porous.* But science, too, reveals and requires true continuity, and in order to account for the propagation of light, etc., fills all those ultimate pores with hypothetical *ether,* itself a continuously extended and highly elastic material substance.

7. Continuous quantity, then, is a real property of bodies. **In what does it formally consist?**

In corporeal substance we may consider many characteristics, all of which are more or less closely connected with that actual extension in space from which we derive our concept of continuous extension. Thus (a) we may consider the corporeal substance in itself; and this of its very nature, as distinguished from spiritual substance, implies entitative parts and parts; (b) we may consider this multiplicity of parts as continuously connected and extraposited in a certain determinate order in relation to each other; (c) we may consider this internally quantified body as actually occupying a definite portion of space.

Now, the mere multiplicity of parts included in the essential concept of corporeal substance in no way corresponds with our concept of continuous quantity. On the other hand, the actual extraposition of continuous parts in a definite order in relation to space implies as *prior* to itself their extraposition in a definite order in relation *to each other*.

Hence we say that the *formal* or *primary* effect of quantity consists in the continuous extraposition of the parts of a substance *in relation to each other* whence flows its connatural aptitude and capacity to occupy space. Hence, quantity may be described as a property which gives to corporeal substance *internal* continuous extension in virtue of which it becomes *capable* of occupying space and *actually* does occupy space unless the ordinary laws of nature are interfered with.

8. That this property must be conceived as a positive perfection not included in the adequate essential concept of corporeal substance is clear from what we have just said. But we may go further and ask, If the *substance* and the quantity of a body are *two distinct things?* Long ago the old Greek philosophers by mere "discourse of reason" arrived at the conclusion that **the substance of a body is one thing; its quantity, quite another.** For, as they said, the *corporeal substance, e. g.,* of a fig-tree or of a crystal of sulphur, is certainly something different from the *property* which extraposits their entitative parts in the *order* which they naturally

take and gives them the *power* of occupying a definitely out-
lined portion of space.

This property would then be an *absolute accident* of corporeal substance, nor could any valid reason be assigned why
it could not be *miraculously* sustained in existence from the
corporeal substance in which it connaturally inheres.

9. **Variability of Volume.**—*External local extension,*
we have said (6), is a connatural result of quantity. Now, is
this external extension—this *actuation* of the quantified body's
aptitude to occupy space—*constant* under all circumstances?
Or is it *variable* within certain limits under the influence of
natural agencies, *e. g.,* heat, pressure, etc.? The latter is the
view of the plain common sense of mankind, and, philosophi-
cally speaking, seems altogether necessary to account for some
of the commonest phenomena in nature, *e. g.,* 'the contraction
and extension of bodies,' 'elasticity,' 'universal attraction,'
'the transmission of sound,' 'heat,' etc., etc. Indeed, if we deny
this variableness of *real* volume, we must ultimately assume the
existence of action at a distance, i. e., across a vacuum "an
assumption which may be made to account for anything; but
it is impossible, as Newton long ago pointed out, for any one
who has in philosophical matters a competent faculty of thinking to admit for a moment the possibility of such action."*

If, then, there are good reasons for maintaining that external local extension as a secondary effect of quantity is *naturally* variable within certain limits, there can be little difficulty in admitting that a quantified body may *miraculously*
exist without any external local extension, i. e., with merely
aptitudinal or *potential* external extension.

10. **Impenetrability** is that *power* by which an actually
extended body maintains its possession of the portion of space
it occupies and hinders another actually extended body from

*Tait & Stewart, "The Unseen Universe," p. 146.

simultaneously occupying it. But here again we must distinguish the *power* from its actual *exercise;* just as we distinguish between the power of thinking and its actual exercise. The *power* of excluding other bodies from the same place is an essential concomitant of quantity; but, though its actual exercise *naturally* follows upon its possession, just as actual local extension is a natural consequence of quantity; yet, there is no ground for denying that its exercise may be prenaturally modified or suspended by the all-controlling power of God. No power can be exercised without His free concurrence, and there is no reason why He should not modify or suspend this concurrence in a particular case, when His Wisdom sees fit to do so.

11. **Space.**—From the actually extended bodies around us, we easily derive the concept of *abstract* continuous extension indefinite in length, breadth and depth, and this we can further conceive as of itself *unoccupied*—a sort of *receptacle* of inexhaustible capacity capable of containing extended bodies. This is the concept of *absolute* or *ideal space.*

In as far as it is conceived as occupied by extended bodies at rest or in motion, it gives us what is called *actual* or *real space,* which may, therefore, be described as the Interval of absolute space included within the ultimate limits of the existing corporeal universe.

Now, as it would be absurd to say with Kant that our concept of space is a mere arbitrary fiction of the imagination, without any sort of foundation in objective reality, so it would be no less absurd to say that space as such, i. e., considered as a mere receptable of extended bodies really distinct from them, and independent of their presence or absence, is something real in itself and actually existing.

The true view avoids both extremes and holds that *what is conceived,* i. e., actual or possible extension, is real and objectively realized or realizable; though it is not realized or realizable *in the manner in which it is conceived,* i. e., as a mere independent capacity or receptacle.

If, then, we must answer the question, **What is space?** we answer that, in reality *actual* space is the total extension of the existing universe, conceived as one continuous container or receptacle of that which occupies it; *possible* or *ideal* or *absolute* space is the total possible extension of all existible bodies, conceived as one continuous container or receptacle in which they would exist and move, if they existed.

NOTE (1).—When absolute space is conceived as eternal, indestructible, limitless, etc., it is clear that these are attributes not of *actual* but of *possible* extension.

(2).—To avoid confusion of thought, we must take care to distinguish accurately between the *concept* of space as above described and the image which accompanies it in the *imagination.* The imagination being an organic faculty can represent objects only in terms of sensual perception, and so cannot represent purely abstract notes, such as mere abstract extension; hence, it pictures space as a sort of phantom substance perfectly permeable and extending indefinitely in all directions.

12. **Place.**—Akin to the idea of space is that of *place.* When a body moves from one portion of space to another, we say it changes its place. It leaves the place it occupied and passes to another; but the place itself remains immovable: we never speak of a place as moving. Place, then, is an immovable portion of space shut off, as it were, from the rest of space by definite bounding surfaces in which the occupying body is contained as in a perfectly-fitting receptacle.

Fixity, then, is a characteristic of place. But how can there be fixity where everything is in motion? For us, there can be only relative immobility, i. e., a constant relation of distance is preserved in regard to certain definite points on the earth or outside of it. Thus New York and San Francisco, though in motion with the earth and with the whole solar system, yet in regard to certain fixed points, *e. g.,* 'the equator,' 'the poles,' etc., are immovable; and this *relative* fixity suffices to verify our idea of place.

The place of a body, then, may be described as, The voluminal interval enclosed within the bounding surfaces which immediately surround it, considered as immovable.

13. A *finite substance* may be said to be **ubicated or** *in a place* in two ways, viz.: (a) *Commensurably,* when the dimensions of the occupying body correspond to and are measured by those of the occupied space so that the whole body occupies the whole place and different parts of the body different parts of the place. It is in this way that *corporeal* substances *naturally* exist in place.

(b) *Incommensurably* when the whole substance is whole in the whole place and whole in each and every part of it. It is only in this way that a finite spiritual substance, *e. g.,* 'the human soul,' can be said to be in place.

NOTE (1).—Hence an actually extended *body* is referred to place by its *quantity,* which occupies a definite determinate amount of space. A finite *spirit,* on the contrary, is related to place not by its quantity (for it has none), but by its energy or *activity,* which can be exercised within certain limits but not beyond them.

(2).—There is another mode of presence in a place, which we know of only through revelation. It may be called *sacramental* ubication and is realized in the Blessed Eucharist. The Body of Our Lord is not referred to place by its *own* quantity or activities, but by the quantity (miraculously sustained) of the bread which has been trans-substantiated. How this is accomplished we do not know. Reason is simply silent in presence of the mystery and has nothing to say for or against it.

(3).—Whatever may be said in favor of the *intrinsic possibility* of an absolute *vacuum,* it seems sufficiently certain that no such thing exists in the *actual* universe; else we could not rationally account for universal attraction, the diffusion of heat, light, electricity, etc.

ARTICLE II.—MOTION.

14. **Change.**—(a) A thing is said to be *changed* when it has become in some way different from what it was before, i. e., when it has gained or lost some perfection. Hence the idea of *change* implies three elements, viz.: a previous condition of the thing, a new condition, the thing itself which has passed from the one condition to the other; or, as they say, a term *from* which, a term *to* which, and a *subject* which passes from the one to the other. In every change, then, we conceive something which ceases to be; something which begins to be; and something which remains constant and common to both terms.

(b) If one *complete substance* wholly ceases to be in order to give place to another and only the same *accidents* remain constant, the change is called Trans-substantiation. If one substantial *form* gives place to another in the same primordial matter, we have what is called a Substantial Change. If the same complete substance remains and the difference regards only its *accidents,* we have an Accidental Change.

(c) Again, when the terms, from one to the other of which, the subject passes, are *contradictorily* opposed—A and not-A—the passage from the one to the other is called an Instantaneous Change; inasmuch, as on merely leaving one term, the subject must necessarily be in the other. On the other hand, if the opposition between the terms is merely one of *contrariety,* and that in a broad sense of the word, i. e., so that there is an assignable mean between them, *e. g.,* '10 deg. C., and 20 deg. C.,' the change is called Successive; inasmuch as the subject, on leaving 10 deg. C., must pass through all the grades of the interval one after another before reaching 20 deg. C. Now this successive change, if *continuous,* i. e., without stop or break from starting point to goal, is what is called Movement or Motion.

(d) But before going on to analyze more fully this idea of motion we must notice one or two axioms which hold true of every changeable Being:—

1st—Every mutable Being is of its nature a potential Being; for it is of its nature in a state of potency as to the possession or privation of a given perfection.

2d—Every mutable Being is, so far forth, an imperfect Being; inasmuch as it either has not the perfection in question; or if it has it is at least capable of losing it.

3d—That a mutable Being may pass from the state of privation to the possession of a given perfection, the *positive action* of an efficient cause is needed; else, we should have an effect without a cause; while, on the contrary, to pass from possession to privation, it would suffice that the causal action which maintained the given perfection in existence be *suspended.*

15. **Motion.**—(a) All change then involves a *transition from potentiality to act;* and, if this transition is *successive* and *continuous,* we have *Movement.* Hence, Aristotle defines motion as 'The act of that which is potential, inasmuch as it is potential.' The Being in process of change has left the state of mere potency, but has not yet arrived at the term towards which it is unceasingly advancing; and, therefore, its motion is but a partial and incomplete actuation of its potentiality in regard to that term. When, then, motion is said to be an *Act,* our attention is called to the prior state of potentiality which is

constantly being left behind; while, the words, **of a Being in potency inasmuch as it is in potency,** remind us that, though our subject has emerged from a mere state of potentiality, its actuation in regard to the term towards which it is tending is not yet complete.

(b) The two characteristics, then, of motion are *succession* and *continuity;* it is the passage of a thing successively, i. e., one after another, through all the parts of the interval between two terms without break or halt. Hence, the difference and the similarity between continuous quantity and motion. They differ in this, that the parts into which extension is divisible exist *simultaneously;* while the parts into which motion is divisible exist *successively.* They are alike in this, that as it is impossible to assign, even in thought, a minimum of extension which is not conceivable as capable of still further division, so it is impossible to conceive a minimum of motion which is not further divisible: a *point,* if we may say so, of *motion,* like a *point* of *extension,* has no entity of its own apart from that of the preceding and succeeding parts which it connects or terminates.

16. **Time.**—(a) As for the perception of continuous extension in the world around us, we rise to the concept of *space;* so from the perception of motion within and without us, we elaborate our idea of *time.* What, then, is time?

Duration, in general, is defined as Permanence or perseverance in existence. Now, we can conceive a Being as existing without beginning, without end and without change or possibility of change in its substance or action so that it is absolutely, and in every sense the same forever without any shadow of difference in its full and simultaneous possession of all-perfect life. This duration is *eternity* in the strict sense of the word; and it belongs to God alone.

On the other hand, we can conceive a thing whose existence is rather a continuous *becoming and ceasing* than an abiding fact, i. e., whose existence is had only by parts, and in such a way that each preceding part ceases to be, just as the succeeding part begins, yet without break or interruption in the continuous succession of Before and After. Such is the *successive duration* of motion which gives us our idea of time.

Now, the whole corporeal universe and everything in it is in a continual state of change or motion. From the perception of this concrete motion we naturally rise to the abstract concept of one uniformly flowing motion whose successive duration is conceived as co-existing with and measuring the various motions of all actual or possible moving things. This is the concept of *absolute* or ideal time.

That portion of this *ideal* evenly flowing successive duration which has been, or is, or will be co-existent with the *actual* motion of concrete existing things is what is called *real* time.

Time, then, as we have already said of space, is neither a mere baseless fiction of the imagination; nor yet, on the other hand, is it an independent entity in itself standing out apart from the concrete motion of actual or possible moving substances. *What is conceived,* i. e., actual or possible successive duration, is real and objectively realized or realizable, but not precisely in *the manner in which it is conceived,* i. e., as a mere successive duration whose onward uninterrupted flow is independent of and embraces and measures the concrete duration of all moving things.

(b)   Wherever, then, there is continuous change or movement, there is successive duration; and, wherever there is successive duration, there is real time; and hence, as each changing moving thing in the corporeal universe has its own changes and motion, so it has its own intrinsic time. But just as we take one fixed standard of extension to measure the extension of other things, so we can take one particular actual motion to measure the duration of all other motion that takes place around us. Hence, as the motion of the heavenly bodies is the most even and uninterrupted we can find, we take its regular succession as the measure of our time.

NOTE (1).—A being is said to exist *in* time inasmuch as it undergoes successive change or motion.

A being which endures unchanged along with other beings which are *in* time may be said to *co-exist with* time. It has and is (all that it has and is) unchangeably without any succession in itself, and its simple unaltered duration is *virtually* equivalent to the imperfect successive duration of all possible changing things.

(2).—The word Present is used in many senses in regard to time. Sometimes we mean an interval of time part of which is past and part of which is yet to follow, *e. g.,* the present century, 'year,' 'day,' etc. Sometimes we mean that small portion of time which passes while we think or say Now. In strictness, however, the present is that indivisible point which has itself no duration, but is conceived as a limit connecting the past and future. "Time speeds onward," says Seneca, "what is past is not mine, nor what is future; all of existence that is really mine consists of a point of fleeting time."

If we find it hard to explain to ourselves or to another, what time is, St. Augustine's words may console us: "What is time? If no one asks me, I know; but if I am asked, and I try to explain, then I know not."

17. Turning now from motion in the abstract to the *actual* world of corporeal things in which we live, we find that it is **a world of ceaseless change and motion.** The *material* of which it is made is in constant circulation, now borne upwards to become living rosebuds or human hearts and brains, and then, as if by an inevitable law, returning to the lowly condition of dead dust. Take any one of the most familiar substances around us, *e. g.,* 'the post to which you tie your

horse'; what a volume it would take to chronicle the changes it undergoes in a single day! How much space it has passed through, as it moves forward with the moving earth! how persistently it has been enticed to move this way and that by the manifold attractions of its fellow bodies! how it has been affected and modified by their chemical activities! how it has expanded and contracted in the heat and cold, etc., etc.!

All these changes that take place in corporeal substance, as such, may be grouped under two general heads, viz.: Substantial and Accidental Changes; and these latter again may be subdivided into Local, Qualitative and Quantitative changes.

A brief word, then on each of these four kinds of change, and we shall dismiss the subject of corporeal motion.

18. **Substantial Change.**—The ultimate inner nature of a Being is manifested to us by its properties and actions, as the source is revealed by the stream. Hence chemistry, as well as the common sense of mankind, makes similarity or difference in specific properties the test of similarity or difference in substance. Now, it is a matter of every-day experience that certain substances may be so transformed as to acquire wholly different properties, so that no trace of their former specific character remains, e. g., to take a most obvious instance, hydrogen burns readily in the air, and oxygen supports combustion better than the air; while the properties of water into which they may be transformed are quite different and even opposite.' Hence, we argue that since the specific properties are different, the sources from which they flow are different; and that, therefore, the substantial natures are different; and consequently that in such transformations we have true *substantial* changes.

Here, then, as in every change, something has passed from one condition to another—something from being one substance has become another—the source of the old *specific* properties has given place to a new one from which new specific properties proceed. Now, that determinable *potential* constituent which remains constant and common in both substances is called *Primordial* or Ultimate Matter, while the old determining *actuating* constituent that has passed away and the new one that has taken its place are called *Substantial Forms.*

Whatever may be said of the character of these two intrinsic constituents of corporeal substance—and we are not concerned to say anything here—their *existence* is a fact which we cannot ignore; there is a Material Cause which remains constant in both terms of a substantial change, and there is a Formal Cause which is different in each.

NOTE (1).—It is not necessary to call attention to the difference between a Mixture, *e. g.,* 'gun powder,' and a Compound, *e. g.,* 'water'; the former is a mere aggregate, or collection of heterogeneous substances; the latter is strictly *one* homogeneous substance.

(2).—When chemistry writes, *e. g.,* 'water as H^2O,' the meaning is not that these substances are *actually* there, which would be contrary to all experience, but that they are *potentially,* or better, *virtually there.* Just as when some misfortune befalls a newly-sown field which destroys the seed, the farmer may complain that he has lost his crop, though, in strict truth, he has lost not an actual, but only a potential or virtual crop.

(3).—Composite bodies have spectra of their own different from those of their components. In the cases where the spectra of the original elements are clearly detected, the conditions are such (extreme heat, etc.) that we are justified in saying that the compound substance, *as such,* has ceased to exist, i. e., that it has been decomposed into the primitive substances from whose substantial transformation it originated.

(4).—Substantial change is effected in two ways, viz.: by *combination* when two substances, *e. g.,* 'H and O,' unite to form a third substance, water, different from either; or by *assimilation,* when a living being transforms by its nutritive powers other substances into its *own*.

(5).—The transformed substances are said to exist *virtually* in the compound, i. e., the compound has been formed *from* them and can be resolved *into* them.

19. **Quantitative Change.**—Actual extension we have already said is a connatural property of all corporeal substances. In virtue of this property and of the cohesive and resistive forces which accompany it, the parts into which a body is divisible are held together in continuous unity and maintain their occupation of a portion of space against each other and against all other bodies. Now, apart from these changes of *real* volume in *living* Beings consequent on nutrition, etc., it is necessary, as we have already said (8) to admit not merely *apparent* but *real* rarefaction and condensation, i. e., of a perfectly continuous solid, in organic substances in order to account, on the one hand, for the possibility of rectilinear motion, and, on the other, for the propagation of light, for universal attraction, elasticity etc.

For either the corporeal universe is a perfect *Plenum* of inelastic particles; and then how account for the possibility of free rectilinear motion? Or there are parts of actual space *perfectly vacant;* and then how account for universal attraction for the propagation of light, etc., across the Vacuua?

Here Quantitative Change, or *real* rarefaction and condensation, is one of the commonest phenomena in nature, and, as might naturally be supposed, accompanies more or less all other accidental modifications of quantified corporeal substances. Indeed, it is clear that an extended substance cannot be intrinsically modified without having its extension in some way or other affected by the change.

20. **Local Motion.**—The passage of a body from one *place* (11) to another is called *local* motion. If the whole body

changes its place, we have what is called Molar Motion. If the whole body maintains the same relative place, while only its continuous parts are rarefied and condensed successively, and so change their relative places, we have what is called Molecular Motion.

Now, apart from the Spontaneous Motion of the animal world—obvious sufficient reason of which is found in faculties of the living Being, which are clearly distinct from the mere change of place—we say that, even in inorganic bodies, local motion is inexplicable, unless we admit the existence, in the moving body, of a real physical quality which is not the mere change of place, but its efficient cause.

Let us roughly illustrate what we mean. Take a baseball lying at rest in the field. It will never move itself, but it has the capacity or potentiality to be moved; and if you once actuate that potentiality, it will, if unhindered, keep the even tenor of its way long after the pitcher's name is forgotten. An *impulse,* or force, or quality has been actuated in it which will bear it on in a straight line forever with a steady velocity, unless some opposing force intervene to stop it or turn it aside.

Now, this impulse, or propelling force is something intrinsic in the moving body which is the immediate efficient cause of its continuous change of place. Hence, local motion, whether molar or molecular, implies an active force actuated in the moving body which is not local motion, but its cause. "Motion," as Silliman puts it, "requires a force to *maintain* it, as well as to produce it."

21. **Qualitative Change.**—All the remaining absolute accidents (Gen. Met. 50) of corporeal substances as such may be classed under one common head as *Qualities, e. g.,* 'shape,' 'color,' 'taste,' 'heat,' 'electricity,' etc. Now, if these things are objectively what our normally disposed faculties perceive them to be—and we cannot deny it without taking up a position

which leads to absolute scepticism—then the existence of Qualitative Changes in the corporeal world is an obvious fact.

That these changes affecting as they do extended bodies in space should be accompanied by local change, molecular or molar, in the modified body, is, as we have said (18), to be expected. Nay, that to every *qualitative* change a certain measure of *quantitative* or *local* change should so exactly correspond, that the measure of one may be taken as the symbol of the other, is but what we should anticipate. But if one should go on to confound the two and say, *e. g.,* that different colors are *merely* different modes of local motion, he would be perpetrating the puerile sophism, that because two things are invariably associated, therefore one of them is the other.

For the rest, we might ask him, how does he know of the existence of the local motion? If he will not trust his senses when they tell him of the objectivity of light, color and heat, why should he trust their testimony to the existence of local motion?

Hence, as we do not object to a chemist using a certain formula for a compound substance, which expresses not what it *is,* but what it *may be resolved into;* so we do not object to a physicist's expressing the various *qualities* of bodies, as far as may be *in terms of local motion,* provided it be understood that the formula represents, not the *quality* in question, but its invariable *concomitant,* or, perhaps, we might better say, *effect.*

22. So much then for the four kinds of change or motion. (Though substantial changes are not strictly Motion, still they imply motion, or successive Qualitative change, preparatory to the education of the new Substantial form.)

Now, as all change implies a transition from potentiality to act, and as such transition can only be effected by *active forces* actually exercising their energies, it follows that there are constantly at work in the corporeal world a variety of active forces as different in their specific character as these changes are.

On the other hand, these active forces could effect nothing, if there were not corresponding capacities or *potentialities* in material substances, reducible to act; the greatest artist cannot make a statue out of mere water.

Hence, recalling what we said in General Metaphysics (67 c) about the efficiency of Secondary Causes, we conclude that the corporeal substances around us are really endowed with a vast variety of *active* and *passive* properties by the *efficiency* and *actuation* of which all the wonderful cosmic changes we behold are produced.

But though all these cosmic phenomena result immediately from the *efficiency* of material forces; yet the measure, harmony, uniformity and constancy—the *finality,* in a word—of the *world's* motion as a whole can find its *sufficient reason* only in an Intelligence which has so adapted these blind activities and potentialities and so ordered their mutual relations that all work together for the universal good (Metaphysics, 71).

23. **The Laws of Nature.**—A law is primarily, A permanent rule of action. Now, ordinary experience shows us that the irrational natures around us follow uniformly and constantly each its own fixed mode of action, and hence, these constant uniform modes of action are called Laws of Nature. That many of these laws are known to us with certainty is also clear.

But we may ask further, **how far are these laws necessary?** As the very *existence* of finite beings is *contingent,* of course their *action* is also, absolutely speaking, a *contingent fact.* But supposing their existence and the existence of a *final* cosmic order *freely* determined by the Creator, how far is their mode of action necessary? To this we may answer again, that *supposing certain conditions present,* the mode of action of irrational beings is necessary, i. e., the laws of nature are *conditionally* necessary. The conditions of which we speak are chiefly—(1) the *absence* of impediment to or interference with the natural action of the agent, (2) the *presence* of the ordinary divine preserving and concurring influence. Hence in a *particular* case the free Omipotence of God can hinder, neutralize, elevate or otherwise modify the action of the creature for wise and worthy ends. Such a particular instance of deviation from the ordinary rule of action of a corporeal being can be recognized as easily as any other obvious fact, and upon proper examination of all the circumstances, can be known to be due to divine interference, on the principle that every effect must have a proportionate cause.

CHAPTER II.

THE INTRINSIC CONSTITUENTS OF CORPOREAL SUBSTANCE.

This chapter may be divided into three articles, viz.:—

I. —The State of the Question;

II. —Unsatisfactory theories;

III.—Hylomorphism.

ARTICLE I.—STATE OF THE QUESTION.

24. From what we have said in the preceding chapter, we may, in general, describe a body as a substance which connaturally possesses continuous extension of three dimensions, and is endowed with certain activities of powers of producing change in other Beings like itself. But reason will not rest satisfied with a mere generic description; it seeks a Real Definition. A knowledge of properties will not suffice: we want to know what the *substantial thing* is to which the properties belong; seeing the stream we wish to know its source.

We are in search, then, of **a theory as to the ultimate inner nature of corporeal substance, as such.** Now, it would seem to be sufficiently obvious that we are not at liberty to construct a theory of the nature of bodies *a priori,* and then to force the facts with which all men are familiar into harmony with it; rather surely, the other way about, the familiar facts are the secure fixed data, while the value of a theory will depend wholly on its capacity rationally to account for them. Yet this plain rule is only too often forgotten. Theories are daily invented and obtruded upon us, in regard to the intrinsic nature of corporeal substances, which, far from explaining, contradict the manifest facts; and when the plain man remonstrates that he with the rest of mankind is conscious of perceiving the facts, he is calmly told, "So much the worse for the facts and for mankind that perceives them: they are mere illusions of sense."

25. Before proposing, then, any theory as to the ultimate forces corresponding to the various changes taking place, and intrinsic nature of bodies, let us set before us clearly and briefly **one or two classes of facts which such a theory is bound to harmonize with and explain.**

(a) We have first, what we may call the Antinomies of corporeal substances, *e. g.,* in one and the same substance, the unity and multiplicity involved in its continuous extension; its elective affinities and antipathies; its inertia and passivity on the one hand and its aggressive activity on the other, etc., etc.

(b) We have cohesion, elasticity, gravitation, universal attraction and the other physical properties common to all bodies to account for.

(c) We have, again, what are called Chemically Simple substances, i. e., those which are not chemically resolvable into specifically different substances, *e. g.,* 'H.,' 'O.,' 'C.,' etc., which though generally alike in possessing extension, divisibility, mobility and many other properties common to all bodies; yet are specifically different in density, affinities, active and passive properties, etc.

(d) Lastly, we have substantial changes (18) of two or more chemically simple substances into a new compound substance wholly different in specific properties from any or all of the components, yet resolvable into them and into them alone by chemical analysis, and so *virtually,* though not *formally,* containing them. "Bear in mind that when we say that water is composed of H. and O., we mean no more than this, that by various chemical processes these two substances can be produced from water. * * * We cannot say that water consists of H. and O. * * * In all instances of true chemical union and decomposition, the qualities of the substances concerned in the process entirely disappear, and wholly different substances with new qualities appear in their place."*

Finally, these substantial changes are not effected at random, but require the combination of certain determinate substances according to fixed invariable laws of Definite Proportions, Multiple Proportion, etc.

26. Independently, then, of any hypothesis, we are safe in making the following **syllogisms as to the ultimate nature of all corporeal substances.**

(a) Properties which are not only different, but diametrically opposite, imply a difference in the substantial sources from which they flow. But the unity and multiplicity, the activity and passivity, etc., which are characteristic of every corporeal substance, etc., are properties not only different but mutually contradictory. Therefore, there is a certain *dualism* or *composition* in the ultimate intrinsic nature of every cor-

*Cooke, "The New Chemistry," p. 98-99.

poreal substance which a satisfactory theory of the nature of bodies must account for.

(b) If in a given class of substances there are certain properties *common* and constant in *every* individual of the class, while certain other properties are *peculiar* and constant in different *groups* of these individuals, then, the inner substantial nature of all these substances is composed of two principles, one of which is homogeneous and the source of their *generic* likeness; the other, heterogeneous and the source of their *specific* difference. But it is a fact, that there are certain properties common to all corporeal substances, and certain others peculiar in different species of them. Therefore, all corporeal substances are composed of two principles, etc.

(c) In every substantial change, we must account for two distinct *substantial* principles, one of which is generic and constant in both terms of the change, the other differential and specific, which in union with the generic common element constitutes a *complete substance* of this or that peculiar species. But all corporeal substances are susceptible of substantial change. Therefore, in all corporeal substances we must account for the existence of two distinct substantial components.

27. To account for this *substantial dualism* in the nature of bodies is a problem which has occupied the attention of thinking men as far back as the history of philosophy extends; and well it may; for the answer to it will express the relation in which the Mind and Matter of which man himself is composed stand to each other.

Setting aside the Idealism which would make the whole substantial universe a mere illusory projection of the Ego upon a background of nothingness, and the Pantheism which maintains that all bodies are nothing but one eternal substance of God evolving, modifying and variously manifesting itself, all views on the subject may be reduced to one or other of the three famous theories: Atomism, Dynamism and Hylomorphism. If antiquity be a fault or newness a merit in a theory, all three have about equal claims on our consideration; for all three come to us from Ancient Greece.

The *Atomic* theory may be said to have been first proposed as a system of Democritus (about 400 B. C.); and Tait tells us that, as to what corporeal substance is, modern Atomism "knows no more than Democritus or Lucretius did." The origin of the *Dynamic* theory is ascribed to Pythagoras (about 550 B. C.); it has never been popular, "rather a hobby of esoteric circles, than an accepted theory in schools of science." *Hylomorphism* dates from Plato and Aristotle (about 350 B. C.). Evolved and perfected by SS. Augustine and Thomas this theory has always held a prominent place in the history of philosophy.

We now proceed to examine briefly these various theories.

ARTICLE II.—ATOMISM AND DYNAMISM.

28.   Both these systems agree in supporting all bodies to be mere aggregations of immutable indivisible units, but they differ in the account they give of the character of these ultimate units. Atomism postulates atoms of *mass;* while Dynamism would construct the material universe out of atoms of mere *force.*

29.   **Pure Atomism,** or as Tyndall calls it, "the mechanically intelligent theory of Dalton," supposes all bodies to consist of very minute, perfectly hard particles, "extended pieces of matter," in fact, "with shape and motion, intelligible subjects of scientific investigation." These particles, or mass atoms, have no inherent forces or activities of their own: they

are merely the passive subjects or recipients of local motion of great velocity and complexity. Tait, for instance, tells us that in a mass of H, at ordinary temperature and pressure, each of these minute particles is moving at the rate of seventy miles a minute and collides with other particles and, therefore, changes its direction 17,700,000,000 times in a second. Where this motion comes from, we are not told, except that it does not come from the particle itself, but is communicated to it from without.

As to the nature of these particles there has been much variety of opinion among atomists. The common tendency at present is to regard them as perfectly *homogeneous,* either all of hydrogen, or all of ether, or of some other kin of Cosmic Vapor, or Cosmic Dust, or Perfect Fluid, which is supposed to fill all space. All the various so-called substances in nature, simple as well as compound, all their differences, and all their physical and chemical properties "result," Herbert Spencer says, "from differences of arrangement (and local motion) arising from the compounding and recompounding of ultimate homogeneous units."

Sir John Herschel describes the whole theory briefly, as "one that resolves the entire assemblage of natural phenomena into the mere knocking about of inconceivably minute billiard balls (or cubes, or tetrahedrons, if that be preferred) which once set in motion and abandoned to their mutual encounters and impacts work out the totality of natural phenomena."*

NOTE (1).—This theory, when it is assumed, as is often the case, to account for *all* the phenomena, material, vital and intellectual, with which we are familiar, is called *Materialism.* It is the starting-point and fundamental assumption of all thorough-going evolution. "As we now understand it," writes H. Spencer, "evolution is definable as a change from an in-

*Familiar Lectures on Scientific Subjects," p. 463.

coherent homogeneity to a coherent heterogeneity accompanying the dissipation of motion and integration of matter."

(2).—The reader will observe the vast difference between the Philosophical Atomism and the Atomic Theory with which he is familiar in the common text-books of chemistry. Of this latter we shall have a word to say presently.

30. Now, setting aside for the moment all vital phenomena, **is this theory, with its inert homogeneous atoms and purely passive local motion, a satisfactory explanation even of the inanimate material world in which we live?** We think not; and, for the following out of many reasons which will naturally suggest themselves to any one who gives any thought to the question.

1st.—It does not answer our question, what are the intrinsic constituents of corporeal substances? It tells us that all bodies are made up of what? Of other little bodies, each of which, as being *an extended piece of matter,* exhibits in its unity and divisibility, i. e., its continuous quantity, in its cohesion and resistive force, the intrinsic dualism of corporeal substance just as truly as a mountain does.

2d.—It explains all the manifold properties and *activities* of things by mere varieties in the position and motion of the *inactive* particles of the homogeneous atomic mass, i. e., its explanation is a denial of what it undertakes to explain. "The Kinetic theory," says W. Thompson, "gives not even a suggestion towards explaining the properties in virtue of which the atoms or molecules influence one another." And, in another place, the same great physicist declares that the theory "is a dream and can be nothing else until it can explain chemical affinity, electricity, magnetism, gravitation, etc.," which it is plain it cannot do; for, no number of inactive zeros, arrange them as you will, will ever give you an active unit.

3d. In like manner it explains away all the substantial differences between bodies by simply denying them. Gold and iron, water and coal-oil, sugar and strychnine, chalk and cheese are simply one and the same substance, with the slight *accidental* difference that the particles are variously grouped and are "knocked about" in various directions and with various velocities. Finally, we are left without *even a suggestion* as to why each chemical element is limited by nature to a select list of admissible companions; and the terms of its partnership (as to definite proportions, etc.) with every one of them are so strictly prescribed that no power in nature can alter them by the most trivial fraction.

31. If one asks how such a theory could ever be accepted, and become popular among reasonable men, the reason may be found:

1st.—In the natural tendency of the mind to reduce all things to some sort of unity and harmony;

2d.—In the tendency, equally strong, in our modern minds to do so in the easiest possible way without any very serious regard to the strictness of our method; hence, as the knocking about of billiard balls is a phenomenon familiar to most people, the formula Matter and Motion is a delightfully simple snythesis of all physical and chemical knowledge;

3d.—Lastly, the fact that it is not unpleasant for a troubled conscience to be permitted to hope that perhaps itself and its bad thoughts and deeds as well as its good ones are mere "modes of atomic motion over which no fellow has any control," may have contributed somewhat to the popularity of materialism.

32. As pure Atomism admits matter only and no force, so **Dynamism** will have *force* only and *no matter*. *Instead* of solid particles with mass, shape and size, it recognizes only mathematical points or force-centers dotted about in space and

influencing one another, not by impact, but by action at a distance. If you can imagine an attraction (or repulsion) without any solid thing which attracts or is repelled; if you can localize this disembodied attraction in a mathematical point, and make it subject to the influence of other similar attractions; you can have some idea of a dynamical force-atom.

If you can make up your mind that such unextended force-atoms actually exist, and that all that we call corporeal substance is a mere aggregation of them; and that the difference between one body (simple or compound) and another, arises from a mere difference in the grouping and interplay of these mathematical force-atoms; then, you are a dynamist.

Your explanation of bodies refines away from the universe everything corresponding to our notion of corporeal substance: you deny extension and all substantial differences and changes: you reduce all our sense-perceptions to illusions; and hence, we cannot accept your theory. Though we may not enter with full sympathy into the first two items of Bossuet's criticism of it, we cannot help agreeing with the last when he says that it is "nova, pulchra, falsa."

33. **We are compelled, therefore, to reject the purely Atomic and Dynamic hypotheses;** because both fail to account for the substantial difference of bodies and for the substantial changes which are patent facts in nature; and because, moreover, the former denies all activities in corporeal substances, while the latter denies its extension and, we might almost say, its very existence. In a word, both fail to account for the essential dualism manifested in every body, great and small.

Yet both have a certain value, as seeking to express half truths. Atomism errs by attending only to the characteristics of bodies which are on the side of the passive homogeneous element in them: Dynamism attends solely to those which are on the side of the active element in them. When you synthesize both theories by assigning substantial sources of both orders of phenomena in the intrinsic nature of corporeal substance as such, you are at least on the way to a true theory of bodies. Now, this is precisely what Hylomorphism does, as we shall try to show briefly in the following article. But first a word on **Chemical Atomism,** as it is called.

34. Chemistry recognizes the existence of some sixty-five or seventy specifically different bodies which, so far at least, have resisted all attempts to analyze them into chemically simpler bodies. Besides these, it recognizes a vast number of other specifically different substances each of which on analysis, i. e., by the destruction of the compound as such, yields two or more of the elemental substances in certain fixed proportions. Now, it is assumed and on good grounds that in the act of synthesis or analysis, each of the combining elements is divided up into the smallest quantitative parts in which it is naturally capable of existing. Immediately before actual combination, these *atoms,* as they are called, are, at first, true substances of the same nature as the original masses of which they are parts, *e. g.,* 'an atom of H is as truly H as a gallon of it.' These specifically different particles under the influence of external agents act and react on one another in virtue of their mutual affinities until at length the nature of both is so altered that we have no longer distinct *atoms* of different substances, but perfectly homogeneous *molecules* of a new substance wholly different in properties from any of the original components. Hence, the chemist knowing the elemental substances from which these products spring names them after their ancestors, and thus expresses every compound substance in terms of two or more of the sixty-seven elements.

35. So far, we are all with the chemist. But should he go on to conclude, that since all bodies can be thus expressed in terms of his sixty-seven elements, therefore, the corporeal universe is nothing but a vast collection of very small bodies

of sixty-seven different kinds and that all compound substances are mere groups of these small bodies; then, we tell him that his conclusion is not philosophical:

1st—Because it explains an obvious fact (substantial change) by gratuitously denying it; and

2d—That, even omitting this decisive objection, his explanation of the nature of bodies is, at best, *penultimate;* for, each of his sixty-seven elemental bodies exhibits all the dualism of an essentially composite substance; and the question is, what are its substantial components?

Of course, it is quite allowable and very convenient for the chemist to express a compound substance in terms of the elements from whose chemical combination it is derived: but it must always be remembered that in this, Chemical Atomism is, as Cooke says, "only a temporary *expedient* for representing the facts of chemistry to the mind:"* and that, as another great modern chemist adds, its symbolism is a device of language, not a representation of actual facts.**

Article III.—Hylomorphism.

36. As has been said, every phenomenon of the corporeal universe asserts the intrinsic dualism of corporeal substance and manifests the presence in all bodies of two essential physical constituents really distinct from each other, viz.: *a homogeneous material principle* which is the source of their divisibility, mass, inertia and other generic properties, and *a differential dynamic principle,* which is the source of their unity, activity, specific properties, etc.

The former or homogeneous mass-principle, is of itself

*The New Chemistry, p. 103.
**Berthelot, Synthese Chimique, p. 167-69.

indifferent, potential, determinable as to being this specific substance or that, and is that constituent of bodies which remains
common and constant in all substantial changes. The latter, or
differential specific principle, determines the specific principle,
determines the specific nature of the substance and varies in
the various substantial changes which bodies undergo. Both
are *incomplete* substances from whose intrinsic union a complete corporeal substance or body of this or that specific nature
results.

Now if you call the former element Primal or Primordial
or Ultimate Matter; and, the latter Substantial Form, you have
in brief the hylomorphic ("matter-and-form") theory of the
nature of bodies.

Of course, many questions remain as to the peculiar characteristics of each of these two ultimate constituents of bodies,
their mutual relations, the passing away of old and the origin
of new substantial forms, etc., etc.; but the existence, in bodies
of a constant and a variable substantial element will not be
questioned by any one who analyzes the idea of substantial
change.

The argument, then, for hylomorphism is based on the
facts and reasoning given above (25, 26), and it is needless to
repeat it here. Substantial changes are a fact. In a substantial
change the *subject* is something substantial, and so are the constituents lost and gained; else, the change would be merely accidental. That the constant *subject* and the variable *terms* are
really distinct is also clear, since the same *matter* is actuated
successively by different forms.

37. As far as the general answer to the question, What
are the intrinsic constituents of bodies? is concerned, we might
safely leave the matter here; but the mind will feel more satisfied if we can determine a little more precisely the character of this Primal Matter and Substantial Form, their relation
to each other, etc. This we shall try to do very briefly, leaving

a large unexplored field for the genius of the philosophic student to work in.

38. As to the ultimate *material* element of bodies. It is not a complete substance, but an *incomplete* constituent of substance, the primal, constant, fundamental subject of substantial changes. It is a positive reality; yet it cannot exist *alone* unactuated by any form any more than extension can exist without a definite shape and figure. It is indestructible except by annihilation: no force in nature can do more than substantially change it; hence, the law, as it is called, of Conservation of Matter, i. e., whatever the change, the *new* being will always give the exact *weight* of the elements from which it is derived. Of itself considered apart from the forms which differentiate it, it is perfectly inert and homogeneous, essentially needing *some* form, yet indifferent to all forms and always in potency and ready to receive the proportionate action which would substantially transform it. It is neither C. nor fruit or flesh, but is successively the material basis of them all. The senses cannot perceive it: imagination cannot picture it: *reason* alone can apprehend it, and is compelled to recognize it as the constant, passive, inert element in the constitution of bodies.

39. As to the *formal* element.

(a) It, too, is clearly a constituent of corporeal substance, not a *complete* substance in itself. It may be described as The ultimate substantial determinant which actuates and differentiates primal matter and, by its union with it, constitutes a complete substance of this or that specific nature. All the specific differences with which we are familiar in the actions, properties and nature of bodies come from differences in their *substantial forms*. As matter passes up the line of corporeal being from the state of a simple elemental body to the condition of living sensitive flesh, it is *informed* successively by a series of substantial forms each of which contains virtually and excels by a new degree the perfections of the lower forms which have gone before it, whose place it takes; just as a higher number contains and excels those below it. Hence, we have a sort of hierachy in substantial forms according to which the various grades of perfection in corporeal substances are determined.

(b)   **In the entire cosmic order we can distinguish four broad generic grades of substantial forms, viz.:**

1st, Those of inanimate bodies; 2d, the vital principle in plants; 3d, the animal soul; 4th, the spiritual soul of Man. Of these four orders of substantial forms, the first three, as being wholly dependent on matter in their action and, consequently, in their existence and origin are called *material* forms. In each of these three orders of forms are included innumerable *specific* diversities in ascending degrees so that the highest species of a lower order just touches the boundary-line which separates it from the lowest species of the order above.

The human soul, on the contrary, as being independent of matter in its higher characteristic operations and, therefore, in its existence, its origin and its destiny is called a *spiritual* form. Hence, in the human body, primordial matter reaches its highest level. Here it is *informed* and constituted a complete substance by its immediate union with a spiritual soul "a little less than the angels," proceeding immediately from the creative hand of God; so that the resultant compound, Man, unites within himself the two great words of Spirit and Matter into which all creation is divided, and, hence, is well styled a Microcosmus or Little Universe.

(c)   The spiritual soul, or substantial form of man, needs, as we shall see later on, the immediate creative action of God to bring it into existence. But, leaving man out of the question, it is clear that in the three lower kingdoms of the irrational world; new substantial forms are constantly coming into existence, while others are as constantly disappearing.

Now, whence do these forms come? whither do they go? how are they produced in matter? An analogy drawn from a common accidental change will help us to understand the answer. Take a cube of soft wax and carefully model it into the shape of a rose. The new shape is something; for, it has cost you labor to produce it, and, if you are only skilful enough, it has given the wax a market value much greater than it had before. Now, whence this new perfection? You will say and rightly that the aptitude or *passive potency* of the wax and the *action* of the artist are sufficient to account for the new figure; or, in technical language, if you prefer it, that the rose-shape has been *educed* out of the *potentiality* of the wax by the action of a competent efficient cause. If, again, I ask you, what has become of the cubic form which the wax originally had and lament that you have annihilated it, you will answer that you have done nothing of the kind, that though it is not actually there—since wax cannot, at the same time, be rose-shaped and cubic—yet it is *potentially* there and can be had back again by a little effort on the part of an efficient cause.

Finally, before leaving our simile, notice (1) that the wax is of its nature *indifferent* as to what shape it may have; (2) that it must always have *some* shape; (3) that it cannot have *two* different shapes, e. g., 'of a rose and a cube,' at the same time; (4) that, while *actually* in any given shape, it is still in *potency* to receive any of the other innumerable shapes which the artist's skill can give it; (5) that the change from one shape to another may require more or less manipulation on the part of the *efficient cause, e. g.,* 'it is easier to change our cube into a tetrahedron than into the figure of a rose'; (6) that the wax needs the action of a competent efficient cause external to itself to effect any change in its shape.

Now we can apply all this to what is called the Passive Evolution of Matter, if we only bear in mind that, in substantial changes, there is question of the *ultimate inner nature* of the body, not of its outer visible accidents.

Primal matter, of itself and theoretically considered, is indifferent to any of the innumerable substantial forms which can complete it as a substance and make it a body of this or that specific nature, *e. g.,* 'C' or 'human flesh.' Yet it never exists alone, but is always actuated by *some* form. It cannot, however, be at once actuated by *two forms;* else, it would be two specifically different substances at the same time. But while actuated by one form it is still *in potency* to receive any other form. Yet it is not always in *proximate* potency to receive *every form, e. g.,* 'matter under the pure elemental forms of C. H. O. and N without intermediate substantial changes, would be but doubtful nourishment for man or beast.' Hence, there is a fixed order in nature, according to which matter is gradually elevated from lower to higher substances. Again, even when matter is in proximate potency (owing to the substantial form by which it is actuated) for a new substantial form, it is not by every *agent* that the new form can be *educed, e. g.,* 'only a horse can transform barley into horse-flesh. Lastly, when in matter thus proximately disposed, a new and higher form takes the place of the lower one preceding it through the action of proportionate natural causes, the new form is not *created,* but *educed* from the potentiality of the matter so disposed. Nor is the old form which passed away *annihilated,* but reduced to *potency,* and it, with all its characteristic properties and activities, can again be actuated by efficiency of proportionate causes.

40. Such, in very brief outline, is the scholastic theory of the nature of bodies. It may seem, at first sight, subtle and hard to grasp, but when we come to examine it closely and, especially, to apply it to the solution of the great problems connected with vegetative, animal and human life, we shall find

that it is forced upon us with overwhelming cogency by the inexorable facts of nature.

CHAPTER III.

Organic Life.

Article I.—Organic Life in General.

41. **Definition of Life.**—A *living* being is one which *moves itself,* which acts upon and perfects itself; one whose action as a living being begins and ends in itself.

The essential characteristics of vital action are, therefore, *spontaneity* and *immanence* as opposed respectively to the *inertia* and *transitive activity* of inanimate things.

42. **Division.**—Hence, we may classify the various *grades* of life with which we are familiar in the world around us under three general heads according to the different degrees of *spontaneity* manifested in their vital action:—

(a) The vital activity may be exercised without cognition of any kind on the part of the living being, *e. g.,* 'a *plant* simply *assimilates* material substances' i. e., changes them into its own living substances and thus develops and reproduces itself.

(b) Or the self-motion may imply cognition and appetition of *individual material objects* on the part of the living being, but without *liberty,* or power of consciously determining the *end* of perceptions, desires, local motion, etc., in regard to the individual material objects around it.

(c) Or finally, the living being may be capable of cognition and appetition of *abstract, universalized* or *wholly immaterial objects,* and, consequently, endowed with liberty and with the power of apprehending and determining the end of its actions. This "perfecta suique potens spontaneitas"—this *self-controlled* spontaneity—is the characteristic excellence of *human life.*

43. **Organic Life;** i. e., *vegetative* and *sensitive* life, is exercised *in* and *by* a material organism. An *organism* is a *natural* material structure composed of various parts (organs) each of which exercises a special function in relation to the life of self-motion of the whole. The organism at first consists of a single cell of protoplasm which nourishes and increases itself by *assimilation* of external substances and then divides so as to form two connected cells. Each of these again in turn increases, divides, etc., until the whole organism of cellular tissue is built up according to a fixed specific type.

44. **Essential Difference between living organisms and non-living bodies.**

(a) In *Origin.* Living organisms are produced only by *living bodies* of their own specific type.

(b) In *Development.* By nutrition and growth they construct and preserve themselves according to a certain morphological type within certain limits of size and during a certain limited time, after which they decay and disintegrate, even though all external conditions remain the same.

(c) In the *variety of functions* exercised by different parts of the same organic body.

(d) In the mutual *interdependence* of the different parts of the organism, so that all the organs *constantly* and *per se* act for *one* ultimate result—the development, preservation and propagation of the whole organic being.

(e) Lastly and chiefly, in the character of the *action* of the organic being, which is *spontaneous* and *immanent* and tends, not to equilibrium or rest, but to continual self-perfective motion.

NOTE.—The formal or dynamic principle of organic life is called a *soul*.

ARTICLE II.—VEGETATIVE LIFE.

45. This is the lowest, and in the visible world the most universal grade of life. The *lowest* because least independent of matter in its exercise, which consists in the development, conservation and propagation of a material organism. The *most universal,* as being common to plants, animals and men. Its chief functions are *nutrition, increase* and *propagation* of the organism.

46. **Nutrition** is that function by which a living organism converts external substances into its own. This implies various operations on the part of the living organism: *absorption* of external substances by roots, leaves, mouth, etc.; *digestion,* or preparation of these raw materials by various elaborate chemical processes; *circulation* of the food thus elaborated throughout the organism; and finally, *assimilation* or conversion of the food into the living substance of the organism. This last is strictly the act of *nutrition* or the *vital* act. The previous preparations may be called Vital actions, only inasmuch as they are accomplished under the influence and directive power of the living organism and for its benefit.

The purpose and necessity of the nutritive activity in the organism is clear. A microscopic germ cannot grow and evolve itself into a perfect plant or animal without assimilation or intussusception of new material.

47. **Growth** or increase is that function by which the living being builds up its complete organic structure according to a definite morphological type out of the nutriment assimilated.

48. **Generation** is that function by which the living organism produces out of its own living substance a *germ* or

seed capable of evolving itself into a new living organism similar in specific nature to the parent.

49. **Vegetative Life,** therefore, requires a dynamic principle in the organism which:

(a) *Modifies, elevates* and *controls* the physico-chemical properties of the anorganic matter absorbed, as it passes through the various channels which fit it for immediate assimilation;

(b) Makes the living organism capable of constant, self-perfective action, *e. g.,* 'development,' 'continual change and renovation of itself';

(c) Enables the living organism to communicate to a special portion of its own substance a *formative* power which makes the microscopic germ capable of building itself up into a complete living organism of the parent type, of preserving and restoring its integrity, and of propagating itself indefinitely.

But such a principle is essentially different from and superior to the dynamic principle in anorganic bodies.

Therefore, there is in every living vegetative organism a dynamic principle essentially different from and superior to the Forms of anorganic substances, i. e., a Vital Principle or *soul.*

NOTE (1).—Hence, a living vegetative organism is essentially different from a *crystal.* In the latter there is no nutrition, growth or generation, as explained above—no *immanent* action of any kind: its development is the result of mere external *accretion,* not of *assimilation.*

(2).—*Organicism* pretends to account for the phenomena of vegetable life by the *mere grouping* and interplay of inanimate atoms. But, no mere arrangement of a multitude of dead particles can account for one constant, spontaneous, immanent, self-perfecting activity. It would not help us at all to account for life to give us a piece of *dead* protoplasm, even if chemistry could succeed in producing it (which it cannot). We can get a whole perfectly-organized dead ox any day in the meat market. What we want is protoplasm with the *power* of nutrition, growth and reproduction, i. e., besides organized matter, we want a special dynamic principle within it, *animating* it, in order to account for the phenomena of vegetative life.

Again, it is not the organism that produces life, but life that produces, develops, preserves and propagates the organism. It is as if a little particle of matter should build itself up into a perfect watch, keeping itself in constant repair and be able to detach from itself little specks of matter, each capable of growing into, and reproducing the parent type indefinitely. *Organization,* therefore, far from being the *cause,* is the *effect* of life.

(3.)—The physical and chemical forces of matter are undoubtedly at work in the living organism, but they can account neither for the organism itself nor for its vital action, unless a special vital principle be admitted which permanently modifies, elevates, controls their action for a fixed end, viz.: the development, preservation and reproduction of a living organism of a specific type. As a matter of fact, all scientists are agreed that no force of chemistry can combine anorganic elements so as to form a single cell of *protoplasm;* much less, a *living cell;* much less, an *organism* capable of developing, preserving and propagating itself. "It is futile to attempt by chemistry to bridge over the chasm between the living and the non-living."—Du Bois Reymond, "Chemistry can never produce a leaf, a fruit, a muscle, an organ."—Berthelot. "All scientific experience tells us that life can be produced from a living being only."—Stewart and Tait. See Maher, Psychology, p. 547 seqq.)

(4.)—Within each living organism there is a non-living liquid (blood or sap) in continual circulation to nourish the organism, and to carry away the material continually being detached from the organism. What is called *organic* or *synthetic* chemistry has succeeded with difficulty in producing some of the non-living elements thus carried upwards or downwards by the non-living stream, *e. g.*, 'formic acid,' 'urea,' etc. This is the utmost that chemistry has been able to accomplish in regard even to the external products of life, and it does so only by means of powerful electric currents or enormous temperatures.

50. In *plants* there are no *organs* of sensation, no evidences of perception, feeling, emotion or spontaneous local motion. Hence, we are justified in saying that **plants have no power of sensation.**

The motions of the sensitive plant, fly-trap, etc., are due to physical contractility of fibre, etc., under the influence of heat, light, friction, etc. The motions of zoospores, antherozoids, etc., have not that irregularity, intermittence and arbitrarary change of direction which indicate *spontaneous* local motion.

51. *A fortiori* the dynamic principle of merely **vegetative life is not spiritual,** i. e., capable of acting and existing by itself apart from matter. For, all the vital operations of plant are essentially dependent on the material organism, i. e., nutrition, growth and generation are exercised in and through the material organism.

NOTE.—Hence, the Soul of the plant is not created by a special action of God, but *educed* from the potentiality of matter by the action of a proportionate natural cause, i. e., by a living being of the same species, and ceases to exist on the destruction of the organism.

52. Natural corporeal substances are specifically distinguished from each other, not by the *mass*-principle in them, but by the *active* or dynamic principle. Plants are natural cor-

poreal substances, and the matter of which they are composed does not distinguish them from other corporeal substances. In fact, it may become C, O, H, N, as simple elements, or any of their combinations. Hence, **plants are distinguished by the dynamic or life-principle in them,** from other corporeal substances. Hence, the vegetative soul is truly a substantial form—the *differentiating* substantial constituent of the living body.

NOTE (1).—Take care not to imagine the plant soul as one *complete* substance indwelling in the organism as in another *complete* substance. In that case the organism would not be a living body endowed with immanent activity. The soul of the living plant must therefore be conceived as a substantial constituent pervading and vivifying the whole organism whence flows the unity, activity and specific properties of the plant.

(2).—In general, therefore, a Soul may be defined as The substantial form of an organized body capable of spontaneous immanent action. We say, *capable* of vital action: because a thing may be a living body even though it does not actually *exercise* any vital function, *e. g.,* 'hybernating animals,' 'frozen fish,' 'frogs,' etc.

53. In each individual plant there is but **one vital principle or soul,** for, *one* vital *activity* manifests one vital *principle.* But in each separate plant all vital activity *constantly, naturally* and *per se* tends to one definite result—the development, preservation and reproduction of one living organism of a fixed specific type. Amid all the variety of parts and functions in the plant, *one* immanent result is steadily aimed at and procured; and this constant ultimate unity of *effect* demands unity of *principle* as its proportionate cause.

NOTE (1).—We said above, each individual plant, because we have many instances of numbers of both plants and animals living together in connected clusters or colonies, *e. g.,* 'corals,' 'mosses,' etc.

(2).—The phenomena that sometimes take place on the separation of parts from a living organism require a word of explanation here. In some cases the separated parts, if cared for in a special way, can continue to exercise indefinitely *some,* though not all, of the functions of the original organism, *e. g.,* 'a graft of a pear tree, if planted in the earth, will die, but if properly inserted in another suitable tree it will live, grow and produce its own species of leaves, fruit, etc.' In other cases the separated parts can live on by themselves and exercise all the functions of the original organism, *e. g.,* 'branches of the vine,' 'poplar,' etc.

The explanation is this. Each organism begins as a simple living cell of protoplasm. This Mother Cell, as it is called, increases by nutrition and divides into two cells; these again increase, divide, etc., until a whole organism of the parent type is built up. These Derived or Daughter-Cells, as they are called, are all *living matter,* but incomplete in themselves and destined to form part of some organ, *e. g.,* 'root,' 'fibre,' etc. In the lower grades of plants and animals the whole organism is very simple, and when such plants have built up all the organs of their simple structure their further growth is but a *repetition* of the whole previous structure. If, then, one of these living *sections, e. g.,* 'of a vine,' is separated, it possesses a complete organism and can put forth roots, etc., and live on alone. The vital principle of such a plant is *actually one,* but *potentially* as *manifold* as there are completely organized *sections* in it, i. e., while the parts are united there is but one vital principle in the whole plant, as is evidenced in the mutual interdependence of all the parts upon each other, and upon the whole; but when the parts are separated each has enough of organization to sustain the vital principle and to live an independent life of its own.

Sometimes no one section is quite complete in itself. It may lack, for instance, the power of putting forth roots and thus acquiring nutriment for itself. But if this deficiency can be artificially supplied, *e. g.*, by properly grafting it on a suitable rooted stem from which it can receive its nutritive material, it can do all the rest for itself. It will assimilate the nutriment and change it into, *e. g.*, pear-wood, produce pears, etc., though grafted on quite a different tree. And here again we have an instance of "anima vegetatrix, *actu* una *potentia* multiplex."

54. **As to the origin of organic life upon the earth,** the doctrine of Abiogenesis or Spontaneous Generation, i. e., the origin of life from the mere grouping and interplay of inanimate anorganic atoms has been sufficiently refuted above (49). No grouping or multiplication of o's, no matter how long you may continue the process, will give you 1; and in the same way no mere grouping of inanimate particles will give you a living, self-perfective organism. Reason cannot admit an effect without a proportionate cause.

Moreover, all the elaborate experiments of Pasteur, Tyndall, etc., have shown to a certainty that, as Huxley says, "the doctrine of *biogenesis,* 'life from life,' is victorious all along the line."

On the other hand, it is certain from Geogony, or the science of the formation of the earth,, and from Geology, or the science of the material substances of which the crust of the earth is composed, that there was a time when organic life did not exist upon the earth, and was in fact impossible.

Hence, all life that has appeared since, from monera to man, is a *caused* thing, an effect, and requires a proportionate *cause*. Very little reflection will show us that the ultimate living cause of life must be itself *uncaused*—a self-existent eternal life.

55. **Organic life is transmitted by generation,** i. e., the production by a living organism out of its own living substance of a new living being specifically similar to itself, i. e.,

of a new being having within itself the power of developing itself into a complete organism specifically similar to the parent type.

Sometimes the new organism may be had by taking cuttings or bulbs from the parent stem. The formation of such parts by the parent organism is called Aggeneration.

Usually, however, the new being produced by *generation* is a highly specialized particle containing within its small dimensions the power of building itself up into a complete organism (a fly or an elephant, an oak tree or a fern) according to the nature of the parent.

Again, there are some cases where the complete life-germ is wholly the product of a *single* organism without any influence from without. This is called Asexual Generation.

More frequently, however, the living germ is the product of *two factors*. One plant, for instance, produces Ovules,, another plant of the same *species* produces Pollen. Neither of these elements separately, but the combination of the two, will give us the complete life germ or seed. Naturally, the new being, as it is produced by two distinct causes, will tend to possess the characteristics of both, a fact which the gardener takes advantage of to produce new *varieties* of the same *species* of flower. The union of pollen and ovule is called Fertilization or Fecundation of the ovule, and it results in an internal substantial modification by which the life-principle of the new plant is *educed from the potentiality of matter*.

NOTE.—We have said that both ovule and pollen must come from plants of the *same species*. If they are taken from plants of different species, the great universal law is that their union will give no result; both ovule and pollen will simply decay. In exceptional cases, when the two species from which these elements are derived are very similar, fecundation may take place, in which case the seed will produce neither of the parent types, but a cross between the two, called a *hybrid*.

These hybrids cannot perpetuate their new type.   As a rule they are altogether *sterile,* or incapable of reproduction.   In the few cases where they produce offspring, these after a few generations either die out or return to one or other of the two original types.   This law, which is absolutely universal in nature, is called the Law of Reversion, and is the great safeguard of the permanence or *fixity* of specific types in nature.

56.   **The fecundated life-germ produced by generation will give us an individual living being of a definite specific type,** possessing in itself the power to build up by slow degrees a fixed type of organism and no other.   The order and the path it must follow in its development are defined for it beforehand, and no power in nature can change them.   You may destroy the germ or embryo, but you cannot alter its powers or its destiny.   "It is possible that at the first moment of their existence all animals resemble each other as spheres of protoplasm, but the specific type of each is fixed from the first and governs all its development.   The embryo of a vertebrate is a vertebrate (potentially) from the start, and never corresponds to an invertebrate."—Von Baer, Agassiz, etc.

NOTE.—Of course *accidental* modifications may result from food, climate and other external circumstances; but they can never *substantially* alter the fixed specific type.

57.   Finally as our life-germ has to build up gradually into, a complete organism, *e. g.,* 'of an oak,' 'a horse' or 'an elephant, it is no wonder that on its passage to perfection it should exhibit many strange shapes and appearances more or less resembling creatures lower than itself.   In some cases these successive changes take place while the new being is still enclosed in the egg or within the organism of the parent.   In other cases the changes take place after the *birth* of the new being, but are all accomplished within the lifetime of a single individual, *e. g.,* 'a butterfly.'   These changes of form are

called *Metamorphoses*. Lastly, we have cases where it would appear that the lives of several successive individuals are required to bring the offspring to the full parental type; so that "the parent finds no resemblance to herself in her offspring till she comes down to the great grandchild"; *e. g.*, 'the medusa.' This is called the phenomenon of Alternate Generation.

But whatever the mode of development may be, it is as fixed for each type as natural law can make it.

58. Not only, then, is Life only from Life, or "Biogenesis," a fundamental law of nature, but "Like from Like," or "Homogenesis," is a law equally universal. All *observations* and *experiments* affirm it. *Reason* itself requires it on the principle that *every effect must have a proportionate cause*. If a living being communicates vitality to a portion of its own substance, that vitality cannot be superior to or of a different nature from that which the parent itself possesses.

Heterogenesis, therefore, or Equivocal Generation, i. e., offspring of a different type from parent, in whatever form it may be proposed, is inadmissible.

ARTICLE III.—SENSITIVE LIFE.

59. **Sensitive Life** implies a living organism capable of perceiving individual material objects, of feeling, desire and aversion and of spontaneous local motion. In the present article we shall consider briefly these *functions* of animal life, and the *nature* of the animal soul from which they proceed.

(i) *Functions of Sensitive Life.*

60. **Sensitive Cognition in General** may be described as a *vital reaction* by which a sentient faculty, in response to an impression received from an individual material object, produces within itself an *intentional representation* (78, below) of the object. Hence, there are four elements to be considered in

sensation, viz.: (a) the sentient faculty, (b) the sensile object, (c) the impression produced by the sensile object in the sentient faculty (technically called Impressed Image or Species), (d) the formal act of perception or the actual representation of the object (technically called the Expressed Image or Species). We may illustrate this by a rough analogy; thus, Given a substance on the one hand, a seal on the other, it is required to stamp the seal on the substance. In the first place, the substance must be in a condition to receive the impression, and the seal must be in a condition to give the impression. Again, the substance of itself is indifferent as to what impression it shall receive; it can receive the impression of this seal, or that, or the other. That it express one rather than the other depends upon which acts upon it or determines it to a particular representation; hence, the seal must act upon the substance in order to produce an impression of itself. But this is not enough. The seal may act forever and produce no image of itself unless the substance *reacts;* but when the substance acted upon by the seal reacts it becomes a *re*-presentation of the seal. If, finally, we can imagine the substance thus *informed* with the image of the seal, as *perceiving,* not the image, but the seal itself which helped to produce it, we shall have a rough illustration which will help us to form an idea of sensation and, indeed, of cognition generally.

61. Applying the preceding analogy to our present subject and remembering that (according to the axioms, "quidquid recipitur secundum modum recipientis recipitur," and "agere sequitur esse") the *impression* received in and the *reaction* of the sentient organ are not merely physical, but *psychophysical* phenomena, we may gather up, the general doctrine of sense-perception in the following brief statements.

(a) In all sensitive cognition the object must be united to the faculty by its *impressed* image or species, else, as the cognitive faculty is indifferent and undetermined of itself, it will not represent any one object rather than another.

(b) Sensation is not the mere *reception* of an impression of the object in the living organic faculty; for, sensation is a vital immanent *action,* while the *mere* impression of the object is nothing more than a transient action of the object by which the faculty *suffers* an intrinsic modification.

(c) The impression received from the object *determines* the vital faculty and thus enables it to produce the *expressed* image or vital representation; for, the formal act of sensation is such that it can proceed from neither independently of the other. The faculty is incapable of producing it without a determination received from the object; and, on the other hand, as we have said above, the mere passive reception of the determination is not a vital act of perception.

(d) The *subjective* image or species is not *that which* is perceived in sensation, but that *by which* the cognitive faculty directly and immediately perceives the object. It is essentially a *formal* sign by which not itself but the thing signified is directly and immediately perceived.

(e) Hence, the fundamental difference between *cognitive* and non-cognitive natures; the latter possesses only their own proper form; the former, besides their own form, acquire also *intentional* or representative forms of the objects of their actual cognition.

NOTE.—"The *organic* constituents of the sentient faculties, generally, consists of the *nervous system.* This is composed of two parts, the central mass and the branches which ramify throughout the body. The central mass, called the *cerebro-spinal axis,* is made up of the brain and the spinal cord passing from it down through the backbone. The brain consists of a soft, convoluted substance of mixed grey and white matter. The spinal cord consists of a column of the white fibrous matter, enclosing a core of grey cellular substance. From the spinal cord between every two vertebrae there issues forth two pairs of *nerves*. The nerves proceeding from the front of the spinal column are called anterior, *efferent* or *motor* nerves, as they transmit impulses outwards, and are the organic instruments of muscular movement. The nerves coming from the back of the spine are called *afferent,* or *sensory* nerves, because by their means the organic impressions which accompany sensations are conveyed inwards from the various external sense-organs of the body. In the several external sense-organs these nerves are arranged and modified in various ways to suit the various psychic faculties and to respond to their external stimuli."

It is hardly necessary to remark that the perfection and differentiation of the nervous system varies according to the grade of the sentient being in the scale of animal life.

62. As we have already said, the sphere of sensitive cognition is limited to *material objects as affected by material indiduating notes.* Hence, the first great division of the sensitive faculties of cognition is into those which perceives material objects external to the sentient subject and those which perceive, retain or recall the sensations of the external senses, or perceive certain other concrete material aspects of external objects which do not fall within the sphere of the five external senses, and yet are necessarily connected with the preservation and perfection of animal life. The former are called *external* senses, the latter *internal.*

63. The External Senses.—These are sight, hearing, smell, taste and touch. The peripheral extremities of the nervous system immediately concerned in the operations of these five senses are, respectively, the *rods and cones* of the retina of the eye, the *Cortian organ* of the ear, the *mucous membrane* of the upper cavity of the nose, the *gustative*

papillae of the tongue and palate, and the *tactile papillae* of the dermis, or under-skin.

64. The *formal objects* of these senses are (following the order above) colored extension, sound, odor, sapidity and extended pressure or resistance.

NOTE (1).—*Temperature* in so far as it is perceived as an objective quality of bodies, may be considered (like softness, roughness, etc.) as a secondary modification of the proper object of touch.

(2).—The five external senses are found only in the higher of more perfect animals. The lower types have only the sense of *touch* and probably of *taste*. Yet even some of these lower types manifest a certain vague sensibility to light and sound which is often spoken of as Dermatoptic Sensibility.

65. As to the *objectivity* of the perception of the external senses, see Logic, n. 104, etc.

66. **The Internal Senses.**—The immediate and direct objects of external sense-perception are individual facts and phenomena *external* to the sentient subject as such. The immediate and direct objects of the *internal* senses, on the contrary, are the present or past sensations, or subjective states of the sentient subject, as well as certain concrete aspects of the objects perceived by the external senses, which, however, do not fall within the sphere of any of the five external senses. These internal senses are four: the *common* or *central* sense, the *imagination,* the *sensuous memory* and the *estimative sense* or *instinct*. The organs of these senses are situated in the hemispheres of the brain.

67. The *central* or *common sense* is an internal organic faculty which perceives, distinguishes and synthesizes the actual operations and affections of the various sensitive organs which ramify from the brain. Thus, the sense of sight may

perceive a certain object as white; the sense of touch, as hard; and the sense of taste, as sweet. When these several data are referred on to the *central* sense, the sentient subject becomes aware that it is in the presence of one external object which is white, sweet and hard, pleasant to sight and taste, but painful to the touch.

As the central sense is thus the *terminus* to which all our external sense-perceptions are referred, so it is also the *source* from which all the sensitive activity of the peripheral senses is derived. "Vis sentiendi diffunditur in organa quinque sensuum ab aliqua una radice communi, ad quam etiam *terminantur* omnes immutationes singulorum sensuum." Hence, when the central sense is rendered inactive, as in sleep, or by nerve-poison, *e. g.,* chloroform, all the external senses become inoperative.

68. *The imagination* is an internal sensitive faculty which retains and reproduces the past experiences of the central and external senses. It may recall these representations singly, or combine them to form entirely new images. Thus it can recall the sensations of sight, sound, etc., which have been experienced, and it can also form new representations by combining them, *e. g.,* 'representations of mountains of gold,' 'walking trees,' 'rivers of blood,' etc.

69. **The causes which determine the imagination to reproduce the sensile representations it retains** are mainly :

(a) The association which exists between the objects whose images are recalled, *e. g.,* 'co-existence or succession in time and space,' 'relations of whole and part,' 'relations of similarity and contrariety,' etc. On account of this association, an object will naturally recall those related to it in past experience ;

(b) The internal condition of the body, inasmuch as it affects the brain. The brain is the organ of this faculty; hence, an impression, however produced on the living brain, similar to that which accompanied a given imaginative sensation, is likely to recall that sensation. Hence, the varied unconnected series of imaginative representations which occur in dreams or in cases of violent fever; hence, too, the predominance of sad or pleasant *phantasms* according to the various states of the nervous system.

NOTE (1).—The state of *sleep,* as we have said, results from the temporary suspension of the activity of the *central* sense (caused either by natural fatigue or by artificial means) and the consequent inactivty of the other sensitive faculties. During the time of sleep the nutritive functions are exercised more regularly and perfectly, and the wear and tear of the nervous system, occasioned by sensuous activity, is repaired. Hence, natural sleep has been described as "vinculum sensorii primi quod fit gratia salutis."

If, however, during this state of sleep, any impression, whether from within the organism or from without, should reach that portion of the brain which is the organ of the imagination and arouse this faculty to action, it will reproduce some of the many images of past experience of which it is the storehouse; and these, in turn, will recall others in a series according to the nature of the present impression and the laws of association, etc., spoken of above. This activity of the imagination partially arouses the *central* sense to action: and as the primary function of the latter faculty in the normal waking state is to refer the various impressions passed on to it from the external senses to the external objects which produced them, so now abnormally stimulated to action and without the influence of the external senses to guide it, it refers the phantasms of the imagination to the external world and "gives to airy nothing a local habitation and a name."

This projection into the outer world of the phantasms of the imagination when it occurs in sleep is called a *dream.*

(2).—In *somnambulism* some of the external senses seem to be open to impressions from without which are woven into the texture of the dream, and this serves to intensify the illusion and to call even the *motor* faculties into play.

(3).—A *hallucination* may be called a *waking dream*. In some case of hyperæsthesia, or exceptional morbid excitement of the nervous system, the representations of the imagination become so extremely vivid as even to counterfeit and overbalance the normal external sensations. The whole sensitive energy of the soul is, as it were, absorbed by the phantasmal image, and the waking sufferer regards it as an *external reality*. It is even said that, at times, the internal disturbance may be so great as to produce modifications in the peripheral organs similar to those that are normally produced by external objects.

(4).—"*Hypnosis* is a species of artificial sleep in which some of the sentient organs are inhibited, while others are overstimulated. When induced by human agency this state involves a dependent condition of the subject which makes him responsive to the *suggestions* (by words or other signs) of the hypnotizer. The secret of this strange power of suggestion is probably to be found in the fact that the last and strongest impression left in the central sense and imagination just before the inhibition and hyperæsthesia are affected, is produced by the commands and personality of the hypnotizer. His image will then occupy all the energies of the imagination and central sense and his suggestions will, as a general rule, be followed and obeyed with almost automatic precision, while the subject remains insensible to all other external impressions."

70. The *sensitive memory* retains, recalls and recognizes, *as perceived before,* the representations of the various internal and external senses. In this it differs from the imagination, that while the latter merely reproduces objects of past experi-

ence, the memory also recognizes them as old acquaintances that have been met before. *Recognition* of past objects of internal or external sense-perception is therefore the characteristic function of the sensitive memory.

NOTE.—"The tendency of an experience to lapse out of memory is in proportion to the feebleness of the original impression and the infrequency of its repetition."

"A past experience becomes unrecognizable in proportion to the length of time and the number and vivacity of the experiences which have intervened since its last occurrence or reproduction."

71. **The estimative sense or instinct,** as it is commonly called, is an internal organic faculty which apprehends certain individual concrete notes of material objects which do not come within the sphere of any or all of the external senses. Thus, "the lamb does not flee because the color or form of the wolf is disagreeable to the external senses, and the bird does not collect twigs for its nest because they are attractive in themselves, but both animals are endowed with a faculty which, under appropriate conditions, is determined by the apprehension of these objects to guide them in the mere execution, without foresight or reflection, of operations beneficial to their specific natures respectively."

72. **The organic character of all the faculties enumerated above is manifest,** as their objects do not transcend the sphere of individual concrete material facts and "phenomena—singularia qualia-quanta." In man, as in the lower animals, these faculties are organic, but their operations are more perfect, inasmuch as they are subject to the guidance of intellect and free will.

73. **The Sensuous Appetites.**—The term *appetite* is used in a very wide sense. It denotes all forms of internal

inclination, comprehending alike (1) the natural tendencies or affinities implanted in all finite beings, even plants and inanimate substances, which impel them blindly towards what is suitable to and perfective of their nature, independently of all cognition on their part; and (2) the attractions and aversions which follow upon cognition in sentient and rational beings.

The former class of inclinations or tendencies are called *natural* appetites, inasmuch as they flow from the very *nature* of the being, i. e., from the dynamic element, or *form* which constitutes it the being it is. To this class of appetites belong the natural tendencies or *nisus* in the various powers and faculties of beings to fulfill the function for which they are by their nature and constitution destined.

The latter class of tendencies are called Elicited Appetites, because they are aroused to vital action by cognition. Elicited appetition is again of two kinds, *rational* or *sensuous,* according to the character of the cognitive faculty by which their objects are perceived and proposed.

74. That the *sensuous* appetite is an *organic* faculty follows from the nature of the *objects* in regard to which it is exercised, viz., those presented by the external and internal senses, i. e., concrete individual material things. As to the *organ* of this faculty, however, opinions are divided. Some hold that it is the *brain,* others, on the contrary, maintain that it is the ganglia and nervous fibres of the *heart.* In favor of the latter opinion it may be said, (1) that it is the common usage of men to attribute the feelings, *e. g.,* of 'love,' 'hatred,' 'fear,' etc., to the heart; (2) that no part of the organism is so much modified by these feelings as the heart, so that as Cl. Bernard has said, it may be considered the organic index of their intensity.

75. The various forms of sensitive appetition may be classified as follows: the object presented by cognition may

be, (1) suitable or repugnant *in itself* simply and just as it stands; or (2) it may be a suitable object difficult to obtain, or a repugnant object difficult to avoid. The former would be the object of what is called the *concupiscible appetite;* the latter, of the *irascible appetite.* In other words, the object of the *concupiscible* appetite is the *good* or *evil* to be attained or avoided: the object of the *irascible* appetite is the *difficulty* to be overcome in attaining the good or avoiding the evil.

The acts of the *concupiscible* appetite are *love* and *hatred, desire* and *aversion, joy* and *sadness.*

The acts of the *irascible* appetite are *hope* and *despair, courage* and *fear, anger.*

NOTE.—*Sensuous Pleasure and Pain.* Sensuous *pleasure* is the satisfaction or repose which the faculties of a sentient being finds in the possession or enjoyment of their proper objects. It is, therefore, an accompaniment of the natural normal exercise of these faculties. In proportion as the energy of the faculty is greater and the object more fitted to call forth and satisfy that energy, so is the pleasure more intense. *Pain,* on the other hand, arises, from *excess* or *defect* in the exercise of a faculty, or from imperfection or unsuitability in the object presented to it.

Both pain and pleasure are therefore dependent on, (1) the natural scope and efficiency of the faculty, its acquired habits and its actual condition of health and energy; and (2) the suitable presence of an object in harmony with the energies of the faculty.

76. **Locomotion.**—Every sentient being is capable of some kind of exterior spontaneous local motion. In fact, it is by the exterior motion that they manifest to us their sensitive faculties of cognition and appetition. Perception of agreeable or·disagreeable objects is followed by desire or aversion; and

this, in turn, gives rise to movement towards or from the object. The special organ of this faculty of movement is considered to be the *efferent* nerves which terminate in the muscles.

NOTE.—The vital movements, *e. g.,* of the heart, lungs, etc., which are effected independently of cognition, are called *automatic;* those which result from cognition and appetition are called *autonomic.* These latter, again, are either *instinctive* or *volitional,* according as they are determined by the *sensuous appetites* (as in *brutes*), or by the *fre will* (as in man).

(ii). *Nature of the Animal Soul.*

77... That the brute animals arounds us possess powers of perception, appetition and autonomic locomotion is the unanimous verdict of the common sense of mankind. These animals have various organs of sense perception more or less similar in structure and function to our own, and, on the other hand, they exhibit in their exterior action generally, all the signs of true perception, feeling and autonomic movement.

The higher animals, at least, also clearly manifest by their actions that they possess the four *internal,* as well as the five *external* senses.

78. Now, if we consider the character of the chief and fundamental operation of sensuous activity, i. e., perception, or cognition, we shall see clearly that it differs essentially from the activities of merely inanimate bodies on the one hand and from those of merely vegitative activities, on the other.

For, on the one hand, all the activities of *inanimate* substances, *e. g.,* their power of attraction, of producing motion, heat, chemical changes, etc., are merely *transitive* i. e., they are capable of producing changes in *other* bodies but not in themselves. As to bodies at a distance, they affect them only, inasmuch as having first affected the intervening media, the energy thus transmitted produces *physical change* in the distant object.

The *vegetative* activities, on the other hand, are merely *immanent;* the *term* of their action is change in the *organism* of the agent, i. e., its nutrition, development, etc.

Cognitive activity, on the contrary, is, at the same time under different respects, *both* immanent and transitive, subjective and objective. The action is *entitatively* immanent and does not emerge from the sentient faculty which produces it; and it is at the same time *representatively* transitive, i. e., it is wholly occupied upon an external object. For instance, the action by which the sense of sight perceives the sun does not issue forth from the eye or produce any change in the sun or in the intervening ether, and yet it is wholly engaged upon an object 93,000,000 of miles away. Hence it is that we speak of the scope which is aimed at and reached by mechanical, physico-chemical and vegetative activity, or the *term* of their efficiency, i. e., the effect produced by them; while the scope aimed at and reached by cognitive and appetitive activity, is called their *object,* i. e., that external thing upon which their immanent action is occupied. Hence, the actions of cognitive and appetitive faculties are *sui generis* and eventually different from and superior to the action of mere physico-chemical or vegetative powers.

NOTE.—Hence, the cognitive act is called *intentional,* i. e., an *immanent* act with a *transitive* or *objective* reference or efficacy.

There is also another aspect of sensitive cognition and appetition which deserves consideration. On the one hand, the objects of our sensations are *extended* material things. These make an extended impression on the extended peripheral sense-organs, and these, in turn, transmit their impressions to the extended nerve-centres, which are the organs of the internal senses, and hence, the objects are perceived, imagined, etc., as individual extended things or as qualities or properties of individual extended things. On the other hand, experience shows us that these objects are perceived as units.

Now, it is a contradiction to say that an extended organ can perceive an extended object as a unit, unless the organ be *informed* by a simple dynamic principle which is itself not made up of parts. Take for instance, a marble in your hand. Your sense of touch apprehends it as one thing. But it is impossible that the different parts of the marble which make different impressions, *e. g.*, on the different tactile papillæ distributed over your hand should be apprehended as *one* thing unless the hand is *informed* by a *simple* perceptive principle.

And this becomes more manifest still, if we go on to consider that while the sight apprehends the marble as a colored thing; the touch, as a cold thing; the taste, as an insipid thing; the smell, as an odorless thing, etc., it is apprehended by the central sense, recalled by the imagination, recognized by the memory, etc., as *one* colored, cold, tasteless, odorless thing.

79. From the preceding considerations it is evident that **no aggregation of merely inanimate, or merely vegetative forces, can give us the cognitive and appetitive faculties** which manifest themselves in the operations of what is called the *animal* kingdom; unless, indeed, we are prepared to admit that a sum of zeros can give us à positive number. An *animal* is, therefore, an organism *informed* by a dynamic principle *sui generis,* essentially different from and superior to the *substantial forms* of merely vegetative or anorganic substances.

80. **Brute cognition and appetition, however, are strictly limited to certain concrete aspects of individual material things.** Even the *estimative* sense never rises above the apprehension of the concrete suitableness or repugnance, here and now, of individual material objects to the actual

needs of the sentient organism. This estimate or instinctive apprehension is the same in all individuals of the same species and differs according to difference of species. Just as each plant builds up its own organism according to a fixed type without cognition of any kind, so "omnis hirunda *similiter* nidificat" guided solely by the concrete sense-perception which excites the impulse to act in a fixed, determinate way according to the specific nature of the sentient being.

NOTE.—Hence, in all the phenomena of animal life there is no trace of any perception of abstract universal truths and principles. There is no progress or change of any kind in the instinctive action of animals. They make no use of instruments, fire, etc., to aid them in their work. They have no scientific, moral or spiritual notions of any kind. "Instinct is perfect in its narrow sphere, but it cannot rise beyond this into the sphere of unlimited thought and contrivance."—Dawson.

81. **Brute cognition and appetition, therefore, is essentially sensuous,** the action neither of the dynamic principle alone, nor of the organism alone, but of the *animated organism* (*psycho-physical* action). Now the *action* of a being manifests its nature, and hence, as the *action* of the brute soul is intrinsically and essentially dependent on the material organism and inseparable from it; the brute soul is therefore, *completely immersed* in the organism which it animates. It is incapable of acting or existing apart from the body and perishes with the disintegration of the latter. Accordingly it does not need *annihilation* to account for its destruction, nor *creation* to account for its *origin*. It is a product of *substantial transformation* effected by *generation* by which an existing vital energy educes from the potentiality of matter a new principle of activity similar to itself.

82. In the animal the vegetative functions produce, preserve and develop an organism adapted for sensation; and,

on the other hand, the sensitive faculties are chiefly exercised for the preservation, development and reproduction of the organism. Again, every modification of the sensitive activity (anger, fear, etc.) involves a corresponding modification of the vegetative activities; and, on the other hand, ill-health, disease, etc., of the organism affect the sensuous perceptions, desires, feelings, etc., of the animal. But such mutual interdependence of the various vital functions, sensitive and vegetative, of the animal organism can only be accounted for by recognizing that **all these various activities have their source in one and the same dynamic principle.** Hence, the brute soul is a substantial *dynamic principle,* or *form,* which immediately actuates *primal matter* and is the ultimate source of all the specific properties and activities of the living, sentient corporeal substance.

NOTE (1).—As to the *divisibility* of the brute soul, the *origin, transmission,* etc.; of animal life, see above, n. 54.

(2).—On the subjects so briefly treated in the present article, see Maher, especially chapters 7, 9, 10 and 12; also the supplementary chapter on Animal Psychology.

ART. IV.—ORIGIN OF SPECIES IN THE ORGANIC WORLD.

83. As we have already more than once seen, the *specific nature* of a corporeal substance is determined by the substantial dynamic principle, or *form,* which actuates and completes *primal matter.* For our present purpose, however, it will suffice to *describe* a species in the living organic world: A collection of living organisms (a) essentially similar in structure and function and (b) productive of offspring by their union with each other, so that the collection can be indefinitely perpetuated in nature by *generation;* and hence, such that the whole collection might have sprung originally from a single

pair. Or more briefly: A collection of individuals of one essentially similar inalienable type, capable of indefinite perpetuation by generation. *Similarity* and *filiation* are therefore the chief *indications* of *specific unity*.

NOTE (1).—*Accidental* diversities of color, size, etc., give us *varieties* within the *same species*. When these are perpetuated by artificial selection on the part of gardeners, breeders, etc., or by other causes, we have *races* or *breeds*. Hence, difference of *race* between parents in no way hinders offspring. But even here, "Domestic varieties, on returning to savage life, gradually, but invariably, assume the characters of the original type."—Darwin.

(2).—The offspring that *occasionally* results from the union of individuals of different *species* is called a *hybrid*. In the rare cases of hybrid fecundity, the inevitable return of the offspring to one or other of the original specific types is called *reversion*. The offspring of individuals of different *races* of the *same species* is called a *mongrel*. The casual appearance in a descendant of such mongrels of one or other of the *external racial* characteristics of either of the primitive parents is called *atavism*.

84. That there is in the organic world such collections of individuals as we have described is a manifest fact, *e. g.*, the various *races* or *breeds* of horses are like each other in fundamental structure and function; they differ essentially in structure and function from other groups of animals, *e. g.*, 'dogs'; and finally, the union of individuals of these different races or breeds with one another is capable of perpetuating the species indefinitely, while their union with individuals of other groups is either not fruitful or produces a hybrid offspring incapable of perpetuating itself. Hence, our description of species is *objective*, i. e., realized in the actual world around us.

85. Most of the *species* both of plants and animals with which we are familiar are comparatively *new* in the history of life upon the earth. From the first appearance of organic life upon the earth to the present time, many *species* of both plants and animals have disappeared and many new ones have been introduced. The question before us is, **How is the origin of these various species of living organisms to be accounted for?** Various hypotheses have been proposed to solve the problem. All the different views on the subject, however, may be classified under two heads:—the theory of *independent formations,* and the theory of *descent* or *derivation.*

86. **The Theory of Independent Formations,** holding to the principle of *causality,* the essential immutability of species and the absence of connecting links by which one species can be shown to have been gradually transformed into another, maintains that the *first* beings (few or many) of each species were produced by the Creator at the period of the world's history when the earth was fitted to receive them and the well-being of the whole would be benefited by their presence.

They would thus have been produced from pre-existing material by the immediate action of the Creator. This action could not strictly be called either *creative,* or *miraculous.* Not *creative,* as it would not imply the production of the *whole* new being out of *nothing,* but the *eduction* of a new *substantial form* in matter, by a proportionate cause. Not *miraculous,* because it would not be *against* any *law* of nature, nor beyond the *course* of nature as designed by the Creator, any more than the creation of matter itself, or of each individual human soul, is *beyond* the *order* of nature.

NOTE.—The vague term Evolution may be applied to this view in so far as the word can express the gradual working out of a predetermined creative plan. In a somewhat similar sense we speak of the *evolution* of the steam engine, of the bicycle, without at all implying that the perfect machines of our day are connected by any bond of *filiation* with their ruder predecessors.

87. **The Theory of Descent or Derivation** maintains, in general, that many organic species are derived or descended from one common parental stock. This hypothesis has been proposed in various forms, differing from one another as to (a) the *extent* of the field covered by the transformation; (b) the *manner* in which the transformation was effected. It will suffice for our purpose, however, to classify the views of *transformists* under the following four heads:—

88. **Monistic Evolution** is simply the extreme *materialistic atomism* alluded to above (n. 29, Note 1). It starts with a vast cloud of homogeneous atoms, each atom standing in a definite position relatively to all others, so that the existing order of the world "lay potentially in the cosmic vapor." To these atoms at a certain definite *time,* a certain definite *measure* of motion in a certain definite *direction,* was communicated; and the actual solar system and all being therein, great and small, living and not living, have been the result. The motion of the homogeneous cosmic dust gave, first, the simple chemical elements, then various chemical compounds, then the simplest living organisms, and these, in turn, advanced from stage to stage, radiate, mollusc, articulate, vertebrate, fish, serpent, bird, mammal, man. There is no telling where the cosmic dust came from, or whence the primitive arrangement of its particles, which yet contained potentially the actual cosmic order. We are not told when the motion came, or why in such a definite measure and direction. There is no substantial difference between bodies simple or compound, between plants and animals, animals and men. There is no such thing as soul, or mind, or free-will. All things are simply groups of homogeneous atoms in motion. There is an accidental difference in the *grouping* of the atoms and in the *mode* of motion; that is all.

89. In the preceding chapter, we have shown (n. 30) that this system is in open contradiction with the most obvious facts of experience which clearly manifest the existence of different substances in the anorganic world. In the preceding articles of the present chapter we have also shown that as Tait says, "to say that even the lowest forms of life can be explained by the mere relations, motions and interactions of inanimate matter is simply unscientific." It is needless, therefore, to attempt further refutation of the system.

It is well to remark, however, that (a) as to its *starting point* it assumes uncaused matter, an uncaused orderly arrangement of the particles of this matter and an uncaused motion of a definite intensity and direction, communicated to this matter at a definite time. (b) In its *progress* it assumes that inanimate matter can produce life, and that lower vital principles can produce higher. (c) *Finally,* it assumes that the irrational and material can change itself into the rational and immaterial and spiritual, and that inert extended matter can give us the intelligent free soul of man. It is, therefore, from first to last, a gratuitous and absurd hypothesis.

90. **Darwinian Evolution** holds that all the forms of life that have appeared upon the earth have sprung from one or two of the lowest types of organisms. Organic life originated with a few specimens of, *e. g.*, amoeba or myxomycetes or something lower still. Offspring differs from parent, and, in this case of course, was an improvement on parent according to the *laws of varation.* As generation followed generation and variations multiplied and were transmitted according to the *law of heredity,* a *struggle for existence* ensued which resulted in *the survival of the fittest* which is another name for *natural selection.* Add to these factors the necessity each living organism would be under to *adapt itself to its environment,* the *use* and *disuse* of different parts of its body according to cir-

cumstances and finally, the *sexual selection* by which the most highly gifted males and females would seek and win each other, and you have all the machinery which the Darwinian theorist requires to obtain from his bit of slime-mould, grass, wheat, the rose, oak, sequoia, etc.; and from his primitive amoeba, oysters, crocodiles, bees, eagles, elephants and men. Of course time was needed to accomplish all these wonderful changes—more time in fact than geology or physics can afford to grant. Of course, too, these changes were gradual, generation after generation slowly accumulating the infinitesimal links of the chain which unites monera with man, and conse quently, the strata of the earth must be stored with fossil remains of the Intermediate or Transitional forms.

91. As to this Darwinian evolution, we say, that it is an hypothesis in manifest contradiction with reason and fact.

(a) It is repugnant to *reason* to attribute stupendous effects to wholly disproportionate causes. Now, Darwinism attributes the production of all the manifold forms of life that have ever peopled the earth to one or two types of the very lowest grade under the influence of the so called laws of *variability, heredity,* etc. But these agencies, if they can be called so, at work to-day with all the ingenuity and skill of man to control and apply them, are wholly incapable of producing more than slight *varietal* changes in living species. Therefore, much less, when left to *chance,* are they capable of effecting *specific* changes, and still less of producing from a few of the lowest forms of living matter all the vast and wonderful variety of plant and animal life which has appeared upon the earth.

The slightest reflection will convince us that Darwin's so-called laws are neither universal laws of nature nor even remotely adequate to accomplish the task which he assigns to them. It is not true, that the accidental *variations* of offspring from parent always imply an improvement on parental characters. It is not true, that parents always transmit to offspring by a law of *heredity,* all the minute points of excellence which they themselves have inherited or acquired. It is not true that only the more perfect among the offspring of each plant and animal are *selected by nature* (whatever that may mean) to survive and propagate the race. *Environment* may *accidentally* affect the organism, but, it is gratuitous and contrary to all experience, to say that it can effect a *specific* change. The moderate *use* of an organ will doubtless strengthen and perfect it, but it is nonsense to talk of the use of an organ *producing* the organ itself.

Realizing the inadequacy of the causes assigned by their leader, later Darwinians are satisfied with simply maintaining that transformism is a *fact,* though we are yet unable to determine the causes which effected it.

(b) We, therefore, take up the second part of our proposition: Darwinian evolution is in contradiction with all known *facts* of the past or present history of life upon the earth. Known facts are: (1) Those which are verified by present observation and experiment. (2) Those which are recorded in trustworthy history. (3) Those which are recorded in the strata of which the earth's surface is composed.

Now as to the *first class of facts.* Present observation and experiment proves: (i) That no *new species* of plants or animals can be produced from individuals of the *same specific type* by the most careful *artificial selection* on the part of gardeners, breeders, etc. Innumerable *varieties* have been so produced, but not a single new *species.* (ii) That no *new species* is produced by the numerous generations of microscopic plants and animals which succeed each other with such astonishing rapidity all around us, "Koch took specimens of the phthisis microbe and placed them in a medium where they could increase and multiply without restraint. He cultivated the microbe most carefully, while modifying its surroundings in various ways to see what would become of it, and whether perhaps it would turn into something else. The stock multiplied prodigiously, but remained absolutely unchanged in species to the end." (iii) That no new species can be produced by *cross-breeding* between *different species*. This is shown by the *sterility* of hybrid offspring and in the rare cases of their fecundity by the ultimate *reversion* of the new offspring to one or other of the original parental types.

As to the *second class of facts*. "The crocodiles, ibises, oxen, cats and various other creatures that were embalmed among the mummies of Egypt were animals such as still live on the earth without having undergone any change. The same fact is shown by the Assyrian sculptures, etc. Here, then, we have proof that external influences acting through thousands of years have failed to modify the living organisms that flourish around us." Williamson, etc. One might catalogue a long list of plants and animals described by ancient writers, sculptured on ancient monuments, preserved in tombs, ruins, etc., but in no case is there a trace of difference between them and those of the present day. Three thousand years is a long time in the life of a species: and one may be permitted in reason to calculate what a longer time would accomplish by multiplying what 3000 years has accomplished in modifying any known species. But three thousand years has done *nothing* in this respect. Therefore, etc.

As to the *third class of facts*. Huxley tells us that "the only perfectly safe foundation for the doctrine of evolution lies in the historical or rather archæological evidence that particular organisms have originated by the *gradual modifications*" of their predecessors which is furnished by fossil remains. Now here is the latest testimony of palæontology on the subject in the words of one of the great *makers* as distinguished from the *retailers* of science—Sir G. W. Dawson writing in 1893.

"Palæontology (i) furnished no direct evidence as to the actual transformation of one species into another; but the drift of its testimony is to show that species came in per saltum (i. e., suddenly and without connection with preceding species) rather than by any slow or gradual process. (ii) In so far as we can trace their history, specific types are permanent in their characters from their introduction to their extinction, and their earlier varietal forms are similar to the later ones. (iii) We are now prepared to say that the Struggle for Existence has *not* been the determining cause of the introduction of new species. The periods of rapid introduction of new forms of *marine* life were no periods of struggle, but of expansion, i. e., periods in which the *submergence* of continents afforded new and large space for their extension and comfortable subsistence. In like manner it was continental *emergence* that afforded the opportunity for the introduction of *land* animals and plants. (iv) Another important palæontological fact is the remarkable *fixity* of certain types of living beings in geological times, especially in the case of many low types of life, through vicissitudes of physical conditions of the most stupendous character and over a lapse of time scarcely conceivable. And this holds true in groups which, within certain limits, are the most variable of all. In the present world, no creatures are more variable than the protozoa, *e. g.*, 'foraminifera and sponges.' Yet these groups are fundamentally the same from the beginning of the palæozoic until now; and modern species scarcely seem to differ from specimens taken from rocks at least half way back to the beginning of the geological record."

As to this last fact (the permanence throughout vast periods of specific types) many instances might be cited. Thus of forty-six species of mammals of the quaternary and glacial period, thirty-nine have survived down to our own times without any appreciable change; the other seven have become extinct rather than changed. The common sand-clam and the short clam now abounding on our shores are identical with those of the crag of the Pleistocene. The oyster is substantially the same today as when first introduced in the Carboniferous. "The corals of the Gulf of Mexico have been the same for over 200,000 years."—Agassiz. Of the trilobites which suddenly appeared in the lower Silurian in vast number and very high perfection, Barrande, the great discoverer and authority on the subject, says, "throughout a series of strata 5000 metres in thickness they remained specifically unchanged until their complete disappearance." And he adds, "The study of the primordial Silurian shows that modern theoretical calculations are quite contrary to facts: so much so, indeed, that the *real* fauna would seem to have been calculated designedly to contradict evolutionist *theories.*"

Darwinian evolution is, therefore, in contradiction with palæontological facts. Hence, even supposing (as Christian evolutionists do) that the first lowly forms of plant and animal life were produced by the Creator in the beginning, and supposing that each human soul, as being a spiritual substance beyond the causality of matter, is directly created by God— even, on this supposition, this second form of the doctrine of *descent,* or Darwinian evolution, is an untenable hypothesis in contradiction with observation and experiment, with the facts of history, with the discoveries of palæontology and with the first principles of rational science, *e. g.,* 'the Principle of Proportionate Causality.'

NOTE.—Some have felt so much the force of the argument from palæontology that they have abandoned the notion of slow insensible changes and have adopted the view that the transition from lower to higher forms was effected suddenly and *by great jumps.* This, of course, saves them the trouble of finding the Missing Links of Darwin's finely graduated chain; but it only increases the violence done to the testimony of actual and historical experience and to the first and most imperative principles of rational science. It was just to avoid this outrage on common sense that the Darwinian hypothesis was proposed, so that by bridging the interval between lower and higher types of life, by a continuous procession of gradually changing organisms, the transition from one species to another might be more easily accepted. It would be too glaring an absurdity, to say, *e. g.,* that a man who had absolutely no money gave at once $10,000 to another, but the absurdity would be less noticed (though not less real) if it were said that he gave it gradually, *e. g.,* in small fracions of a cent at a time.

A **third form of derivation theory** would suppose that the Creator, at certain periods when new forms were to be introduced, either directly transformed pre-existing species into new ones, or in some way enabled them to produce the germs of new species. This is certainly possible hypothesis inasmuch as a proportionate cause of the new species is assigned. Yet the philosopher must consider it as arbitrary and gratuitous—an interference with the ordinary laws of organic nature—and hence, far less philosophical than the theory of *independent formations* which are a part of the order of the nature, not an interference with it.

93. **The fourth form of the derivation theory** supposes that in the beginning God created all specific forms of plant and animal life that have ever appeared upon the earth, but in a condition suited to the circumstances of the time. Outwardly they would all appear more or less alike, just as, in the embryonic stage, all animals now resemble one another. In one, however, there was the Substantial Form or dynamic principle of a horse; in another, the form of an eagle, etc. These higher forms could not at first develop themselves into full perfection,

owing to the conditions of the time. Each could only reach some low stage of embryonic development and reproduce its kind before passing away. Gradually as conditions changed each specific type in succeeding generations would be enabled to manifest its innate specific power either by slow imperceptible degrees, or suddenly and "per saltus." In this view again there is no violation of the law of causality. Species are distinct from the first, only the embryonic development which is now accomplished in one individual life would then have taken perhaps thousands of individual lives to reach its maturity.

The objection to this view, and it is a strong one, is that it is hard to see why the Creator should create high specific types in circumstances in which it was impossible for them to attain their natural perfection. Moreover, there is no animal known to palæontologists which would represent, *e. g.*, "a horse" at any period of its present embryonic development.

NOTE (1).—This last theory differs from *Darwinian* evolution in two essential points: (i) Darwinism supposes nothing to start with but the simplest forms of almost undifferentiated living protoplasm. This acted upon by external physical agencies would give all the varied life of the past and present world. This theory, on the contrary, supposes that the different organisms are, from the first, differentiated by different dynamic principles, but that the organisms were unable to attain their full development until suitable surrounding circumstances occurred. (ii) Darwinism holds that the human soul is merely a development of the animal life-principle. This theory, on the contrary, holds that the human soul is in every case a spiritual substance directly created by God.

(2).—"The term 'evolution,' has been employed in so many senses, as to have become nearly useless for any scientific purpose."—Dawson. The word is used in all the senses considered above, and in many more. When, then, a man says he is an Evolutionist, or asks you if you admit the doctrine of Evolution, you will do well to ask what he means by the word, where his evolution begins, where it ends, how it is accomplished, etc.

(3).—What has *revealed religion* to say as to the origin of species? Very little. (i) God is the Author and Creator mediately or immediately of all finite beings. (ii) Each individual *human* soul is directly and immediately created by God. (iii) As to the origin of the *first human body*, Holy Scripture says that God formed it from the earth. Hence the words *literally* imply an immediate action of God in the formation of the first human body. Now it is a canon of all interpretation that the words of a document are to be taken literally, unless there is a cogent reason for taking them in a figurative sense. In the present case no such reason exists. Therefore, etc. Again, it is a rule of interpretation in the Church, that it is not permissible to interpret a statement of Scripture in a sense opposed to that in which it has been unanimously understood from the beginning by all the great doctors and theologians of the church. But the Scripture narrative of the formation of the body of Adam has always been taken in the *literal* sense of the words by the great doctors and theologians. Therefore, etc.

Hence, as the matter is so closely connected with some of the fundamental truths of revelation, *e. g.,* the unity and original state of the human race, etc., it would be rash and imprudent on the part of a Christian to admit that the first human body was in any way evolved from a brute organism; all the more so, as there is not a shadow of a scientific reason for doing so.

(4) Why have so many scientific men (they will be found to be, generally speaking, the popular *retailers* rather than the great *makers* of science) accepted the theory of Evolution?

The reasons given above (n. 31) will hold here also. (i) A want of grasp of logical and metaphysical principles. The law of Proportionate Causality is lost sight of in hasty efforts to classify isolated facts. (ii) A desire, it would seem, to push the Creator as far back as possible from the affairs of the world He made and governs, if not to get rid of the thought of God altogether.

In this connection it is worth while to draw attention to two significant passages quoted by Lord Salisbury in his address, as president of the British Association, delivered at Oxford before the assembled scientific representatives of America and Europe, August, 1894. \

Lord Kelvin, "the greatest living master of science among us" is quoted as saying: "I feel profoundly convinced that the argument of *design* has been greatly too much lost sight of in recent zoological speculations. Overwhelmingly strong proof of intelligent and beneficent design lie around us, and if ever perplexities, whether metaphysical or scientific, turn us away from them for a time, they come back upon us with irresistible force, showing to us, through nature, the influence of a Free Will and teaching us that all living things depend on one Everlasting Creator and Ruler."

Prof. Weismann, a prominent evolutionist authority, is quoted as follows: "We accept Natural Selection, not because we are able to demonstrate the process in detail, not even because we can imagine it; but simply because it is the only explanation we can conceive * * * without assuming the help of a *principle of design*."

For a clear and authoritative exposition of Evolution and allied topics see the article by Herman Muckermann, S. J., in the Catholic Encyclopedia.

94. Objections.

(a). From *Palaeontology*.

(i).—Geology shows that the order in which the various forms of organic life were introduced was one of gradual progress from lower to higher types. But this proves that higher types are descended from lower.

Answer (1).—T. maj. N. Min. Fallacy, Post Hoc; ergo Propter Hoc.

(2).—T. maj. D. min.; If transitional forms connect the various types, this would give *probability* to some *rational* hypothesis of descent, c. min. If no such forms exist, the mere fact of ascending series of types would justify any hypothesis of descent, n. min.

(3).—N. maj. An ascending series would be protozoa, cœlenterates, echinoderms, worms, molluscs, arthropodes, tunicates, vertebrates. Now all these *sub-kingdoms* are found in the lower palæozoic and all are found together in all the eras. Nor is there an ascending series in the *classes* of these sub-kingdoms, except reptiles, birds and animals of vertebrates. Nor is there an ascending series in *specific* representatives of these classes. The trilobites, cuttle-fishes and ganoid fishes of the Silurian and Devonian—the amphibians of the Carboniferous—the reptiles of the Mesozoic, etc., are, as a rule, far superior to the corresponding types of later times.

(ii).—Geology gives us *transitional forms, e. g.,* ganoid fish of the Devonian join teleost fish and reptiles. Ichthyosaurs (swimming reptiles), Dinosaurs (walking reptiles), Pterosaurs (flying reptiles), show the connection between fish, birds, amphibians, etc.

Answer.—These are the Transitional Forms required to prove descent, N. assert. You might as well say that our *bat* is a bird on its way to become a mouse.

These are distinct specific types intermediate between other species, and permanent in their own, just as the *bat* is, C. assert.

NOTE.—The forms just mentioned may be called *generalized* types suited to a mixed land and water and aerial existence, such as the condition of the earth at the time of their introduction required. But there is no trace of genealogical connection between them and more specialized forms.

(iii)—At least we can trace the transformation of the *horse* from a little four-toed animal about the size of a fox in the Eocene.—(See Leconte, Compend, p. 361).

Answer.—N. assert. The best palæontologists, even among those who favor the doctrine of *derivation, e. g.,* Gaudry, etc., reject this argument for transformism. The various animals mentioned as ancestors of the horse are too different in structure to suggest connection by descent; and the Transitional Forms to bridge over the intervals are, as usual, missing. "If the horse is evolved out of Hipparion, myriads of individuals must have existed to effect this gradual change." —Williamson, etc. If we begin with Anchitherium or Miohippus, three-toed animals, as Marsh and Cope do, the difficulty remains the same.

NOTE.—The Plasticity of species, within the limits of *varietal* changes, is very great, *e. g.,* 'pigeons,' 'dogs,' 'horses,' etc. Geologists justly complain of the tendency among fossil discoverers and naturalists, for every trifling difference in structure, to multiply *species;* while the animals in question may well be merely *varieties* of the same species.

(iv)—The geological record is incomplete, and therefore, it furnishes no argument against evolution. (See Leconte, *passim*).

Answer (1).—"The geological record is much more complete than is generally supposed. Over long periods of time and many lines of being, we have a nearly continuous chain of facts, and if these do not show the desired tendency, the fault is as likely to be in the *theory* as in the record."—Dawson.

(2).—This is a strange method of argument. Evolution depends on Palæontology as its "only perfectly safe foundation." The "foundation" refuses to support the airy superstructure. Therefore evolution is "exact science," etc.

(b)   From *Anatomy*.

(i).—*Similarity of structure* shows descent from a common stock. But all plants and animals are similar in structure, *e. g.,* 'the limbs of a fish, a bird and a horse.' Therefore, etc.

Answer (1).—The argument may be retorted. *Dissimilarity* of structure shows descent from different stocks. But all species of animals differ in structure and function from their neighbors, e. g., 'the limbs of fish, bird, etc.,' as above.

(2).—*Specific* similarity in structure and function shows descent from a common stock, c. maj. *Generic* similarity shows, etc., n. maj. But all animals are *specifically* similar in structure, n. min.; all animals are *generically* similar, t. min.

NOTE.—The fallacy here is in the transmission from the *abstract* to the *concrete*. We can form the abstract concept of a backboned warm-blooded four-limbed being; and this concept, so far as it goes, represents all such things. But when we come to the actual concrete world we find that the abstract notes are realized in essentially different ways. The abstract similarity is modified in the concrete by decided differences as essential as itself.

(ii).—In many organisms we find certain organs *atrophied, rudimentary* organs—useless to their possessors, but fully developed and useful in other animals, *e. g.,* 'the wings of the apteryx,' 'ostrich,' etc. Now, such rudimentary organs show genealogical relationship between their possessors and those organisms in which they are found fully developed.

Answer.—To say that these so-called rudimentary organs are *useless* is altogether gratuitous. "There is no organ of the body, however small, however seemingly unimportant, which we can presume to neglect. It may be that the balance of assimilation and nutrition, upon which the health of the whole organism depends, hinges upon the integrity of such obscure structures: and it is the maintenance of this balance which constitutes health; its disturbance, disease."—Schafer.

NOTE.—The law of the Correlation of Parts for the Perfection of the Whole governs all perfect work in nature as in art. To construct, *e. g.,* a vertebrae of some *particular* specific type, the general *parts* essential to all vertebrates must be arranged and developed in subordination to the idea of *this particular whole.* Some of the *parts* will be more developed, some less, than in other species of the class, in order that the *whole* may be a perfectly balanced structure; and any modification of any of these parts, for better or for worse, will injure the whole. Hence, it is misleading to speak of the normally developed parts of any specific type as Rudimentary. They *would be* rudimentary in other types, just as the *spring* of a lady's watch would be *rudimentary* in a town clock.

(c) From *Embryology.*

(i)—Every day the most varied organisms are evolved out of similar cells of protoplasm. Therefore, all organisms have arisen from a primeval, undifferentiated mass of protoplasm.

Answer.—From cells similar in *origin, internal energy* and *outward* appearance, n. anteced. Similar in outward appearance but different in origin and internal energy, t. anteced.

(ii).—*Ontogenesis* is a summary of *phylogenesis.* But the history of the embryonic development of each individual of a higher species exhibits a series of transformations from a simple cell through all the types of life inferior to its own.

Answer.—N. major. It is a mere fanciful and gratuitous assertion. Also, n. min. Von Baer, on whose authority

Haeckel tries to base this assertion, calls it flatly a *falsification of science*. So, too, the greatest biologists, *e. g.,* Milne-Edwards, "There is never a complete likeness between any adult animal and the embryo of another at any period of the latter's development." Thus at a certain period the vertebrate embryo has something of the appearance of an arthopode; but closer examination shows "that the vertebrate has its nerve-centers in the *dorsal side;* the arthropores, in the *ventral.* Indeed, all the organs are oppositely situated."—Von Baer.

NOTE.—It is the dynamic principle within that differentiates one form of life from another, and this is fully manifested only in the mature definite stage of a being's development. Hence the present objection, as well as those drawn from metamorphosis, alternate generation, etc., do not really touch the question.

(d) From *Philosophy*.

The theory of Immediate Formation is an interference with, while that of Evolution is in accordance with, the laws of nature.

Answer.—As to the first part of this assertion, see n. 86. As to the second part, it must be clear from what has been said that fixity and immutability of species is the law of nature as revealed to us by the facts of present, historical and geological time. Hence, the transformation of species would be an interference with law, and as such a true miracle.

PART FOUR.

RATIONAL PSYCHOLOGY.

1. **Rational Psychology** is, The science of the human soul, i. e., of that principle in man by which he lives, feels, thinks and wills. Here, however, we take account only of those vital acts which are *characteristic of man* and distinguish him from all other living things in the visible world around us. We start, then, with the data which consciousness (our own, and that of other men), expressed in their life and language, furnishes as to the characters of the vital acts of *thought* and *volition;* and from these we reason back to the *nature* of the ultimate principle from which they proceed, its relation to the body, its origin, etc. From what the soul *does* we gather what it must *be*. Thus, our natural knowledge of the essence, origin, destiny, etc., of our souls is not arrived at by *intuition*, but by *deduction*.

The subject may be divided into two Chapters:—

I.—Intellect and Will;

II.—The Nature of the Soul.

CHAPTER I.

INTELLECT AND WILL.

ARTICLE I.—INTELLECT.

2. We have already shown in Logic (n. 113) that there exists in a man a cognitive faculty far higher and nobler in its

grasp than sense, whose perceptions, as Huxley is forced to admit, "are neither sense-perceptions nor modifications of them," inasmuch as it not only apprehends individual material things under abstract universal essential aspects altogether different from concrete singular accidental representations to which organic faculties are necessarily restricted, but it occupies itself, chiefly and in preference to all others, with objects which lie wholly beyond the range of sense, *e. g.,* 'truth,' 'moral beauty' and 'goodness,' 'rights and duties,' 'perfect happiness,' 'the future,' 'the possible,' 'causality,' 'eternity,' 'infinity,' 'God.'

3. This faculty is the **intellect** whose chief functions we have already enumerated and considered from certain special points of view in Logic. Assuming therefore, what has been said elsewhere, we shall consider briefly in the present article the chief points of philosophical doctrine in regard to the *objects,* the *origin* and the *spirituality* of our intellectual knowledge. And that the present matter may be more easily connected with what has gone before, we shall treat our subject under three separate heads, viz.: *ideas, judgment, reasoning.*

i. Ideas.

4. The *formal object* of a cognitive faculty is that special note or character in things which is requisite and suffices to make them objects of the faculty in question, i. e., capable of being perceived and represented by it. Now, as we know from General Metaphysics, the human intellect apprehends the abstract note of Being: and hence, whatever is proposed to it, whether by intuition or reasoning or authority, as A Being, A Something, can be apprehended and represented by it as such.

Being, therefore, is the **formal object of the intellect.** Hence, there is nothing in the whole range of *being,* actual or *possible, substantial or accidental, necessary or contingent,* which cannot be more or less perfectly apprehended by the human mind at least analogically or under some transcendental or broad generic aspect, i. e., only Absolute Nothing is absolutely *unknowable*.

5. **The proportionate object of the human intellect** in man's present state comprises those beings which are *primarily, immediately,* and *directly* presented to and perceived by it, "ea quae *primo* et *per se* cognoscuntur," those objects which are first apprehended by the intellect and represented by it according to their own proper notes and characters.

Now, it is a matter of experieence that the first immediate and direct objects of our intellectual knowledge in our present state are the abstract universalized *quiddities* or essential notes of the material objects perceived by the senses and represented in the imagination.

Thus, the child's first judgments are about material things. In abstract reasoning we recur to material objects to illustrate our highest and most immaterial concepts. The words used to express externally, and the phantasms in the imagination which accompany our loftiest spiritual thoughts, are originally derived from material phenomena. Finally, those deficient in any sense from birth are without direct immediate knowledge of the objects corresponding.

Nor is it less evident that our *intellectual concepts* of these material objects are wholly different from merely sensuous representations of them. Thus, if I describe a circle on the blackboard, your sight perceives, and your imagination pictures, the mere concrete external characters of *this* particular circle, its color, size, position, etc.; while intellect forms the concept of what constitutes *a* circle, anywhere and everywhere, independently of all relations of time, space, color, etc. *Sense* perceives the individual accidental contingent; *intellect,* the universal essential necessary in regard to the same material objects. **Cfr. Logic, n. 118.**

6. **That the intellect can form these abstract universal concepts of material things, is beyond doubt.** "Contra factum non valet argumentum"; we *have* the universal ideas of *a* circle, *a* substance, *a* metal, *an* animal, etc., derived somehow from the contemplation of individual concrete objects. These ideas do not represent mere individuals or mere collections of individuals; but they answer the question *what* is a circle, *an* animal, etc., i. e., they represent the *quiddities* or essential notes of these objects. We *know,* and cannot help knowing, *e. g.,* that it is not a matter of mere customary association confirmed by heredity, but an objective necessity, independent of all our thoughts about it, that a circle is a figure in which, everywhere and eternally, the diameter is to the circumference as 1:3.14159.

7. **As to the origin of these abstract, universal concepts of material things.** To be able to see the universal in the individual, the necessary and eternal in the contingent and transient, is truly a marvelous power. But in order to explain it, there is no need to *deny* its existence, as *Empiricists* do; or to have recourse to the doctrine of *innate ideas;* or merely *subjective forms,* as Cartesians and Kantians do; or to postulate an *immediate vision of the divine ideas,* as Ontologists do. Of these theories we shall speak briefly in a few notes at the end of this article. The *scholastic* explanation is substantially this:

(a) As we have said above (Cosmol. n. 60, 61), four elements must be accounted for in the cognitive act, viz.: the *object,* the *faculty,* the *action* of the object on the faculty, and the vital *reaction* of the faculty by which the object acting on it is perceived and represented.

(b) Man is endowed with cognitive faculties of two essentially different orders, viz.: *sense* and *intellect.* In the material objects, primarily and immediately presented to us, the *formal object* of *sense* is the individual concrete fact or phenomenon, *e. g., 'this* Something,' *'this* Movement,' *'this* Circle.' The intellect, on the contrary, "intus legit," and apprehends and represents these objects as *quiddities deindividualized,* abstracted from individuation, universalized, *e. g.,* 'being,' 'movement,' 'circle.'

(c) Now this *proper proportionate* object of the intellect is not and cannot be presented to it, either by the individual object, or by any concrete sense-perception of it which merely represents the individual object according to the impression received from it; though, indeed, the abstract Quiddity expressed, *e. g.,* by the common noun *circle* is *potentially* in every individual circle.

(d) To reveal this abstract essence or nature in the individual object, the intellect is endowed with an *active* power (intellectus *agens),* which, when a concrete phantasm of a material object is pictured in the imagination, spontaneously *deindividualizes,* abstracts from individuating notes, universalizes the essence or quiddity (generic or specific) of the object represented, and thus makes it a proportionate object of intellectual apprehension, capable of determining the *perceptive* power of the intellects (intellectus *patiens* or *possible)* which *reacts* by perceiving it and representing it in abstract spiritual *concept* (the *direct universal idea).* Logic, 118.

"The process, then, in brief, is this: An individual material object is perceived by the *external senses,* and an individual concrete representation of it is formed in the *imagination;* and here the work of the lower powers ends. Since, however, in man the sensuous faculties of cognition have their source in a soul endowed with *intellectual* power, this latter now issues into action. The presence of the *phantasm* is a condition of rational activity, furnishing, as it were, the raw material on which it works; and when this is present the intellect, by its own active and passive powers, generates the *concept* which represents the abstract de-individualized essence or quiddity of the external material object."

NOTE (1).—This *abstractive* power of the intellect is often called the Light of Reason. For as light renders *visible* the color of bodies, so this power makes *intelligible* the abstract essence realized in the concrete individual object. Hence, the special function of this intellectual activity is described as Illuminatio, Depuratio, Abstractio Phantasmatis.

(2).—The intellectual concepts elaborated in the manner described above are (i) *abstract,* i. e., the object is represented apart from individuation, (ii) *quiddiatative,* i. e., the mere *nature* or *essence* (generic or specific) of the object is represented, (iii) *universal,* i. e., *one* nature is represented which is *capable* of being realized in and univocally predicated of *innumerable* different individuals. That we have such concepts of material objects has been shown in logic.

Now, such concepts are wholly beyond the power of organic faculties. For an organic faculty represents an object according to the impression which the latter makes upon the living organ, and as all objects in nature are individual, they can only produce impressions of themselves as such, *e. g.,* a circle of an inch in diameter cannot produce in matter, whether living or not, an impression that will represent every possible circle. On the other hand, it would be as impossible to re-present a universal concept in a material faculty as it would be to draw a universal circle on the blackboard. The human intellect, therefore, which, as a matter of fact, is capable of forming universal ideas, is necessarily a *supra-organic,* or *spiritual* faculty.

(3).—The more perfectly the individual material object is represented by the sensuous phantasm the more perfect and comprehensive, *ceteris paribus,* will the intellectual concept be. Hence, as our first sense-perception of an object is generally very imperfect and incomplete, so our earliest intellectual concept of it is generally indistinct and represents it only under some transcendental or broad generic aspect, *e. g.,* as 'a being,' 'a corporeal substance,' 'an animal,' etc.

(4).—The account of the origin of our universal ideas given above (i) supplies all the elements of the act of cognition, (ii) harmonizes with the actual state of man in which the soul is united to the body for the advantage of both, (iii) accords with experience which proves that the action of the imagination must precede and accompany the action of the intellect, and that sound senses and a sound brain are *conditions* of normal thought, (iv) and finally safeguards the *objectivity* of science by tracing back the origin of our intellectual concepts to actual existing things.

8. **Self-consciousness.** When once aroused to action in the manner described in the preceding paragraph, the intellect not only apprehends the quiddity of the external object, but at the same time becomes aware of its own act of cognition and of itself as the agent eliciting the act.

This self-consciousness may be more or less explicit. It may be a mere spontaneous concomitant of the act by which the external object is apprehended, or it may be a deliberately *reflex* operation in which the cognitive energy is directed rather upon itself and its own action than upon the external object with which it is engaged. In the former case it is called *direct* or concomitant consciousness; in the latter it is called *reflex* consciousness.

That the mind, in most of its intellectual operations, is *concomitantly* conscious of its action and of itself is a matter of ordinary experience. In our normal intellectual operations —perceptions, judgments, reasonings, etc.—independently of any deliberate reflexive effort, the mind is usually conscious of itself and of its action, or, in other words, of *itself as acting,* or of *its action as its own.*

But it is in the deliberately *reflex* act of self-consciousness that itself and its operations, and the distinction between itself and its operations, are most distinctly apprehended by the intellect. While I am thinking, *e. g.,* what course I shall take in regard to some serious matter proposed to me, I am spontaneously, and without any deliberate introspective effort, aware that *I am thinking* about the matter, but I do not attend to the exact course of my thoughts or explicitly distinguish between my thought and my thinking self. By an effort of attention, however, I can watch closely the progress of my thinking and notice with what degree of clearness and distinctness I apprehend the question before me, the relative force of the various reasons pro and con, etc. In this case I clearly distinguish between the process of thought and the thinking mind. The former is seen to be a *series of passing acts:* the latter, an *abiding principle* of action.

In this reflex act, therefore, (i) the *distinction* between the *permanent thinking mind* and its *transient states,* or acts of thought, is vividly brought home to us; (ii) we have as full a certainty of the *existence* of this permanent thinking mind as we have of the existence of its transient acts, or states; (iii) Finally, we clearly apprehend the perfect *identity* between the mind *reflecting* and the mind *reflected upon.*

Now, a self-perceptive power which can set itself and its own present action before itself, as an immediate object of cognition, cannot be an organic power. An organic power is one into which matter enters as an essential element, i. e., it is the *compound* of matter and soul that perceives, feels, etc. But no material faculty can double back, or reflect upon its whole self and its action, *e. g.,* 'the eye cannot see *itself* and its own *act of vision';* 'the tip of a finger cannot touch *itself* and its *own sensation of touch,'* etc. Only a *simple* energy which *sub-*

sists in itself and *acts by itself* independently of matter, can thus apprehend itself and its own action. This wonderful power of self-consciousness is, therefore, an evident proof of the *spirituality* of the human soul.

NOTE (1)—To those (*e. g.,* Taine) that deny that we have this power of self-consciousness the only answer is "solvitur reflectendo." The same answer must be given to those (Sully, etc.) who say that "all introspection is retrospection." To those (Spencer) who hold that our consciousness of a permanent mind within us, distinct from its transient state and acts, is merely "an inevitable illusion," we can only say that it is a doubtful philosophy which accounts for evident facts by denying them. A child "examining his conscience" is one of those stubborn facts that no eloquence of denial can explain away.

(2).—As to the objects immediately perceived by the self-conscious mind: (i) Self-consciousness immediately perceives only the acts of the soul, not its *inner nature* or *essence,* which is known only by a more or less elaborate process of reasoning. (ii) The *primary* object of self-consciousness is the *intellectual act* and hence, *intellectual agent;* but, as this simple intellectual agent is also endowed with other powers (which are simultaneously occupied with the same material object as the intellect), its consciousness of itself makes it aware of its various cognitive and appetitive operations, and of the body which it *informs* and which co-operates in some of these operations, and finally, of the individuating notes of the object whose abstract *quiddity* alone is directly apprehended by the intellect. (iii) Self-consciousness, therefore, apprehends the *Ego,* or complete human person, as a compound of soul and body with various perceptive and appetitive powers, some of which are intellectual and spiritual, while others are sensuous and organic.

(3).—Self-consciousness aided by memory clearly *perceives* the *abiding* identity of the *person* who is self-conscious, but this perception does not *constitute* personal identity, any more than seeing a house makes the house; and just as the house continues to exist when we cease to look at it, so a sleeping man is a person, though he is unconscious of himself. (Gen. Metaphys, n. 48.)

(4).—When a man says, *e. g.*, 'I am not *myself* today,' the word *self* is clearly used in a loose sense to express the *state* of the real substantial self. He means simply *my* present *state* is not *my* normal *state,* indicating at the same time the *identity* of the *Ego* and the *diversity* between its normal and its present *state*. This loose use of the word Self has given rise to the inaccurate and mischievous expression, "Double or Multiple Personality." The change in his subjective moods and states, resulting from certain morbid nervous conditions, may indeed sometimes induce in the sufferer himself the illusion that he is different persons at different times; but we may not take insanity to illustrate the normal mental life.

9. *Positively immaterial or purely spiritual objects.* That man is capable of forming ideas of such objects is a *fact* manifested universally in human speech and actions, and clear to each one from the testimony of consciousness. Even those who deny the *existence* of such objects, clearly show that they have some sort of ideas of them.

Now the question is, (i) how do we form *clear* ideas of such objects, and (ii) how do we come to know that there are objective realities corresponding to these ideas?

As to the first question: Given, on the one hand, the abstract ideas of external objects and the perceptions of consciousness, spoken of in the preceding paragraphs, and, on the other, the analytic and synthetic power of the intellect, we can form concepts which *clearly* represent purely spiritual objects. Thus, from our intellectual perception of external material objects and of the facts of consciousness, we can form the general ideas of 'being,' 'substance,' 'cause,' 'power,' 'intelligence,' 'free volition,' etc. We also know immediately what a 'limit' *e. g.* of power is, what 'extension' is, etc. We know, too, what a 'negation,' or 'absence,' means. Now we can unite these various positive and negative notes in one concept and form the idea of *an unextended substantial being, unlimited in power, intelligence, etc., uncaused, incapable of change, unending etc.* This is a *clear* and *proper* conception of an infinite spirit i. e., it represents such a being and no other, i. e., no material or finite object. It is called an *analogical* concept, inasmuch as the various abstract notes elaborated and combined to form it were originally apprehended in finite objects.

As to the second question—*Direct intuition* gives us knowledge only of external material objects: *Reflex intuition* reveals to us the existence of a substance endowed with the power of intelligence and free will, but not the inner *nature* of that substance. We have, therefore, no *intuitive* or *immediate* knowledge of purely spiritual objects as such. Our knowledge, therefore, of the existence of such objects is acquired either by *reasoning* or from *authoritative testimony.*

Note.—The fact that the human mind can and does form ideas of such purely spiritual objects is the strongest proof of its own spirituality. An organic faculty, as we have said before, can only give a concrete representation of an individual material object proportionate to the impression produced in the living organ by the object.

ii. *Judgment and Reasoning.*

10. There is nothing special to add here to what has already been said in Logic about the nature of these mental acts, except briefly to call attention to the supra-sensuous or spiritual character of the judicial act in general.

Now to form the simplest *particular* judgment, *e. g.,* 'this iron is hot,' the mind must apprehend the *predicate* as an ab-

stract de-individualized note, before it can intelligently affirm
that it belongs to the subject. In common judgments, *e. g.*,
'gold is a metal,' both *subject* and *predicate* are apprehended
as *universal*. Hence, to say nothing of the act of *comparison*
and the perception of the *relation* between the two terms, the
apprehension of the *universal,* implied in every judgment,
clearly shows that it cannot be a sensuous act.

But it is in what are called *necessary* judgments that the
supra-organic character of the judicial act is most strikingly
manifested. Thus in the axioms of geometry, metaphysics,
ethics, etc., *e. g.,* 'things which are equal to the same things are
equal to each other'; 'A thing cannot at the same time be and
not be'; 'Ingratitude is wrong'—in all these cases the mind
clearly perceives and affirms that these truths *hold* and *must
hold* universally and forever, always and everywhere, and this
not through any blind instinct, but from an *intelligent insight*
into the nature of the two terms compared and united by the
judicial act. Now, this everlasting necessity and universality
cannot be apprehended by sense which reaches only the individual, contingent, mutable fact.

If, finally, we consider the power of the mind to link together intelligently long series of such judgments, grasping the
connection and relations between them and moving forward
with the security of perfect insight from the known to the unknown in regard to the most abstract and immaterial objects
of knowledge, *e. g.,* mathematics or metaphysics,—such a power most evidently demonstrates the *spirituality* of the intellect.
To deny this would be to deny the foundation of all science,
i. e., the principle "agere sequitur esse"—"the nature of a being is revealed by its actions."

NOTE.—It is necessary to insist strongly on the fact evident to us from consciousness, that in our intellectual judgments, it is not a question of one idea "inevitably recalling"
another, but a question of the mind holding two terms dis-

tinctly before it and seeing a valid motive which justifies it in affirming a *relation* of agreement or disagreement between them.

It is true, indeed, that the perception of an object may recall the image of another associated with it in past experience. Thus, *e. g.,* 'a street dog seeing a small boy pick up a stone, barks an expression of pain and runs away.' Here the sight of the boy stooping for a stone recalls the memory of other facts connected with it in past experience, *e. g.,* of a stone thrown, a pain felt, etc. But this power of recalling associated experiences is not what we mean by the intelligent judicial act which consciousness testifies, a man is capable of. The *associated images* come up spontaneously and automatically from the first fact of the series to the last without any *insight* into the *relations* between the terms. Not so in our judgments and reasonings. Here, the terms are united not blindly and automatically, but on account of sufficient evidence (intrinsic or extrinsic) of the relations existing between them.

1. So far, then, we have seen that the intellectual acts enumerated above are essentially distinct from those of organic faculties and require a supra-organic or spiritual power in the being who is capable of eliciting them. In maintaining that the intellect is a spiritual faculty we do not, however, imply that it is in no way dependent on the organism. In our present state in which the soul is united to the body, the action of the imagination which is an organic faculty must precede and accompany the action of the intellect; and hence, we admit an *extrinsic* dependence of the intellect upon the organism. But it would be just as reasonable to conclude that, because the eye needs an object in order to see it, therefore, the object is the eye; as to argue that because the intellect needs the presence of phantasms in the imagination, in order to elaborate its spiritual concepts, therefore, the imagination is the intellect. Healthy

cerebral action (like sound external senses) is a *condition,* not an efficient or coefficient *cause* of thought.

St. Thomas thus sums up the fundamental difference between sense and intellect:

(a) Sense perceives only the individual; the intellect conceives the universal.

(b) Sense perception is limited to the corporeal: intellectual knowledge embraces the immaterial and spiritual.

(c) Sense cannot reflect upon itself and its own action: intellect can.

NOTE.—(a). **The Hypothesis of Innate Ideas.** A common characteristic of all those philosophers who have adopted in one form or another the hypothesis of innate ideas, is an extremely keen appreciation of the vital difference between sensation and thought. Supra-sensuous mental products, such as the ideas of being, unity, the true, the good, necessary truths, and the like, cannot, these philosophers maintain, in any way have been derived from sensuous experience. They must consequently, have been *innate* or *inborn* in the mind from the beginning. Such, in a word, is the case for this theory.

There are numerous fatal objections to it. (i) it may be rejected as a gratuitous hypothesis. Man's intellectual knowledge can be satisfactorily accounted for by the combined action of sense and intellect; hence, the assumption of innate ideas is unwarranted. (ii) There is no evidence of the existence of any of our ideas antecedent to experience. (iii) All our earliest ideas are of objects known by sensible experience, and to these we always turn to illustrate our loftiest and most abstract conceptions. But these facts are obviously in conflict with the supposition of a supply of ready-made cognitions from the beginning.

(b) **Empiricism.** The Sensationist, or Empiricist theory of knowledge stands in the completest opposition to the views of the supporters of innate ideas. Starting from the assumption that sensuous and intellectual activity are essentially the same in kind, its aim is to make it appear that universal and abstract concepts, necessary judgments, self-consciousness and all our higher spiritual cognitions are merely more complex or refined products of sense. Universal concepts are either confused with the concrete phantasms of the imagination, or their existence is boldly denied. All our cognitions, in fact, are declared to be merely more or less elaborate sense impressions. This indeed is the fundamental defect of empiricism. It ignores the active energy of intellect with which the mind is endowed, and, consequently, it can give no adequate account of our higher intellectual operations. Hence, it denies their existence against the testimony of our consciousness.

(c) **Ontologism.** This theory holds that we have an immediate knowledge of God and of His divine ideas, and from this intuition of the divine ideas, we acquire our intellectual knowledge of the essences of things and of necessary truths. (i) Now, this is a purely fanciful and gratuitous hypothesis. (ii) It is, moreover, a pernicious hypothesis, as attributing to our natural powers what is the very climax of supernatural power, i. e., the intuitive vision of God. (iii) Finally, it is against the evident testimony of our consciousness, which clearly denies the existence in us of any such direct and intuitive knowledge of God or of the divine ideas.

Article II.—The Will.

(i). *Will in General.*

Will or rational appetite is the power of loving, desiring. enjoying that which is apprehended by the intellect as good. The range of this rational power of desire and enjoyment is, therefore, co-extensive with that of the intellect. Now, the intellect as it apprehends *being* in general, so it apprehends *the good* in general. **The formal and adequate object of the Will is,** therefore, *the good* as apprehended by the intellect.

Hence, an object which would embrace in itself *all good,* if presented to the Will as such, would satisfy all its capacities and be *necessarily loved* and desired by it. On the other hand, an object however perfect in itself, if presented to the Will as lacking anything of the absolute good apprehended by the mind, will not satisfy all the Will's capacities, and hence, cannot *necessitate* its love or desire.

The Will, therefore, can embrace all the good presented to it as such by the intellect, whether material or immaterial, whether of ourselves immediately or of those whom we should love, unlimited in extent, endless and unfailing in duration.

That we have within us such a power of longing for, striving after *ideals of e. g.,* 'knowledge,' 'power,' 'peace,' 'moral goodness,' 'beauty,' 'wealth,' etc., which no sense-representation can picture is the testimony of each one's consciousness. Man "looks before and after and pines for what is not" to be found in any accumulation of material or finite objects. He can, moreover, and he frequently does reject objects the most attractive to sensuous desire, for the sake of immaterial spiritual good, *e. g.,* 'virtue,' 'duty,' 'the honor of God,' etc., which can be apprehended only by the intellect.

This power of desiring the *unlimited,* the *everlasting,* in every order of *good,* is at once the cause of man's unrest, the stimulus of his progress, and the simplest proof that there is in him a source of supra-organic spiritual energy.

(ii) Free Will.

13. "We have now arrived at that fundamental and far-reaching truth, **the freedom of the Will.** This great philosophical truth, the *physical liberty of man,* branches out into all departments of *Philosophy* and determines the whole theory

of human life and morality, which is the practical outcome of speculation. If a man does not possess Free Will, if he cannot by his own inherent personal energy oppose himself to the current of influences which bear upon him, whether in the form of inherited character, or early training, or of present motives, then he is really nothing more than irresponsible machine. The mechanism may be most ingenious, the agencies at work innumerable; but if his conduct is always the inevitable resultant of the forces playing upon him, there is no essential difference in kind between the acts deliberately willed by him and the movements of the madman, the brute or the rain cloud.

14. "By free will, or physical liberty, or the control of the Will over its own actions is meant that endowment by which an agent, in regard to certain objects presented by the intellect, when all the conditions requisite to elicit a volition are present, is able either to put forth or abstain from that volition. Liberty, thus, implies that volitions are *freely* elicited by the *Ego* or Person and are not the necessary outcome of his nature *plus* the attractions of the moment.

"Now, many of man's acts are not free. Control over our thoughts ceases during sleep; and even when awake, independently of automatic movements, such as breathing, winking, etc., we perform many acts not clearly realized in consciousness. A long train of thought may thus have passed through our mind before we, by an act of self-consciousness, advert to the fact, and become aware that, although hitherto it has been indeliberate, henceforth it is free, and we are responsible for it."

The question at issue, then, is not whether *every* action of man is free, but whether *any* is so. Or, to put it otherwise, Is the consenting act of the Will always completely determined by the pre-requisites for a volition except the Will itself? Does that act *necessarily* follow? Determinists or Necessarians answer in the affirmative: Libertarians or Indeterminists say, No.

"We allow most readily, first, that a great part of man's daily action is indeliberate; secondly, that when he acts deliberately and exercises his power of free choice, he is greatly influenced by the weight of the motives attracting him to either side; and finally as a consequence of this, we allow that a being possessed of a perfect knowledge of all the forces operating on a man would be able to prophesy with the greatest *probability* what course that man will take. But on the other hand, we assert emphatically that there are many acts of man which are not simply the resultant of the influences working upon him; that he can, and sometimes does, set himself against the balance of aggregate motive, natural disposition, acquired habit; and that, consequently, prediction with *absolute certainty* as regards the future free conduct of man is impossible from mere knowledge of character and motives.

15. "The arguments usually adduced to establish the Freedom of Will proceed upon three different lines, the psychological, the ethical, and the metaphysical.

(a) **Psychological Argument.** "The first proof is that from the direct testimony of consciousness. It has been justly asserted that consciousness is the ultimate court of appeal in the science of mind. Consequently, if careful and repeated introspection reveals to us, as the clear declaration of consciousness, that we are free in the exercise of volitional acts, such an averment must be admitted. Now, consciousness most unmistakably affirms in the movement of deliberate decision that we choose freely. Therefore, we have freedom of choice, or *Free Will*.

"If a man asserts that he is aware of no internal experience of free choice, then argument with him is useless. We can only appeal to the impartial mind anxious to attain truth.

If any man within his own mental life discovers no phenomenon of the kind indicated, we cannot by any logical contrivance introduce it thither. But, if internal observation assures him of the reality of this fact which we know to exist in our own case, and which the ethical and other judgments of mankind at large prove to be universal among rational men, then he may rest convinced on the highest evidence that may be presented to his intellect that he is endowed with Free-will.

(b) **Ethical Argument.** *"Duty, Obligation, Responsibility, Merit,* all imply *moral* liberty. If we *ought to* abstain from a forbidden gratification no matter how pleasant it would be to us, if we are to be *responsible* for our deliberate consent to it, if we are *meritorious* and *deserving* of *approval* for resisting it, then assuredly we must be possessed of Free-will, we must be capable of yielding, just as well as of refusing to yield, and our act can not be the mere inevitable outcome of our circumstances, internal and external.

"In other words, if Determinism be true the entire human race have been hitherto under a most stupendous delusion. For, the universal consent of mankind, as expressed in the languages, literature, and laws of all times, emphatically affirms that there is such a thing as *real moral obligation,* as *accountability,* as *merit,* and the rest. All men place a distinction between certain acts done indeliberately and similar acts done deliberately and freely, which implies that the latter are free and the former are not.

"The denial, then, of Free-will is not merely a rejection of the most manifest declarations of consciousness in a question upon which this faculty is the highest judge, but it is a repudiation of the universal conviction of mankind corroborating that testimony."

(c) **Metaphysical Argument.** Will is rational appetite; an appetite which embraces nothing of necessity, except what is apprehended as absolutely good and *desirable in every respect.* The Rational Will can be irresistibly drawn only by that which reason proposes as so universally attractive that it contains no lack of good, no dissatisfactory feature. As long as the thought of an object reveals any lack of good, any disagreeable aspect, the Will has not that which it is naturally longing for, *perfect good;* and it is able to reject this object. Appetite is in truth merely tendency towards good; and an object which contains any deficiency is the reverse of desirable so far as that feature is concerned. If, then, attention is concentrated on this point and withdrawn from those which are attractive, the object loses its enticing force. But, during this present life, no object presents itself to the intellect as attractive under *all* aspects when we *advert* to its value. As regards *finite* goods, it is obvious that, either in the difficulty of their acquisition, or the uncertainty of their possession, etc., there is always something on account of which they are undesirable, and for which man may turn away from them to seek the infinite good—God himself. At the same time it is equally clear that man is not at present drawn inevitably in this latter direction. The inadequate and obscure notion of God possessed in this life, the difficulty of duty, the conflict of man's pride and sensuality with virtue, all make the pursuit of our *true good* disagreeable in many respects to human nature, so that we can only too easily and freely abandon it. The clear apprehension of an Infinite Good, such as is given in the Beatific Vision of the blessed in Heaven, would of course remove this freedom. The blessed cannot help loving God above all things; we, however, though necessitated to seek after the good in general, are physically *free* to reject any particular form of it presented to us.

"Free-will is, therefore, a result of man's possession of a spiritual faculty of cognition whose object is the *universal,* and which can conceive unlimited and unalloyed good. Consequently, where such a power does not exist, as in the case of brute animals, liberty is absent."

16. **The physical liberty of the Will** established by the preceding arguments implies such a dominion of the Will over its own action that upon the presentation of any particular limited good, as such, by the intellect, and with all other requisites of action (*the Divine Concurrence* included) present, it can elicit or suspend its act of volition according to its own choice. Free-will is therefore essentially an *elective* power, an active power of *self-determination*. Its action is determined, not by any necessity of its nature, or by force of acquired habit or present disposition, or by the object or the motives presented to it by the intellect, but *by itself* here and now endowed with the power of *self-control*.

Now such a power cannot belong to an organic faculty. An organic faculty *must receive* the impression of the object acting upon it and *must re-act* in proportion to the impression made upon it.

NOTE.—(a) The power of *willing* or *not willing* a given object or action is called *liberty* of contradiction. The power of choosing one or another of various eligible objects is called *liberty of specification*. The power of choosing between a morally good act and its contrary, i. e., an act of vice, is called *liberty of contrariety*. This last kind of liberty implies an imperfection in the intellect, which presents what is, in reality, wholly bad and undesirable, as under a certain aspect, good and eligible.

(b) **Moral liberty** is *freedom from obligation*. Thus a man is not *morally* free to tell a lie, though he has *physical* liberty to do so.

(c) "A *voluntary* act is an act that proceeds from the will with a knowledge of the end to which the act tends." The term *voluntary* has therefore a wider extension than the term free. All *free acts* are *voluntary acts,* but not all *voluntary* acts are free.

17. Notes for the solution of objections against the freedom of the Will.

(a) A free volition is not an Uncaused or a Motiveless act. The *cause* is the free Will: its *motive,* some form of good apprehended by the intellect and *freely* chosen by the Will.

(b) Consciousness testifies not merely that our volitions are spontaneous and voluntary, but *also* that they are free. We are conscious that many of the acts of the will are under its control.

(c) To assert that all causation is *necessary* is to reject the clear testimony of consciousness and the universal conviction of mankind.

The will does not *create* physical energy, but directs and applies it.

(d) We do *not* consider the deliberate acts of our neighbors to be the *inevitable outcome* of their character and circumstances, else the words *responsibility, self-control, merit,* etc., would have no meaning. Nor does this make it impossible to forecast men's future conduct sufficiently for the purposes of social life and business. For, (i) many of man's acts are *indeliberate,* and hence, the result of his character and circumstances. (ii) In many of his *deliberate* acts he is, as a matter of fact, guided, though not *necessitated,* by his character and circumstances. (iii) Men of virtuous lives habitually resist the temptations of pleasure, self-interest, etc., while a man accustomed to yield to a particular temptation will very probably yield again, though of course *freely,* when it recurs, etc. Hence, *general* uniformity in individual conduct is quite reconcilable with the possession of free Will.

(e) *Statistics* do *not* show any *constant* proportion between certain external circumstances and the commission of certain crimes. And even if they did, it would only show that such circumstances were *proximate occasions* and *strong inducements* to the commission of these crimes, not that they *necessitated* them.

(f) It is most true that God knows all our free future actions, but He knows them just as they will be, i. e., as *free actions* of the Will. God's knowledge of such acts no more *necessitates* them than my knowledge of what you are now freely doing necessitates your doing it.

18. **The Control of the Will over the other Faculties.**

(a) It can *apply* the intellect, the internal and external senses, and the motor powers to *action*.

(b) In regard to the *judgments* of the *intellect,* when the connection between subject and predicate is not apprehended as evident, our Will may find some real or apparent good in our adopting a particular view on the question. In such a case it can fix the attention of the intellect on the reasons for that view and on the objections against any other, and compel assent to the proposition of its choice, as useful, prudent, pleasurable, etc.

(c) In regard to the *sensuous appetite,* the Will can control it *indirectly,* inasmuch as it can control the application of the external and internal senses to such objects as would excite sensuous desire or aversion.

CHAPTER II.—Nature of the Human Soul.

Article I.—Substantiality and Simplicity of the Human Soul.

By the words **Human Soul,** we understand *the subject of our mental life, the ultimate principle by which we think and* *will.* We now proceed to expound and justify our doctrine regarding the nature of the reality corresponding to this term.

19. **The Human Soul is a Substantial Principle.** This proposition merely asserts that the ultimate principle of our mental life cannot be an *accident.* A *principle* is that from which something proceeds. A *substance* we have already defined as *a being which exists per se,* which subsists in itself, in opposition to an *accident,* which is a being that cannot so subsist, but must inhere in another being as in a subject. Now, the ultimate principle of our mental life must be a substantial principle. States of consciousness, mental modifications necessarily presuppose a subject to which they belong. Ideas, judgments and reasonings cannot inhere in nothing. Volitions cannot proceed from nothing: they must have a source from which they flow. This ultimate substantial principle, whatever its nature may turn out to be, which is the subject of our conscious states, we call the *Soul.*

20. **The Human Soul is a Simple Substantial Principle.** By affirming the simplicity of the soul we deny that it is extended. Our argument runs thus. Every extended substance consists of extraposited parts. But the subject of our conscious acts cannot consist of such parts. Therefore, it is not an extended substance. The major premise is evident. The minor is proved by a multitude of mental facts of which we will indicate a few.

(a) *The Simplicity of Intellectual Ideas.* Every one's experience teaches him that he is capable of forming various abstract ideas, such as those of 'Being,' 'Unity,' 'Truth,' 'Virtue.' and the like, which are of their nature simple and indivisible. Now, acts of this sort cannot proceed from an extended substance, for instance, 'the brain.' This will be seen by a little reflexion. In order that the indivisible idea of, say, 'Being,' proceeds from such an extended substance, either different *parts* of the idea must belong to different parts of the brain, or *each* part of the brain must be the subject of the whole idea, or the whole idea must pertain to a *single* part of the brain. Now, the first alternative is absurd. The act by which the intellect apprehends *truth, being,* and the like, is an indivisible thought. It is directly incompatible with its nature to be allotted or distributed over an aggregate of extraposited parts. The second alternative is equally impossible. If different parts of the extended substance were each the principle of a complete idea, we should have at the same time not one, but several, ideas of the subject. Our consciousness, however, tells us this is not the case. Lastly, if the whole idea were located in one part or element of the extended substance, either this part is itself composite or simple. If the latter, then our thesis—that the ultimate subject of thought is unextended—is established at once. If the former, then the old series of impossible alternatives will recur again until we are finally forced to the same conclusion.

(b) **The Simplicity of the Intellectual Acts of Judgment and Inference.** A similar line of reasoning applies here. The simplest judgment supposes the comparison of two distinct ideas which must be simultaneously apprehended by one unextended agent. Suppose the judgment, 'science is useful,' to be elicited. If the subject which apprehends the two concepts *science* and *useful* is not unextended, then we must assume that one of these terms is apprehended by one part and the other by a second; or else that different parts of the extended subject are each the subject of *both* ideas. In the former case, however, we cannot have any judgment at all. The part *a* apprehends *science,* the different part *b* conceives the notion *useful,* but the indivisible act of comparison requiring a single agent who combines the two ideas is wanting, and we can no more have the affirmative predication than if one man thinks *science* and another forms the concept *useful.* In the second alternative, if the parts *a* and *b* each simultaneously apprehend both *science* and *useful,* then we should have, not one, but a multiplicity of judgments.

The simplicity of the *inferential* act of the mind by which we seize the logical sequence of a conclusion from premises is still more irreconcilable with the hypothesis of a composite subject. The three judgments—every *y* is *z* : every *x* is *y* : *therefore,* every *x* is *z*—could no more constitute a syllogism if they proceeded from an extended substance than if each proposition was apprehended alone by a separate man.

(c) *The Simplicity of the Act of Volition.* The same line of argument as in the case of judgment establishes the simplicity of the soul from the unity of principle manifested in the acts of the *Will.* One, indivisible, immanent act of free choice cannot be elicited by an extended faculty composed of different extraposited parts.

(3) *Memory.* Through memory we are aware of our own *abiding personal identity.* We know with the most absolute certainty that we are the same persons who yesterday, last week, fifty years ago, had some vivid experience. But this would be impossible were the material organism the substantial principle in which these states inhere. The constituent elements of the latter are completely changed in a comparatively short time; and transient mental acts which did not inhere in a *permanent* subject could no more give us memory than could the disconnected cognitions of successive generations of men. Only a simple principle persisting unchanged amid successive states can afford an adequate basis for the faculty of remembrance. The condition necessary for the act of recollection is the identity of the being whose former states are recalled by memory.

21. The activities of our mental life are intelligible. Therefore, only by referring all our ideas, judgments, voli-

tions, memories of the past, etc., to one simple substantial principle as their source and center.

We have thus demonstrated the *simplicity* of the substantial principle which is the source of mental phenomena and we have shown that it cannot be an extended or a composite reality.

Article II.—The Spirituality of the Soul.

22. We have proved that the human soul must be a substantial principle and, moreover, that this principle must be of a simple and abiding nature. We now pass on to demonstrate that the soul is *spiritual* or *immaterial*. The attribute of spirituality is sometimes confounded with that of simplicity, but it is important to carefully distinguish these two terms. By saying that a substance is *simple* we mean that it is not composed of parts. By affirming that it is *spiritual* or *immaterial*, we signify that in its existence and in some of its operations it is independent of matter. The principle of life in the lower animals is an instance of a *simple* principle which is nevertheless *not* spiritual, since it is absolutely dependent upon the organism, or, "completely immersed" in the body.

23. **The Human Soul is a Spiritual Substance.** The human soul is the subject of various *spiritual activities*. But the subject of *spiritual* activities must be itself a *spiritual being*. Therefore, the soul must be a spiritual being. The minor premise is merely a particular application of the axiom that the operation of an agent follows its nature—*actio sequitur esse*. As this being *is,* so will it *act*. An act cannot transcend its cause. If, accordingly, any activities or faculties of the soul are spiritual, then the soul itself is spiritual. For the proof of our major premise—that we are endowed with activities of a spiritual or immaterial kind—we have only to refer to the conclusions established in the preceding chapter.

We will, however, here recall some of the facts which bring out in the clearest manner the truth of our thesis.

(a) *The Spirituality of the Faculty of Thought.* We are capable of apprehending and representing to ourselves abstract and universal ideas, *e. g.,* 'truth,' 'unity,' 'man,' 'triangle'; we can form ideas of purely spiritual beings, *e. g.,* 'of God'; we can understand necessary truths; we can apprehend possibilities as such; we can perceive the rational relations between ideas, and the logical sequence of conclusions from premises. But we have shown that such operations as these are spiritual phenomena which must accordingly proceed from a spiritual faculty. They could not be acts of a faculty exerted through or intrinsically dependent on a bodily organ. A power of this kind, (i) can only *react* in response to physical impressions, and (ii) can only *form representations* of a concrete character, depicting contingent individual facts. But universality, possibility, logical sequence, general relations (i) do not constitute such a physical stimulus, and (ii) can not be re-presented by an organic faculty. Accordingly, these higher mental functions must be admitted to be of a spiritual character: they thus transcend the sphere of all actions depending essentially or *intrinsically* on a material instrument. Since, then, our intellectual activity is of a spiritual character, the soul itself must, therefore, be a spiritual being.

(b) *Self-consciousness.* In the act of self-consciousness there occurs an instance of the complete or perfect reflexion of an indivisible agent back upon itself. I recognize an absolute identity between myself thinking about something and myself reflecting on that thinking Self. The mind reflecting and the mind reflected upon is the same: it is at once *subject* and *object.* Now, an action of this sort stands in direct and open conflict with all the most fundamental characteristics of matter. One part of a material substance may be made to act upon another, one atom may attract, repel or in various ways influence another, but that precisely the same portion of matter can be agent and patient in its own case is repugnant to all that either common experience or physical science teaches us. If, then this unity of agent and patient, of subject and object, is so contrary to the nature of matter, assuredly an activity whose action is intrinsically dependent on a corporeal organ cannot be capable of self-reflexion. To such an activity self-consciousness would be impossible. Consequently, there is a spiritual power within us, and the substantial principle from which it proceeds must be intrinsically independent of the body.

(c) *The Will.* The argument based on *voluntary* action may start from two distinct points of view.

(i) A merely sentient agent—one whose whole being is immersed in material conditions—can only desire sensuous good. On the other hand, to a spiritual creature which is endowed also with inferior faculties, both sensuous and supra-sensuous good is adapted. Therefore, the aspirations of the latter are unlimited, while those of the former are confined within the sphere of material well-being. But our own consciousness, history, biography and the existence of poetry and romance, all overwhelm us with evidence of the fact that man is moved by supra-sensible good. Love of justice, truth, virtue and right for its own sake are motives and impulses which have inspired some of the greatest and noblest works chronicled in the history of the human race. Consequently, there must be in man a principle not completely subject to material conditions.

(ii) Again. We are *free*: we are capable of active self-determination and in the act of free choice we can deliberately reject all that is attractive and gratifying to sensuous desire, and can choose instead that from which the body shrinks. But an *organic* power cannot thus control and coerce the exercise of its own activity.   To do so would be to act against its own nature.

24.   *Notes for the solution of objections.*

The *Materialist hypothesis* as to the nature of the soul is expressed in different terms by different writers, *e. g.,* "Thought is a secretion of the Brain."—Cabanis; "There subsists the same relation between thought and the brain as between bile and the liver."—Vogt; "There is every reason to suppose that consciousness is a function of nervous matter."—Huxley; "Consciousness and nervous action are subjective and objective faces of the same thing."—Spencer; etc.

There is, however, this fundamental agreement between all these writers, that "Soul and Body are not two distinct realities, but merely two 'aspects,' 'sides,' 'faces,' or 'phases,' of one and the same thing," i. e., *intellect* and *will* are organic faculties; the human soul is not a *spiritual* substance distinct from the *material* organism.

Now, it will be observed as we proceed that one radical vice pervades all the arguments (so far as they are arguments and not mere reckless assertions) adduced in favor of the materialist hypothesis, i. e., the mistake of confounding *conditions* with *causes.*   Legible print and good light are *conditions* requisite for good reading, but they are not the *cause* of the reading.   In the same way, a certain state of the brain may very well be a *condition* of normal *thinking* and *willing,* but in no state, short of becoming an unextended immaterial faculty, can the brain be the *cause* of our thoughts and volitions, as has been clearly shown in the preceding paragraphs.

Hence, the folly of what has been called the Double-Aspect theory, i. e., that mind and body are not two distinct realities, but merely two aspects, sides, or phases of one and the same thing—matter in motion.   Even if the reciprocal correspondence between every form of *mental state* and definite *neural processes* were established—utterly hopeless though the prospect of such result be—absolutely nothing would have been done towards reducing mental activity to a mere aspect of nervous changes. The two sets of facts are separated, as Spencer confesses, by "a difference which transcends all other differences." To talk of the unextended spiritual soul and the material body as "subjective and objective sides of the same fact," as a "two-sided cause," or a "double-faced unity," is merely a childish attempt to deceive ourselves with nonsensical or sophistical terms, just as it would be to talk of a "circular square."

Another thing that must be borne in mind in order to interpret aright many of the facts which are urged as objections against the *spirituality* of the soul, is the *relation of the human soul to the human organism.* The soul is not a *pure spirit* indwelling in the brain as in a palace or a prison. It is a substantial dynamic principle united to the body as Substantial Form to Matter. It is the source of various powers or activities some of which can only be exercised by the *compound* of soul and matter; others, by the soul *alone.* To the former class belongs the *vegetative* and *sensitive* powers of man; to the latter, the *intellectual.* Now, as in an *animal,* the vegetative powers subserve the sensitive; so in a *man* the vegetative and sensitive operations subserve, the intellectual activity of the *one simple dynamic principle* from which all these various powers proceed. The exercise, therefore, of its intellectual activity will naturally be more or less influenced by its vegetative and sensitive operations, and hence *organic* conditions will indirectly and remotely influence intellectual activity. Philosophy, therefore, far from slighting, will gladly welcome every fact that helps to illustrate in detail the relation between organic processes and mental states. Only let us be sure of our *facts* and gather *rational conclusions* from them.

With these simple principles in mind let us consider briefly the chief arguments for Materialism, drawn from Anatomy, Physiology, Pathology, etc.

(a) *Anatomy and Physiology.* "*Intellectual ability* varies in proportion to the size of the *brain,* its weight, chemical composition and the complexity of its convolutions. Therefore, the intellect is the brain."

Ans. (i) T. anteced.; n. concl. The most the antecedent would prove, if it were true, would be the *extrinsic* dependence of the intellect on the internal and external senses, of which we have spoken above, n. 7.

Ans. (ii) N. anteced. In point of *absolute* weight the brain of the elephant far exceeds that of man; and that of the boy that of the full grown man. In *relative* weight of brain several of the smaller birds are superior to man; and in this respect, too, the child is superior to the mature man.

In regard to the proportion of *phosphorus* in the brain, fish, sheep and geese are at least man's equal.

Finally, as to the multiplicity, complexity, etc., of the *convolutions* of the brain, the elephant, the ass, and the sheep would be superior to man.

Long ago St. Thomas said that the human organism has the most perfect brain, but science has as yet failed to say in what *precisely* that perfection consists.

(b) *Pathology.* "A power whose action can be disturbed and almost rendered impossible by indigestion, slight lesions of the brain, alcohol, opium, etc., and which can be restored by a dose of medicine, a surgical operation, etc., cannot be a spiritual power. But the intellect is such a power. Therefore, etc."

Ans. N. maj.; t. min.: n. concl. The intellectual activity of the soul is dependent on the *imagination,* as a reader on his book. Every disturbance of the brain, therefore, which is the organ of the imagination, will thus indirectly affect the operation of the intellect. This, however, is an old-fashioned truth; and the most modern physiology can do little more than note the fact of which the oldest philosophers were well aware.

"Almost everything needed for an exact science of the relations between changes in the brain and changes in our sensations is lamentably deficient."—Ladd. Complete insanity is found to co-exist with a perfectly normal condition of the brain, as far as science can judge; and, on the other hand, normal and even brilliant intellectual activity is often manifested by those suffering from serious cerebral lesion.

(c) *Psychological Heredity.* "The intellectual and moral qualities of parents are inherited by children. But only the material elements of man are derived from his parents. Therefore, intellectual and moral characters are merely material qualities."

Ans. D. maj., *directly,* i. e., as *spiritual* qualities, n.; *indirectly,* i. e., *physiological* qualities are inherited from which follow *aptitudes* for certain *sensitive* operations which in their turn *extrinsically* affect intellectual action, c. D. min., material elements affected by the physiological conditions of the parents, c.; material elements unaffected by the physiological conditions of the parents, n.

NOTE.—Bodily conditions, as we have said, indirectly influence the exercise of the soul's spiritual activities. On the other hand, a man's intellectual and moral life affects the sensitive and vegetative operations of the soul and in this way the very texture of the bodily frame. For the rest, the early teaching and example of parents, rather than the bodily qualities transmitted to their children, is the chief influence in the formation of the mental and moral character of the latter.

(e) In regard to *psycho-physics* and *cerebral physiology,* in general, two cautions are necessary; (i) The intellect is a *spiritual* faculty, and hence, even if science should one day show that certain definite cerebral processes invariably preceded and accompanied certain definite intellectual acts, it would only show that such cerebral modifications were the organic factors in those *sensitive* acts which are the *extrinsic* *conditions* upon which the exercise of intellectual activity, in our present state, depends. (ii) The sweeping assertions, so frequent in materialistic works on cerebral physiology, are in the actual state of science mere groundless conjectures. Thus we are told that "all *mental phenomena* have *exact equivalents* in specific forms of the *nerve-commotion* of the living brain." On this Professor Ladd, one of the highest living authorities in this line of study, remarks: "Our first impression on considering the foregoing * * * is that of a certain surprising audacity. The theory, standing on a slender basis of real fact, makes a leap into the dark which carries it centuries in advance of where the light of modern research is now clearly shining."

Every lover of knowledge will surely welcome all facts which help him to understand the relations between the matter and spirit of which he is composed. But here, as elsewhere, the student must be warned against mistaking any writer's day-dreams and conjectures for objective facts of nature.

Article III.—Immortality of the Soul.

25. So far we have proved that the human soul is a *simple, spiritual, substantial principle*. These truths, though of interest in themselves, derive their chief importance from their bearing on the question of a future life. It is clearly perceived that if the immortality of the soul be once established a scheme of future rewards and punishments is corollary which necessarily must follow. Consequently, the most violent Psychology and the most desperate Logic are pressed into the service of Materialism. The great poet of the school, Lucretius, openly confessed that the aim of this philosophy is to relieve men from anxiety regarding their condition after death, and the more candid of his modern disciples scarcely conceal their agreement with this view.

26. **Immortality of the Soul.** *Immortality* means literally *freedom from death*. By *death* is meant the cessation of life in living things. Such cessation of life might conceivably be brought about in either of two ways: *annihilation* of the living being or *corruption* of its vital principle. *Annihilation* means the reduction of an object into absolute nothingness. A being is, strictly speaking, *annihilated* only when it so ceases to be that nothing of it remains. An object is said to be *incorruptible* when it is incapable of perishing either by dissolution into the constituent parts or elements which may compose it, or by the *destruction* of *the subject* in which it inheres or upon which it depends for its existence.

Corruption from the philosophical point of view may thus in scholastic language be of either of two kinds—*corruptio per se* (essential corruption) or *corruptio per accidens* (accidental corruption). In corruption *per se* there is a dissolution of the being into its component principles, as in the *death of a man* or the *combustion of firewood*. A Being is said to suffer corruption *per accidens,* when put an end to *indirectly* by the destruction of the *subject* on which it depends, *e. g.,* an *accident* perishes in this way, when the subject in which it inheres is broken up or changed in such a manner as to be no longer a fit support for it, as in the case of the disappearance of the shape and color from a ball of melting snow or butter.

Now we hope to prove: (a) that the human soul is both *per accidens* and *per se* incorruptible; (b) that it can be annihilated neither by itself nor by any other creature; (c) that it will live at least for some time after separation from the body; (d) that God will never annihilate it.

(a) *The Human Soul is an Incorruptible Substance.* We have already demonstrated (i) that the soul is a substantial being; (ii) that it is a *simple* being; (iii) that it is *spiritual* or not intrinsically dependent on the body in its action or existence. But a simple substantial being is incapable of corruption *per se;* for it is not composed of component parts or principles into which it might be resolved; and a spiritual substance is exempt from corruption *per accidens,* since it does not intrinsically depend on the body for its existence. Therefore, the human soul is incapable of corruption in either of these alternative ways. *Incorruptibility* is thus a consequent of *spirituality.*

(b) The Human Soul cannot be Annihilated either (i) by Itself or by (ii) any Created Being. Annihilation is the reduction of something to nothing. But this result cannot be the effect of any *positive* action, for every positive action must terminate in a positive reality. A positive act, other than that of creation, can only *change* the state of the materials upon which it operates. Any action, accordingly, whether of the soul itself or of another creature, could at most effect merely a change or modification in the soul. Annihilation is possible only by the withdrawal of the conserving or creative power which sustains the being in existence. Now, as creation and conservation in existence pertain to God alone, He only can cease to preserve; and, therefore, He alone can annihilate.

(c) The Human Soul is not Annihilated at Death.

(i) *Proof from the Moral Law and the Sanctity and Justice of God.* God has inscribed in our rational nature His *Moral Law,* commanding us to do right and to abstain from wrong; and, as an infinitely wise, just and holy Legislator, He must have fortified this law with a *perfect sanction.* But there is not such a perfect sanction in this life. Therefore, the soul must exist at least for some time after death.

Our own conscience gives us the most intimate and perfect assurance that we are under such a *Moral Law.* The study of the laws, literatures, religions of the various nations of the world; investigations into the customs and moral ideas of savage tribes; the researches of the science of Philology, all conspire to afford irresistible evidence of the universality of ethical conceptions which reveal the moral law.

But without a sufficient sanction such a law would obviously be incomplete and inadequate, and, therefore, incompatible with the character of a perfect, wise and just Lawgiver.

That a sufficient sanction is not to be found in the *present life* is a fact of common observation. The goods and ills of this world are often distributed inversely in proportion to desert. Many self-sacrificing, virtuous men meet with continuous suffering and trial, and during the whole course of their lives, whilst many wicked men have enjoyed prosperity up to their very last moments. Now, this cannot be the final outcome of life. An infinitely holy and just God cannot permit this. He cannot allow that it be ultimately better for those who break His law, who violate the precepts of reason and degrade that nature in which they are like unto Him, than for those who seek to observe His commands and to conform their conduct to the arch-type of holiness. Therefore, there must be a future existence of the Soul, in which the present deficiencies of the practical order shall be set right.

If there is not such a retributory state, then—there is no use of concealing the fact—the moral life of man, the seemingly grandest and sublimest reality in the universe, is founded on an irrational hallucination, and many of the noblest acts that have ever been achieved, and which all mankind conspire to applaud, are simply unspeakable folly.

(2) *Proof from man's desire of perfect happiness.* A natural and universal desire in harmony with the dictates of reason could not have been implanted in man's nature by a perfectly wise and good God with the intention of its universal, necessary and final frustration. But unless the life of the human sould be continued after death, such is the case. Therefore, the soul will not perish at death. Our major premise is too obvious to require proof. It is inconceivable

that a God of infinite wisdom and goodness could have set in man's nature a truly rational desire, designing it to be inevitably and universally rendered vain. This implicit tendency towards perfect beatitude, this striving after the possession of an infinite good, is an intelligent yearning. It is a desire rooted in the rational nature of man, in that element of his being which makes him specifically human. It is a longing universal throughout the race, expanding with mental and moral development and attaining its grandest and noblest form in those men who conform their lives to the loftiest ideal of virtue. It would, then, have argued both folly and cruelty in the Author of our nature to have created this desire and purposed it for inevitable and universal frustration.

The minor premise is also easy to establish. Our own internal experience, our personal observation of other men, the history of the human race, all bear witness to the truth that man's yearning after happiness can never be satisfied in the present life. Health, strength, beauty, wealth, intellectual gifts fall to the lot of a very few, yet even where they are all combined we know that there may be found, not merely absence of perfect happiness, but even painful discontent and acute misery. Anything capable of satisfying the desire of happiness is, in the present world, beyond the wildest hopes of the vast majority of the human race. Unless, then, we are prepared to predicate both folly and cruelty of God, we must maintain a future existence in which this desire can meet its proper object. There must be a state where this unfilled yearning can be satiated.

(3).—*Proof from the universal judgment of mankind.* A third argument for the reality of another life, upon which much stress has been always laid, is the fact that, morally speaking, in all times and among all nations there has been found a belief in a future life. Now, such a conviction in direct opposition to all sensible appearance must spring from man's rational nature, and must be allowed to be true, unless we are prepared to affirm that man's rational nature leads him inevitably into error. To assert this is virtually to adopt the position of absolute scepticism. Consequently, we are bound under the penalty of intellectual suicide to admit the trustworthiness of this universal belief.

(d) **God will not annihilate the Soul.** We have now proved that the soul will certainly not perish at death, that it is of its own nature incorruptible and that it can be destroyed neither by itself nor by any created being; it only remains to be shown that God will never annihilate it. God acts with wisdom in all His works. But there is no wisdom in making a Being capable and necessarily desirous of living forever and then annihilating it after a definite period of duration. Therefore, God has not done so. But He has made the soul innately and intrinsically immortal and desirous of immortality. Therefore, he will never annihilate it. We gather God's Will from His works; His intentions in regard to His creatures from the natures He has given them. But, by its very constitution and nature, the human soul is fitted to live forever. Therefore, God will not contradict the connatural requirements of this Being which His wisdom planned and His power called into existence, but will preserve it in existence forever.

27. Notes for the solution of objections.

(a) "The soul is *born* with the body, *grows* with the body, *decays* with the body and therefore *perishes* with the body.

Ans.—The soul is not derived, like the body, from the parents. Being a *spiritual* principle, it must be, as will be shown in a later article, immediately *created* by God.

It does not *grow* in the sense of being quantitatively increased, but, extrinsically conditioned by the efficiency of the brain and sensory organs, it gradually unfolds its intellectual and moral capabilities.

It does not *decay* with bodily disease, although since its sensuous operations are immediately dependent on the instrumentality of the organism, they must naturally be affected by the health of the latter.

The arguments can also be inverted. In many instances the mind is most powerful and active in the decrepit frame of the old, and in spite of dreadful havoc from bodily disease.

(b) The activity of the intellect is conditioned by that of the imagination and the external senses—organic faculties. Therefore, since the latter are extinguished at death, so must the former be.

Ans.—While the soul is united to the body in the present life, its intellectual activity is extrinsically conditioned by the exercise of its sensuous powers, c.; when separated from the body its intellectual activity is so conditioned, n.

NOTE.—The mode of *action* of a being is conditioned by its mode of *existence*. In the present life the spiritual soul is united to the body as Substantial Form to Matter; and its energy is distributed in various lines of action (vegetation, sensation, intellectual cognition and volition). The good of the whole being requires that there should be a hierarchical order among these various activities. The lower faculties must therefore subserve the higher, and the higher must be in some way dependent on the lower. As the man must pass through the various stages of childhood and growth, so the human spirit "a little lower than the angels," must begin its career in union with matter, and learn its first intellectual lessons from the information supplied by the senses. In the ordinary course of nature, however, the time must come when it is separated from the body, and goes forth with the knowledge acquired in this life and treasured up in memory into a new world and new conditions. The spiritual powers of knowledge and volition are more intense than is possible in this life, as all the energy of the soul is now concentrated in these activities. The *natural* objects of its knowledge are (besides the things it learned while united to the body itself), its fellow-souls and a more perfect knowledge of pure spirits and of God than can be had here. These objects of knowledge, with the mind's innate power of analysis, synthesis, reasoning, etc., give abundant scope for the exercise of intelligence and will. This implies nothing supernatural or preternatural: it is simply the soul's connatural state in its new conditions, apart from all consideration of rewards and punishments.

(c) Against the argument from the *desire of happiness*.

(i) Many natural desires are vain, *e. g.*, 'man's longing for health,' 'wealth,' etc., 'the love of life in the brute,' and the like.

(ii) This desire will at all events be vain in lost souls.

Ans.—(i) The desire of happiness is distinct in kind from the impulses with which it is here compared. It is *universal and necessary*. It is the great radical rational tendency which manifests the end of man as a human being. The other impulses that can be cited, however, are all *particular* appetites toward some special form of happiness. No one of them is necessary, or an inevitable outcome of man's nature.

As regards the instincts of the lower races of animals—in the first place, they do in a great part attain their end; and secondly, they cannot properly be compared with the rational desire of man. The brute has not an intelligent apprehension of what is meant by a continued existence. Consequently, though it is impelled to avoid pain or destruction for the time being, it cannot be said to desire immortality. Brute existence may attain its end though all the lower animals die, whilst if this all-comprehensive desire in man is doomed to universal disappointment, it must be held that in the highest order of being upon the earth there is an enormous failure, anything like which is not to be discovered elsewhere in the universe.

(ii) The desire of beatitude is undoubtedly frustrated in the lost. This desire, absolute and radical in every human soul, shows indeed the natural capacity and destiny of the being. But the attainment of the object which shall satisfy it depends, as conscience testifies, on the free fulfillment of certain conditions during the present life. The lost soul is, by its nature, capable of forever existing. It has deliberately refused to fulfill the conditions necessary to attain to a happy eternity. It justly deserves to go without the good it has thus wilfully rejected. Its existence in that state of privation of the object it necessarily longs for is an internal affirmation of the sacredness of right and justice, of the foulness of moral evil and of the sanctity and supreme Majesty of the Divine Law-giver.

(d) The argument from *universal belief* is attacked on the ground that some peoples and many individuals, both philosophers and non-philosophers, do not judge there is any future life. It may be observed in answer that when the proof from universal consent is invoked it only implies a *moral* universality. As regards the nations or tribes who have been asserted not to believe in a future life, advancing knowledge does not confirm such a statement. The greatest care is required in interrogating savages regarding their religious opinions. Inaccuracy in this respect has often caused the ascription of atheism to tribes later on proved to possess elaborate systems of religions and hierarchies of gods. Future annihilation, asserted to be a cardinal doctrine of Buddhism, is by the vast majority of the disciples of that sect understood to be, not a return to absolute nothing, but an ecstatic state of peaceful contemplation.

(e) It is often asserted that there is no proportion between an *eternal* punishment and a *transitory* offence.

Ans.—There is no proportion in *duration* between the offence and punishment, any more than between ten years' imprisonment and an attempt on a sovereign's life, c.; there is no proportion in equality and fitness, n. Deliberate rebellion against infinite justice, goodness and holiness by a being bound absolutely to obedience and loyalty in gratitude for everything which he possesses is a crime suitably atoned for only by such a penalty. Deliberate refusal to fulfill the conditions on which a certain end is appointed to be attained is justly punished by the privation of that end. However long or short, therefore, the time of probation may be, a *final* state of rebellion should mean a *final* state of punishment: final rejection of the conditions required for the attainment of the end should mean *final* privation of the end.

(f) A word finally in reply to certain scholastic difficulties. (i) "The soul," it is said, "is the *form* of the body. But a *form* cannot be separated from the subject which it actuates." The solution lies in the fact that the human soul is not a form educed from the body and intrinsically dependent on the latter.

(ii) "The soul is created to inform the body; hence, the reason for its existence disappears with the destruction of the body." The answer is that an immediate and secondary end of the soul's existence is to animate the body: the primary end, however, is to glorify God by its intelligence and will.

(iii) "The soul being the form of the body, its union with the latter is *natural;* its separation would, therefore, be *unnatural,* and so could not endure." We reply that the separation would not be *unnatural* in the sense of being *impossible;* but we readily admit this state to be *non-natural,* in the sense of not being in complete harmony with the nature of the soul; hence, the propriety of the resurrection of the body.

Article IV.—Unity of the Soul.

28. Plato allotted to the human body three really distinct souls. Some modern authors teach that there is in man, dis-

tinct from the rational sentient soul, a vital principle the source of vegetative life. This is the theory of *vitalism*. Others make the rational soul numerically different from the common principle of sentient and vegetative activities. In opposition to these various hypotheses the scholastic doctrine holds that in man there is but one dynamic principle, the rational soul, which is, however, capable of exerting the inferior modes of energy exhibited in sensuous and vegetative life.

(a) That *the rational soul in man is at the same time the subject of his sensuous life* is proved by various considerations.

(i) We have the testimony of consciousness to the most perfect identity between the soul which *feels* and the soul which *thinks*. Introspection assures us that it is the same being which understands or reasons and which is the vital principle of our sensation.

(ii) I can compare intellectual operations with sensitive states, and affirm the former to be more painful, more pleasant, etc., than the latter. But this can only be effected by the two compared states being apprehended by one and the same indivisible agent.

(iii) The intimate interdependence of thought and sensation is inexplicable if they are activities of diverse principles. In particular, no reason can be assigned why it is of objects apprehended through sense that the first intellectual concepts are elaborated by the understanding.

(b) We have next to demonstrate that *the principle of vegetative life in man is identical with the rational sentient soul*.

(i)—The intimate union and mutual interdependence subsisting between the sensuous and vegetative activties cannot be accounted for on the supposition that two distinct principles are at work. Organic changes and sensations arise simultaneously. Fear, hope, joy, anger may instantaneously and powerfully affect the action of the heart, stomach, liver, lungs, or the state of the nervous system generally; while conversely, the atmosphere, narcotics, the action of the stomach, of the liver, circulation, and, indeed, nearly all physiological functions may modify the color of our sensuous life. In a word, the two classes of activities condition each other.

(ii) If the rational soul in man were a new entity indwelling in a living body already animated by a sentient or vegetative soul, man would not be a single individual. He would no longer be essentially *one,* but *two* beings.

NOTE (1)—The solution to a difficulty often raised in various forms may be indicated here. It is argued that a *corruptible principle* must be really distinct from an *incorruptible* one. But sentient and vegetative souls are admittedly corruptible. Therefore, the rational spirit in man cannot be identical with the source of his inferior life; or if it is, then it must be mortal. To this we can answer, it is quite true that a soul or vital principle capable of *merely* sentient or vegetative activity perishes on the destruction of the subject which it informs, and is accordingly corruptible, but this is not the case with the principle of the inferior species of life in man. Sentiency and vegetation are not in him activities of a *merely* sentient subject. They are, on the contrary, phenomena of a rational soul endowed with certain supra-sensuous powers, but also capable of exerting lower forms of energy. There can be no reason why a superior principle cannot virtually and superabundantly contain such inferior faculties. Scholastic philosophers, accordingly, have always taught that the virtue of exerting organic functions is inherent in the human soul, but that these activities are necessarily suspended whilst the soul is separated from the body. In the case of man, therefore, the active source of sentient and vegetative life is not a corruptible principle.

(2).—It is sometimes urged that the existence of a *struggle* between the rational and sensitive powers shows that both proceed from diverse principles. The true inference, however, is the very opposite. It is one indivisible soul which thinks, feels, desires and governs the vegetative processes of the living human being, and precisely because the source of these several activities is the same they mutually impede each other. Violent exercise or any kind of activity naturally diminishes the energy available for another, if both activities flow from the *same sources*. If, however, the two kinds of activities flow from *different* sources, there is no reason why one should impede the other.

Article V.—Union of Soul and Body.

29. Various theories have been advanced regarding the **nature of the union between soul and body.** The most celebrated are: (1) that of Plato, (2) Occasionalism, (3) Preestablished harmony, (4) the doctrine of Matter and Form. The first three are all forms of exaggerated Dualism: the last alone recognizes and accounts for the essential unity of man.

30. **Ultra-Dualistic Theories.** (a) According to Plato, who historically comes first, the rational soul is a pure spirit incarcerated in the body for some crime committed during a former life. Its relation to the organism is analogous to that of the rider to his horse, or of the pilot to his ship. Since it is not naturally ordained to inform the body, the soul receives nothing but hindrance from its partner. This fanciful hypothesis, it is needless to say, does not receive much favor at the present day. (i) There is not a particle of evidence for such a pre-natal existence; and (ii) the doctrine would make man not one, but two beings.

(b) *Occasionalism* represents soul and body as two opposed and distinct beings between which no real interaction can take place. It is God alone who effects changes in either. On the *occasion* of a modification of the soul He produces an appropriate movement in the body; and *vice versa*. All our sensations, thoughts and volitions are produced by God Himself, all our actions are due, not to our own, but to the Divine Will. The doctrine of Occasionalism, however, is not confined to the interaction of soul and body. *No* created things have, in this view, any real efficiency. God is the *only* operative cause.

(i) This theory renders purposeless the wonderful mechanism of the various sense-organs. (ii) It is in direct conflict with the testimony of consciousness to personal causality in the exercise of volition and self-control. (iii) It is refuted by the experience of our whole life, that our sensations are excited by the impressions of external objects, and that our volitions do really cause our physical movements, (iv) Finally, Occasionalism involves the gratuitous assumption of a continuous miracle.

(c) The theory of *Pre-established Harmony* substitutes for the never-ceasing miracles of Occasionalism a single miraculous act at the beginning. Soul and body do not really influence one another, but both proceed like two clocks started together in a divinely pre-arranged correspondence.

The objections to this theory are substantially the same as to the last. In both, moreover, the union between mind and body is *accidental,* not essential; and we have in man really *two* beings.

(d) Another theory, that of *Physical Influx,* would make the union of soul and body consist in their mutual interaction. The account, however, is either merely a statement of the *fact* that they *do influence* each other, or an explanation which would dissolve the substantial union into an *accidental* relation between *two* juxtaposed beings.

31. **Scholastic Doctrine.** The true doctrine is the Peripatetic theory. This explanation was formulated by Aristotle, and later on adopted by St. Thomas and all the leading Scholastic philosophers. The Soul is described by these writers as the *substantial form* of the body, i. e., a dynamic principle which, by its union with the matter that it actuates, constitutes a complete substance of a determinate species,—a human being, *a man.*

Now, we have already proved that there is in man, a vital principle to which is due the *natural unity* of activity comprising the phenomena of his life. But, such a principle must be the *substantial form* of the living human being. For, since every *action* of an agent flows from the *nature* of that agent—the principle which is the source of the natural activity of a substance must be determinant of its being and nature. Consequently, as the soul is the source of all vital activities, it must be the determining or actuating principle of the living being. The soul is thus a substantial principle upon which the very being of the substance depends. In other words, by its union *with* its material co-efficient, the soul constitutes the complete living human being. That is, the soul or vital principle is the substantial form of the living body.

Furthermore, the rational soul must also be the *only* substantial form of man. For man is *one,* complete, individual substance; specifically, distinct from all other substances. Were the human body, however, actuated by more than one substantial form, man would be, not *one,* but an *aggregate* of individuals, since each substantial form would constitute with matter a complete substantial being of a determinate species.

NOTE.—The chief difficulty urged against the thesis of the present paragraph is based on the spirituality of the human soul. It is said that since intellect is a supra-organic faculty intrinsically independent of matter, it cannot be a faculty of a principle which is the *form* of a body. In reply we admit that intellect could not be a faculty of a form *completely dependent* on a material co-efficient. But, there is no impossibility in a substantial principle which, although it informs a living body, yet being endowed with a spiritual faculty, transcends and exceeds the sphere of a merely organic form. There is no contradiction, as we have before shown, in a spiritual principle possessing capabilities of an inferior as well as of a superior order. Moreover, we have proved that the human soul is *de facto* the source of both classes of faculties.

32. As to the manner in which the soul is *present* in the body, it is enough to remark that the *simplicity* of a spiritual substance, just as that of intelligence and volition, does not consist in the minuteness of a point. The soul is an immaterial, substantial source of energy which, though not constituted of separated extraposited parts, is yet capable of *informing,* and of exercising its virtue throughout an extended subject. Such a reality does not, like a material entity, occupy different parts of space by different parts of its own mass. In scholastic phraseology it is described as present throughout the body which it informs, not *commensurably* but *definitely*. Its presence is not that of an extended object the different parts of which fill and are *circumscribed* by corresponding areas of space, but of an immaterial source of energy present ubiquitously throughout the living body.

The soul, since it is the substantial form of the body, vivifying and actuating all parts of its material co-efficient so as to constitute with it one complete living being, must by its very nature be ubiquitously present in the body. For it is only by this immediate *presence and union with matter* that it can actuate and vitalize it. On the other hand, since the soul is an indivisible spirit, wherever it is present, it must be there in its entirety; consequently, the entire substantial soul is present in the whole body and in each part. Those functions of the *com-*

pound, however, which require a special organ, can only be exercised in that part of the body which constitutes the special organ, *e. g.,* 'eye,' 'ear,' etc. This is expressed technically in the phrase, "The whole *substance* of the soul is present in every part of the living body, but the whole *activity* of the soul cannot be exercised in every part of the body."

NOTE.—The higher spiritual acts of intellect, etc., are intrinsically independent of the organism, i. e., no bodily organ co-operates in eliciting them; yet there is no great inaccuracy in saying that the soul thinks *in the brain,* inasmuch as the brain is the organ of the imagination and sensuous memory on whose functions the exercise of intellectual activity extrinsically depends.

ARTICLE VI.—ORIGIN OF THE HUMAN SOUL.

33. **Mode of Origin of the Soul.** Of philosophers holding erroneous ideas regarding the origin of the human soul, some have conceived it as arising by *emanation* from the Divine substance, others as derived from the *parents.* The former theory starts from a Pantheistic conception of the universe, and is in conflict with the simplicity and absolute perfection of God. The hypothesis that the soul is transmitted to the offspring by the parents—and hence, called *Traducianism*—has taken a variety of forms. Some writers have maintained that the soul of the child, like its body, proceeds from the parental *organism;* others that it comes from the *soul* of the parents.

Traducianism, whether understood of a *corporeal* or *incorporeal* seminal element, is an inadmissable theory. As regards the derivation of the rational soul of the child from the *body* of a parent, it is obvious that such a supposition is based on a materialistic conception of the nature of the soul. *Nemo dat quod non habet;* a spiritual substance cannot proceed from a corporeal principle. The derivation, however, of the rational soul from the soul of a parent is equally absurd. Every human soul is a simple spiritual substance. Consequently, the hypothesis of any sort of seminal particle or spiritual germ being detached from the parental soul is absurd. Finally, if the soul of the child were generated or evoked out of the *potencies of matter,* it would not be a spiritual being endowed with intellect and will and intrinsically independent of matter.

34. Opposed to these various theories stands **the doctrine of creation,** according to which "each human soul is produced from nothing by the creative act of God." By *creation* is meant the calling of a being into existence from nothing, the production of an object as regards its entire substance. Now, a spiritual substance, if produced at all, must be produced by creation. But, the human soul is a spiritual substance, whilst at the same time it is of finite capacity, and therefore a *caused* or *contingent* being. But, because of its contingent and limited nature it cannot be *self-existing,* it must therefore have received its existence from another being. On the other hand, inasmuch as it is a *spiritual* being intrinsically independent of matter, it cannot have arisen by any process of substantial transformation; for, if it did so arise, it would necessarily be a composite substance consisting of Matter and Form. Finally, since God alone, Who exists of Himself, and Who alone possesses infinite power, can exert the highest form of action, calling creatures into existence from nothing, the production of the human soul must be due immediately to Him.

NOTE.—Objections urged against the doctrine of the creation of the soul are (i) Like end must have like origin; but the human soul is immortal, therefore it must never have had a beginning. (ii) The theory of creation involves a continuous exercise of miraculous power on the part of God.

Answer (i)—We simply deny that the end of a creature must be like its beginning in the way asserted. God alone is without beginning, but He can will to exist whatever is not intrinsically impossible, and He may will it to last forever. Consequently, there can be no absurdity in His creating from nothing a simple incorruptible substance which He designs never to perish.

(ii)—A miracle is an interference with the laws of nature, but in the given case, the creation of souls, when the appropriate conditions are posited by the creature, is a law of nature.

35. **Time of Its Origin.** When does the human soul begin to exist? Plato taught that previous to its incarceration in the body the soul had from all eternity resided among the gods in an ultra-celestial sphere. In that ideal land it contemplated Truth, Goodness and Beauty, as they are in themselves; and its present cognitions are merely faint, cloudy reminiscences of the knowledge it once possessed. The theory of *Metempsychosis* or Transmigration of souls, has been held under one shape or another by many Oriental thinkers. These doctrines, however, in all their forms are gratuitous and absurd hypotheses. There is not a vestige of argument in their favor; no memory of any such previous existence; no knowledge of any kind, much less of any personal fault committed in a previous state. On the other hand, they misconceive soul and body as two complete substances mutually hostile to and independent of each other, accidentally and not substantially and naturally united in man. Lebnitz considered human souls along with all other Monads to have been created simultaneously by God at the beginning of the world. All souls were conserved in a semi-conscious condition inclosed in minute organic particles, ready to be evoked into rational life when the fitting conditions are supplied. Proof of course is here out of the question. No sufficient end can be conceived for the sake of which such an unconscious life could be vouchsafed to the soul; and consequently, it must be rejected as a useless and incredible hypothesis.

The true doctrine as to the time of the origin of the rational soul is that which teaches that it is created precisely *when it is infused into the body.* There are two tenable views as to the exact moment of this event. One holds that the rational soul is created and infused into the new being at the instant of conception; the other, supported by St. Thomas, assigns a somewhat later period for this occurrence. The advent of the rational soul occurs, St. Thomas maintains, when the embryo has been sufficiently developed to become the appropriate material constituent of the human being.

NOTE.—The argument by which we have established that each individual rational soul owes its origin to a Divine creative act, proves *a fortiori* that the *first* of such souls must have thus arisen. Since even the *spiritual* soul of a human parent is incapable of itself effecting a spiritual soul in its offspring, it is evident that the merely *sentient* soul of a brute could less still be the cause of such a result. Again, the human soul, as we have shown, possesses the spiritual faculties of Intellect and Will, and is, therefore, itself, a spiritual principle intrinsically independent of matter; but such a being could never arise by mere continuous modifications of a vital energy intrinsically dependent on matter. In a word, all the proofs by which we established the spirituality of the higher faculties, and of the soul itself, demonstrate the existence of an impassable chasm between it and all non-spiritual principles, whether of the amoeba or the monkey. The special intervention of God must therefore, have been necessary to introduce into the world this new superior order of agent.

ARTICLE VII.

UNITY AND ANTIQUITY OF THE HUMAN RACE.

36. **Unity of the Human Race.** Under this head we have two questions, (i) as to *specific unity* and (ii) as to *unity of origin.*

(a) *Specific Unity.* All races of men are essentially similar in anatomical and physiological characters, and permanently fruitful intermarriage can have place between individuals of all the various types. Therefore, etc. All races of men possess intelligence, free will, the power of speech, the social, ethical and religious instincts, etc. Therefore, etc. "Dolichocephalous or brachycephalous, great or small, orthognathous or prognathous, man is always man in the full sense of the word."—Quatrefages.

NOTE.—The peculiarities of the different races, *e. g.,* 'color,' 'size and shape of skull,' 'character of hair,' etc., are merely accidental modifications resulting from environment, climate, food, physical and moral conditions of life, etc., and transmitted by heredity.

(b) *Unity of Origin.* Full certainty that all the various races of men are descended from the same primitive parents is given only by the authority of the *divine revelation.* However, the comparative study of the traditions, customs, religions, folk-lore and languages of the various races, furnishes a very powerful positive argument in favor of unity of origin.

NOTE (1).—As to the objection that it is impossible to account for the vast population which filled the earth, within less than a thousand years after the flood, if all were derived from the family of Noah, it is enough to say, "assume that between the age of 25 and 50, each married couple become the parents of four children, and a single couple propagating itself at this rate could in a thousand years give a population twice as great as there is now upon the earth."

(2).—"We cannot admit that the difficulties in the way of *migration* offer a valid reason for disbelieving that mankind originally came from one spot on the earth. These difficulties are nowhere greater than in the Pacific Ocean, and yet the Pacific Ocean affords abundant proof that these difficulties do not hinder the spreading of the inhabitants from one group of islands to another. The great similarity in the language, customs, traditions and religions of Polynesia, from the Sandwich Islands to New Zealand, will not allow us to suppose that these Islanders are of different races."—Waitz. "The Polynesians started from the Archipelagoes on the eastern coast of Asia. None of these migrations date back beyond historic times. The chief migrations took place a little before or after the Christian era."—Quatrefages.

37. The Antiquity of the Human Race. The Bible does not give any fixed date for the origin of man. Arguing from such data as the sacred text affords, commentators have made various attempts to determine the age of the human race. The *maximum* assigned would be 6000 to 8000 years B. C.; the *minimum,* about 4000 B. C. The opinion commonest among orthodox commentators at present would place the date of man's first appearance on earth at between 8000 and 10,000 years ago. Our *natural* sources of information on this subject are *geology* and *archaeology* on the one hand, and *history* on the other.

(a) *As to Geology.* Geologists tell us that the first *certain* proofs we have of the existence of man would place his appearance at or about the close of the *glacial* period. But how far back are we to date the close of the glacial period? Taking the erosion of the Niagara gorge as our chronometer (according to Lyell, etc.), the maximum length of time since the birth of the Falls, contemporaneous with the end of the Ice Age, is 7000 years. This is the latest result of the careful calculations of C. K. Gilbert, of the U. S. Geological Survey. These calculations are corroborated by the observation of Winchell, Wright and other high authorities.

(b) *As to History.*—Apart from the Old Testament narrative, the best Egyptologists place the origin of Egyptian history and civilization between 3000 and 4000 B. C.; Baby-

Ionian history dates back between 2000 and 3000 B. C.; Phoenician, about 1600 B. C.; Assyrian, about 1500 B. C.; Indian, about 1200 B. C. China has no authentic history before the beginning of the eighth century, B. C.; but as a matter of conjecture, Klaproth, Lassen, etc., place the beginning of Chinese history about 2000 B. C.

From the preceding brief remarks it is seen that neither geology nor history requires or permits us to assume a higher antiquity for man than that roughly assigned by Biblical chronology.

NOTE.—As to the *primitive* state of the human race, all historical evidence is in accord with the teaching of Genesis. All peoples, savage and civilized, have in their traditions some reminiscences of a primitive "golden age" of the human race. Egypt and Babylon, whose authentic history antedates that of all other nations, affords no indication of any early period of barbarism. "All authorities agree that however far we go back, we find in Egypt no rude or uncivilized time out of which civilization is developed."—G. Rawlinson.

We may conclude this brief article with a few quotations from Dawson's latest work, The Meeting Place of Geology and History. "The absolute *date* of the first appearance of man cannot perhaps be fixed within a few years or centuries, either by human chronology or by the science of the earth. If the earliest men were those of the river gravels and caves, men of the 'mammoth age,' or the "Palæolithic period,' we can form some definite ideas of their possible antiquity. They colonized the Continents immediately after the elevation of the land from the great subsidence which closed the pleistocene or glacial period, in what has been called the 'continental' period of the post-glacial age. We have some measures of the date of this great continental elevation, and know that its distance from our time must fall within about eight thousand years. * * *

"There is but *one species* of men, though many *races* and varieties; and these races and varieties seemed to have developed themselves at a very early time and have shown a remarkable fixity in their later history. There is a reason to believe, however, from various physiological facts, that this is a very general law of varietal forms which are observed to appear rapidly or suddenly and then in favorable circumstances to be propagated continuously. * * *

"The precise *locality* of the origin of man * * * must have been in some fertile and salubrious region of the northern hemisphere; and probability as well as tradition points to those regions of southwestern Asia, which have been the earliest *historical* abodes of man.

"The man of Cro-magnon and his contemporaries are eloquent of one great truth. They tell us that primitive man had the same high cerebral organization which he possesses now, and we may infer, the same high intellectual and moral nature, fitting him for communion with God and leadership over the lower world. They indicate also, like the mound-builders who preceded the North American Indian, that man's earliest state was the best—that he had been a high and noble creature before he became a savage. It is not conceivable that their high development of brain and mind could have spontaneously engrafted itself on a mere brutal and savage life. These gifts must be remnants of a noble organization degraded by moral evil. They thus justify the tradition of a Golden and Edenic Age, and mutely protest against the philosophy of progressive development as applied to man."

PART FIVE.

NATURAL THEOLOGY.

---

1. Theology is the *Science of God*. **Natural Theology** is, The Science of God attainable by *unaided human reason* in man's present state. Now, we may say in general that there are four ways in which one can arrive at a knowledge of any Being.

(a) From the most hasty and obvious glance at an effect as such, we can gather the *existence* and some imperfect confused notion of the *nature* of the cause.

(b) From a careful investigation of the character of the effect we can gain a fuller and more distinct knowledge of the cause; and thence, by analysis of certain prominent attributes which we find with certainty to belong to it, we can conclude to certain other less obvious attributes which it necessarily possesses.

(c) We may further learn many things about the nature of the cause from trustworth *testimony*.

(d) Lastly, we may see the cause itself immediately and intuitively as it really is.

It will suffice for our present purpose to group the various kinds of knowledge that we can have of God under the above four heads.

(a) There is the concept of God which arises almost spontaneously in the minds of all who have attained the use of reason, from the most casual reflection on themselves and the world around them. This idea represents God as a Mighty, Intelligent, Personal Being distinct from and above and beyond the moving universe, who has made it all that it is, on whom it depends, who rules and controls it, to whom it belongs, and who notes the actions of His rational creatures, and will one day judge them, and rewards their observance and punish their breaches of the moral law which He has imprinted in their hearts. This is the ordinary *popular* idea of God.

(b) There is the idea of God which the philosopher can attain to by careful analysis of the note of First Uncaused Cause of all contingent beings. Such a Being must be self-existent, necessarily existing, infinite, eternal, etc., etc., and contain in itself in a manner compatible with its character of self-existence, all the perfections of its effects. This may be called the *scientific* idea of God.

(c) There is the knowledge of God which we may acquire through His own free supernatural *revelation*.

(d) Lastly there is the knowledge of God which is had by the Blessed who see Him face to face.

The two last kinds of knowledge of God are *supernatural,* and do not come within the sphere of Natural Theology. Here we are concerned to know what knowledge of God man can acquire by the right use of his natural reason, i. e., what reason can demonstrate about God from the data furnished by nature.

2. **Our natural knowledge of God** is derived from the consideration both of the external world, and of the human soul. The external world manifests chiefly the Wisdom, Power and Providence of its maker; the human soul manifests the inner attributes of the Divine Life. The material and

spiritual worlds are thus, as it were, two mirrors in which are reflected, though imperfectly, the image of the Creator. Hence, our natural knowledge of God is mediate and *analogical, not intuitive,* nor representing the Divine Nature as it is in itself purely and simply. The perfections found in creatures are but faint images of the perfections of the Creator, yet they truly shadow forth the character of their Author, and from them we are enabled to gather a concept of God, which, however incomplete, still truly represents His Nature and Attributes as far as it goes. But before our concepts of the perfections found in nature, *e. g.,* power, wisdom, life, liberty, etc., can be applied to God, they must first be purified from all imperfection and enlarged and elevated so as to be in accord with the character of the self-existent eternal First Cause of them. Hence we must distinguish three steps, as it were, in this adaptation of our concepts of nature's created perfections to God:

(a)   We *affirm* that these created perfections image and shadow forth the Divine perfections of their cause;

(b)   We *deny* that these perfections are in God in the same manner as in creatures, i. e., limited and mixed with imperfection;

(c)   We conceive the Divine Essence as having in itself in a supreme unlimited degree whatever is perfect in creatures without any admixture of imperfection.

In a word, we may say that the whole treatise before us is founded on the two self-evident Principles of Causality and Contradiction. The First Cause *must* possess such and such perfections, because He is the ultimate adequate cause of all contingent Being; He *cannot* possess these perfections in such and such a way, because it would be contrary to His character of self-existent.

With this brief preface as to the character of our natural

knowledge of God, we go on to our subject, which we shall divide into three Chapters, viz.:

I. —*The Existence and Nature of God.*

II. —*The Life of God.*

III.—*The Action of God in the Created Universe.*

CHAPTER I.

EXISTENCE AND NATURE OF GOD.

ARTICLE I.—THE EXISTENCE OF GOD.

3. As we shall see presently, actual *existence* is the very *essence* of God. The proposition "God exists" is therefore analytical, immediately evident *in itself,* just as the proposition "the whole is greater than the half." Nevertheless, since we have no immediate perception of the Divine Essence this proposition is not immediately evident *to us.* For us it is knowledge arrived at by more or less simple demonstration. We see God's works and from them we reason back to His existence. But although we come to the knowledge of God's existence by reasoning, our certitude of His existence is not necessarily the result of a *formal* scientific demonstration. A natural proof sufficient for perfect certitude offers itself, as it were, spontaneously to every human mind. "The existence of God," said Cardinal Newman, "is as certain to me as the certainty of my own existence, though when I try to put the grounds of that certainty into logical shape, I find a difficulty in doing so in mood and figure to my satisfaction." Hence, process of formal demonstration, when made use of, find in the mind already a conviction of God's existence, and only serve to set forth in detail the bases of this conviction and so confirm and strengthen it.

4. The proofs of the existence of God are of two kinds
—*direct* and *indirect*.

The *indirect* proofs show that our knowledge of God's
existence is a necessary outcome of man's rational nature.
These proofs are taken from the universality and constancy of
this knowledge, and of the moral and religious activity based
upon it. The arguments drawn from these facts is often
spoken of as the *moral* argument for existence of God.

The *direct* proofs present God to us as the only ultimate
Sufficient Cause of the physical effects we perceive within and
around us. In this case we may direct our attention either to
certain evidently *essential* characteristics of ourselves and the
other beings around us, *e. g.,* dependence and contingency of
existence, and thus we have what is called the *metaphysical*
argument; or we may consider merely the purpose, design,
finality exhibited in the construction of individual things or
in the whole cosmic order, and we have what is called the
physical or *teleological* proof of the existence of God.

Besides these, there is what might be called the "historical" proof, i. e., preternatural manifestations of the Divine
power in physical and moral miracles, answers to prayer, signal
punishment of evil and rewards of virtue, etc., witnessed to by
the most unimpeachable human testimony.

In the present article we shall confine ourselves to three
simple arguments selected from the three classes of proofs—
metaphysical, physical and moral—of which we have spoken.

(i) Metaphysical Argument.

5. Everywhere around us we perceive effects proceeding
from causes, while of the causes which fall within range of
our experience, many are evidently themselves effects of prior
causes, i. e., we are clearly conscious of the existence of *dependent, contingent, caused* beings. But the existence of
contingent, dependent, caused things—be they few or many—
necessarily implies the existence of an *uncaused* Being (one or

manifold) which is self-existent, and the ultimate and proportionate sufficient reason of all produced things. Therefore, outside of the series, however numerous, of contingent things, an independent, self-existing Being who is the ultimate and proportionate sufficient reason of all caused perfections, whether of *mind* or *matter*—God—exists.

The *major* is a matter of self-evident internal and external experience. To deny it would be to deny all change, all activity in the universe. Thus all the wonderful results of human intelligence, will and energy, are *new* things; each human soul is a *new* thing; the human race itself is a *new* thing; all the marvelous forms of plant and animal life are *new* things, and we can put our finger on the point of time where they first appeared; the whole present cosmic order is something *new* which science tells us *began* to be and will *cease* to be. Now, all these *new* things are *effects* for which an ultimate proportionate *cause* must be assigned.

The *minor* is hardly less evident. For the ultimate cause (one or manifold) of all the *new* beings, substantial or accidental, that have come, and are constantly coming, into existence around us, is either uncaused and self-existent or produced by a prior cause. In the former case, the self-existent Being whose existence we are asserting, is conceded. If the latter alternative is chosen, the same question recurs as to the producer of this produced cause, and must inevitably recur until we arrive at an *uncaused self-existent* First Cause. Insufficiency, adequately to account for its own existence, and consequently, for the existence of the effects which proceed from it, is an essential note of every contingent, produced cause; and hence, however you multiply such causes—to infinity even if you will—as they never lose their essential nature, so they never lose their radical insufficiency to account for their own existence or the existence of the effects to which they give rise. To say that if the number of *caused causes* were conceived to be infinite, they would be sufficient to account for all

existences, independently of a *self-existent cause,* would be—
not to speak of other absurdities—the same as saying that an
infinite number of *zeros* equal *one.* Insufficiency for existence
is the very groundwork of their nature, and no sum or product
of them can get rid of it. Hence, the truth of the old scholastic
saying, "if a self-existent being did not exist it would be a
metaphysical impossibility that anything should exist,"—a
formula which expresses at once a fundamental law of being
and a necessary law of thought.

6. Thus then, if it be once admitted that *anything* exists,
even a transient thought or feeling, there is no escaping the
conclusion that a self-existent being exists. But now before
going further, let us try to get a clear idea, once for all, of
what self-existence means. It means:

(a) That such a being cannot, without a contradiction of
thought, be conceived as non-existing. For, if it were so conceived, it would be conceived as at the same time self-existing
and not self-existing; as receiving its existence either from
itself as non-existent which is a manifest contradiction, or from
some other pre-existing Being, and then it would be a produced
Being, not a self-existent First Cause. Therefore, a self-existent Being is a *necessary* Being, i. e., one that cannot *not*
exist, one that is inconceivable as non-existent (Gen. Met.
n. 79).

(b) The existence then, of such a Being is *unreceived,*
and consequently belongs to its intrinsic nature or essence.
Nor can its existence be conceived as an entity distinct from its
essence. It must be conceived as the intrinsic constituent of
its essence (Gen. Met. n. 37). Hence, actuality, existence constitutes the ultimate radical essence of a self-existent Being,
and any concept that would represent its essence as a potentiality distinct from existence, would be self-destructive and
contradictory.

(c)   Again, since there can be no actually existing Being which is not *this* determinate, individual Being, it follows that all that pertains to the *mode* of existence of a self-existent Being, belongs to its essence; and is as *necessary* as its existence itself.   Hence, as we cannot conceive the essence of such a Being as non-existent, neither can we conceive its determinate *mode* of existence as other than it is.   In fact in such a Being, essence, mode of existence and existence are one and the same necssary entity, and cannot be conceived apart, and are, therefore, equally incapable of non-existence or mutability.   Hence, a self-existent Being is one without beginning, end, or capacity for change, i. e., *immutable* and *eternal* in the strict sense of the word.

(d)   Again, since nothing indefinite can exist, a self-existent Being must be either finite or infinite in actual entity or perfection.   But such a Being cannot be conceived as finite. Therefore, it must be *infinite* in actual entity or perfection. For its actuality cannot be limited from without, because it is self-existent.   On the other hand, if it were limited from within, then we should have to conceive its essence as *limiting* its actuality, or concrete existent reality, to a given circumscribed sum of notes to the exclusion of other possible perfections, i. e., its essence would necessarily be conceived as a receiver measuring and confining actuality or existence within a certain limited sphere of perfection.   But that which limits, measures, confines, must be *conceived* as distinct from, and prior, at least in thought to that which it limits.   Consequently, in the hypothesis that a self-existent Being is self-limited and finite in actuality, its essence must be conceived as distinct from existence, as not self-existent, i. e., our ultimate concept in the analysis of things, would give us not existence, but mere potentiality, which is a contradiction (Gen. Met. n. 38-77).

Again, it could be argued that, since self-existent Being is the sufficient reason of all other actual and possible Beings, it must contain in itself, in a manner in keeping with its nature, i. e., independently, necessarily, eternally, the perfections of all those Beings, else they would not be actual or possible. But thus to possess the perfections of all actual and possible Being is to possess a perfection than which no greater is conceivable. Consequently, such a Being must be infinite in perfection.

(e) Furthermore a first, self-existent Being cannot be a *composite* Being, i. e., made up of either quantitative or essential parts. For a compound is posterior to and dependent on the parts of which it is composed and the force which binds them together. A *compound,* again, is conceivable as resolved into its components, and therefore, as non-existent. Lastly, a *compound,* as being made up of parts, consist of a sum of essentially perfectible, and therefore, imperfect elements. But no sum of such imperfect entities will give us absolute infinite perfection. Now as we have just seen a self-existent Being is ultimate, independent, inconceivable as non existent, absolutely infinite in perfection. Therefore, it cannot be compound. Briefly, we may say that *simplicity* is a pure perfection; *composition,* an imperfection; therefore, the former must be affirmed, and the latter denied of a self-existent Being.

NOTE.—From the preceding analysis it follows (i) that a self-existent Being must be a *substance,* since no *accident* can be an ultimate or independent Being. (ii) It cannot be an *incomplete* substance else it would not be wholly perfect in itself. (iii) It must be a *simple spiritual* substance, since all corporeal substances are both essentially and quantitatively composite, and lacks the perfections of thought and volition. (iv) It cannot be conceived as a *subject* of inherent *accidents;* else its substantial essence would be conceived as *perfectible,* and lacking in itself the perfections which such imperfect accidents confer, and therefore, finite in entity and perfection. Hence, in a self-existent Being, its knowledge, volition, etc., cannot be conceived as they are in us, i. e., as superadded variable accidents, but as wholly *identified* with its substance.

(f)   Again, self-existent Being must be *one* and *only one* in number, i. e., *unicity* is a necessary consequence of self-existence. A self-existent Being is an infinitely perfect Being. But a plurality of infinitely perfect Beings involves a manifest contradiction; for, as being self-existent, necessary, etc., their perfection would be *univocal;* while on the other hand, as being individually distinct, each would have a perfection of its own, peculiar to itself, and constituting its *individuality,* and therefore not possessed by the others: But the sum of all these particular and individual perfections would be greater than any of them singly, and consequently none of these supposed self-existent Beings would be infinitely perfect. Again, all of them would have to be supposed *omnipotent,* yet none of them would be independent in its external action, or in its dominion over all contingent Beings, i. e., they would have to be conceived as omnipotent and not omnipotent at the same time.

(g)   Lastly, this one self-existent Being must contain in itself in a manner proportionate to its simple, infinitely perfect nature, all perfections of all caused Beings. They have all they have from it, and it can give only what it has got in an equivalent or a nobler degree. All caused perfections are ultimately the effects of its action, and the action of a Being cannot produce anything greater than itself, though it may, and usually does, and in the case of a self-existent Being, *must* produce effects less perfect than itself. Consequently, as we find life, mind, free-will, and personality in the universe, the self-existent Being must be a living personal Being, with knowledge and liberty. Moreover, since this Being is infinitely perfect, it has knowledge and freedom in the highest degree, and since it is a necessary being, it has these perfections necessarily, eternally and immutably.

7. Thus, then given the existence of any Being, however short lived and insignificant, we are inevitably led by the necessary laws of thought and being, into the presence of one simple, self-existing, eternal, immutable, infinite, spiritual substance—a Living, Personal God. Of these and other attributes of the Divine Nature we shall speak in detail presently; here, we have been concerned merely to show that they are necessarily involved in the concept of self-existence, just as self-existence is necessary to account adequately for the existence of Contingent Being. All we want to insist upon, however, is that, given the world we live in, a *self-existent Being* must be admitted.

NOTE (1).—It is legitimate to argue from a Distributive to a Collective sense, i. e., to deny a given predicate of a whole collection, when the predicate denied is in every way, both wholly and partially, excluded from each and every individual of the collection, e. g., neither *a* nor *b*, nor *c*, etc., has any money, therefore the whole group has no money.

(2).—A caused Being may suffice *proximately* to account for the existence of other Beings produced by it; but not *absolutely* and *ultimately,* as its own existence is dependent and received.

(3).—The Law of Causality does not mean that *every* Being must have a cause, but that every *new* or *contingent* Being must have a cause; nor does a self-existent Being mean a *self-caused* Being.

(4).—Of course, we cannot *imagine* a self-existent, eternal, infinite Being, nor can we form an *adequate concept* of such a Being, which represents it just as it is in itself; but we can form a *clear* and more or less *distinct* concept of it which suffices to distinguish it from the most perfect finite Being, and thus far, at least, it is neither *unknowable* nor *unbnown.*

(ii) **Physical Argument.**

8. Self-existence is the Middle Term which the philosopher chiefly employs to demonstrate the conclusions which his reason can reach in regard to God. Yet, though his method of argumentation is not very subtle or abstruse, it can hardly be supposed to be the one followed by the great multitude of men, women and children of all times, and stages of culture, in reaching their conviction of the existence of God. There is an easier and more obvious way, open to all who have the use of reason. The *order* of the physical world without and the moral world within man, brings home to him with almost immediate evidence, the existence of a Supreme Intelligence which disposes and controls all the activities at work in nature and to which man himself is accountable for his actions.

The *teleological* argument may be formulated briefly thus: In the universe around us, on earth, in sea and sky, we find innumerable blind, unintelligent activities—mechanical, chemical, physical and vital—co-ordinated and adjusted so as to work together uniformly, constantly and harmoniously for the attainment of definite ends, particular and universal. But the ultimate sufficient reason for this co-ordination and adjustment of such activities can only be found in a Supremely Intelligent Being who rules the material universe with wisdom and power. Therefore, above and distinct from the ordered world, there is a Supremely Intelligent Being who controls it, i. e., God.

As to the *major;* each particular natural science bears its witness to the universality of law, order and purpose everywhere in nature. Astronomy, chemistry, physics, anatomy, physiology, natural history, etc., may be called sciences of the *order* displayed in the various fields of nature. Telescope and microscope, the more perfect they become, reveal to us more fully the mathematical exactness with which order is followed and purpose accomplished, as well by the motions of mighty planets as by the functions of infinitesimal animalculæ. Indeed, the great lesson which the advance of physical science teaches us is that all natural agents known to us, and all *parts* of each work together for the good of all. Each acts blindly and by a necessity of its nature; yet all these manifold unintelligent activities, amid unceasing changes, are so balanced and adjusted and harmonized as to result in a *cosmos,* where order and purpose are visibly *executed,* however they may have *originated.*

Minor.—To bring this result about, to *originate* this complex, constant *dynamic order,* the special laws which govern the activities of each of the innumerable unintelligent agents at work, must be taken into account, and so adjusted, harmonized and co-ordinated, that while the good of individuals is attained, this is subordinated to more universal and loftier ends. Now, thus to co-ordinate and harmonize the blind activities of nature, manifests an *art* or "knowledge of how to do things," beside which the the highest human art is dwarfed and insignificant. Hence, if it is considered a triumph of mind to *understand* even the little our greatest scientist do, of the order of nature, surely the Being who *originated* the marvelously complex order of the universe must be admitted to be *intelligent.* (Gen. Met. n. 82-84, also n. 71). But this intelligent cause of the order of the universe is either a self-existent or a produced Being. If the former alternative is chosen, the existence of God is admitted; if the latter, the metaphysician of the preceding paragraph will take up the argument and carry it on to its conclusion.

9. To put the same argument in another form:

(i) The order of the *inorganic* world around us, *e. g.,* the regular motion of the bodies of which it is composed, the supply and distribution of light, heat, air, water, soils, etc., upon the earth so admirably adapted for the support of plant and animal life, etc.—is a *new* thing, and therefore, a *caused* thing. Hence, even assuming that our system has resulted from the condensation and division of a primitive rotating nebula, "the more purely a mechanist the speculator is, the more firmly does he assume a *primordial molecular arrangement,* of the which the actual phenomena are the consequences."—Huxley. Or as Mill puts it, "the variety in the effects depends partly upon the amount of force applied, and partly upon the diversity of the primitive collections." Supposing, then, that say twenty or thirty million years ago the chemical elements of the fiery cloud were so grouped with such a definite amount of motion in such a definite direction that "competent physico-mathematical skill could predict" the order manifested today in the inorganic world, we are led to ask *who* or *what* grouped those chemcial particles in that wonderful "primordial arrangement," and communicated to them just the proper amount of motion, and in just the proper direction, to give us our present solar system with all its mechanical, physical and chemical harmonies?

That primitive order cannot have been the result of the "forces of matter" else it would not have been a "primordial arrangement," but the result of a *previous ordered grouping* of the elements, whose origin would have to be accounted for. It cannot have been *essential* to matter, else it could not have been changed for the present arrangement. The only explanation, therefore, that can be accepted without doing violence to reason, is to admit that the order manifested in the inorganic world owes its origin, whether nebular or otherwise, to an *intelligent* cause.

(ii) If the mere forces of matter are inadequate to account for the order of the *inorganic* world, much less can they account for the order manifested in the structure, functions, activities, instincts, etc., of the *organic* world of plant and animal life. See Cosmology, Chap. 3.

(iii) Finally, *Man* himself is to himself the most obvious proof of the existence of an Intelligent Creator. Endowed with the power of perceiving the order displayed within and around him, and conscious of his own powers of intelligence and will and of the "absolute validity of the law of causation," he concludes with the fullest certainty that himself and the universe he dwells in are the work of a Supreme Intelligence.

NOTE (1).—*Nature* is nothing but the collection of contingent agencies at work in the universe; hence, it is true to say that nature *executes* the order of the universe, but not that it *originated* or designed it. In the same way the "laws of nature," as the phrase is commonly taken, simply mean the uniform manner of acting of those individual agencies when left to themselves. Nature, then, is a sum of agents, each with its own laws, or constant manner of acting. Such a collection will never give us the ordered world in which we live without adjustment and co-ordination and subordination of those various activities for the attainment of manifold particular and universal ends; and for this, Mind is needed.

(2).—The teleological argument is not founded on *analogy,* but on the principle of *causality,* i. e., The order and finality apparent in the inorganic and organic worlds must have a sufficient cause, and this sufficient cause must be an Intelligent Power.

(3).—When it is objected that there is much purposelessness and failure in the universe, we must remind our opponent that he is assuming that he knows the relations of the object he calls purposeless, to all other creatures in the universe, which is certainly a large assumption for the human mind to make. A man need not understand the precise part each wheel and axle of a machine is destined to play, in order to be certain that it is constructed with a purpose. And as to failure in nature, it is well to remember the saying of Huxley, that to contemporaries, doubtless, in the carboniferous, the waste of vegetation would have appeared extravagant, while

the ordered chemistry of nature was surely and silently forming the coal-beds on which so much of the material progress
of later times depends.

(4).—We do not care to maintain that the order manifest in nature leads us *immediately* to the knowledge of an
infinite Intelligence, though it certainly does so mediately and
inferentially. All that we are concerned to defend here is that
given an innumerable multitude of unconscious, necessarily-
acting agents whose activities are yet so exquisitely balanced
and adjusted and controlled that they all, small and great,
uniformly and constantly, meet and fit into each other in an
endless circle of harmony and purpose—given this fact, we
say, which is as obvious as any physical fact in nature, a proportionate Intelligent and ordering Power is required to account for its existence. Even Hume himself is forced to admit
this: "The whole frame of nature," he says, "bespeaks an
Intelligent Author, and no rational inquirer can, after serious
reflection, suspend his belief for one moment with regard to
the primary principles of theism * * * All things in the
universe are evidently of a piece. Everything is adjusted to
everything. One design prevails throughout the whole. And
this uniformity leads the mind to acknowledge one Author."
And Kant: "Roused from all mental suspense, as from a
dream, by one glance at the wonders of nature and the majesty of the cosmos, reason soars from height to height till it
reaches the Supreme Author of all."

(iii) Moral Argument.

10. A judgment on a matter of the utmost importance
to man, which has prevailed constantly and uniformly among
all peoples, at all times, and in all places, which has outlasted
all changes in human institutions, and is, as it were, a distinctive characteristic of man in every condition of civilization
or savagery, which no effort of the lower nature which it
bridles and checks can ever wholly suppress, which is firmest

in the highest and purest of our race, and which becomes clearer and more inevitable the more it is scientifically investigated—such a judgment must be admitted to flow spontaneously from our rational nature itself, and therefore cannot be erroneous. But such is the judgment of mankind as to the existence of a Supreme Being on whom all things depend, and to whom man himself is accountable for his actions. Therefore, this judgment must be considered as a primary truth of reason, and cannot be false, if we are to place any trust in man's cognitive faculties.

When we see a phenomenon occurring regularly and constantly we say there is a law of nature which rules it. The affirmation of the existence of God has all the constancy of a law of nature. It is, therefore, a necessary law of intellectual and moral gravitation in humanity towards its source and centre, God.

The minor of our argument states a fact which is testified to by all competent historians and travelers, and by monuments, languages, customs, etc., of all nations. "Religion," says Ticle, "is a universal phenomenan of humanity." "There is no evidence," says Tyler, an unwilling witness, "sufficient to warrant the assertion that there exists anywhere any race of human beings without religion." "There is no necessity," says Livingstone, speaking of the Bechuanas, "to tell the most degraded of these people of the existence of a God or of a future state, the facts being universally admitted." Of the negroes of the slave coast of Africa, Baudin writes: "In their religious systems the idea of God is fundamental; they believe in a Supreme Primordial Being, the Lord of the universe." Archbishop Vaughan is witness that the aborigines of Australia believe in a Supreme Being; and among our own Indian tribes the belief in the *Great Spirit* is practically universal. But there is no need to multiply quotations in regard to modern races. Wherever civilized man meets his savage brother, and knows enough of his language and character to enter into easy communication with him, he always finds in him that "Sensus Numinis" which proves an intellectual and moral kinship between them. Hasty assertions are often made, but fuller knowledge invariably proves them to have been unfounded. "Not many years ago," says Max Muller, "it was supposed that the Zulus had no religion; at present our very Bishops have been silenced by their theological inquiries. A more striking instance still is that of the Andaman Islanders. They cultivate no crops, raise no cattle, have no knowledge of metals, or even of how to make a fire. Writing is quite unknown to them. Their dress consists of a paste of clay, with which they cover their bodies, allowing it to dry and form a sort of carapaca. The few implements they use are of the rudest pattern and made of stone, shells or wood. They were long thought to be completely destitute of religious or moral ideas, and to represent the lowest type of humanity in existence, or rather a sort of missing link between ape and man. Better knowledge of them, however, has shown that they believe in one God who is the Creator of the world, all powerful, full of pity for those who suffer, who punishes the wicked after death, and rewards the good with an eternal recompense. They believe also in the resurrection of the body, in original sin, etc., etc. They are strict monogamists, and most exact in all that regards truthfulness, honesty, fidelity, mutual respect, etc.

As to the ancient nations, Plutarch tells us: "You may find cities without walls, or literature, or laws, or fixed habitations, or money. But a city destitute of temples and gods, a city without prayers and oracles, and sacrifices to obtain good, and turn away evil, no one has ever seen." Of the Chinese, De Harlez tells us: "The primitive religion of the Chinese was, and continued to be, the most spiritual and the most perfect form of monotheism ever known through ancient times outside the pale of Judaism." Of ancient

Egypt, Chevalier says: "The higher we ascend towards the origin of the Egyptian nation the clearer we find in their primitive purity the principles of the natural law; * * * the adoration of the one only God, Creator of the world and man."

In the long list of the great masters of science, from Plato and Aristotle to Kelvin and Pasteur, it would perhaps be impossible to find one who did not openly confess his conviction of the existence of God. "Many excellent people," says Lord Rayleigh, "are afraid of science, as leading toward materialism * * * It is true that among scientific men, as in other classes, crude views are to be met with as to the deeper things of nature; but that the life-long beliefs of Newton, of Faraday, and of Maxwell are inconsistent with the scientific habit of the mind is surely a proposition which I need not pause to refute."

"To treat of God is a part of natural science. The whole variety of created things could arise only from the *design* and *will* of a necessarily-existing Being." Newton.

"The heavens, the sun, the planets, proclaim the glory of God."—Kepler.

"Overpowering proofs of intelligence and benevolent design lie around us, showing us through nature the influence of a Free Will, and teaching us that all living things depend upon one, ever-acting Creator and Ruler."—Kelvin.

"We find that all knowledge must lead up to one great result, that of an intelligent recognition of the Creator through his works."—Siemens.

"We assume as absolutely evident the existence of a Deity, who is the Creator and Upholder of all things.'"—Tait and Stewart.

We will conclude with a quotation from the recent work of A. R. Wallace, who may fairly claim to be joint-author of the Darwinian theory: "There are at least three stages in the development of the organic world, when some *new cause* *or power must necessarily have come into action.* The first stage is the change from inorganic to organic, when the earliest vegetable cell first appeared. The next stage is still more marvelous, still more *completely beyond all probability of explanation by matter, its laws and forces.* It is the introduction of sensation. The third stage is the existence in man of a number of his characteristic and noblest faculties. * * * These three distinct stages of progress from the inorganic world of matter and motion up to man, point clearly to an unseen universe, *a world of spirit,* to which the world of matter is altogether subordinate."

Thus, therefore, we find everywhere, as universal in time and place as humanity itself, a firmly-rooted belief in the existence of a Supreme Personal Being, the author of the universe, to whom man offers homage and feels he is responsible. The concept may be vague and indistinct and even distorted. But yet it is there, and whatever counterfeit may have taken the place of the Divine Reality, the very counterfeit bears witness to the spontaneity of the judgment of mankind that above and beyond the world there reigns a Supreme Invisible Being on whom it depends, and who is all-powerful to save or to destroy.

The universality and spontaneity of belief in a Supreme Lord and Master being thus established, it is easy to trace it back to its true origin. The cause must be as universal as humanity. But there is only one such case—rational nature itself, yielding to the evidence of objective truth. No influence of disordered *will* or *passions* can account for belief in a Being who forbids and punishes their indulgence. *Education* will not account for it, for education is as various and changeable as the various races of men. *Ignorance* will not account for it, for ignorance is not universal; Plato, and Cicero, and Newton, and Clerk Maxwell, and Pasteur, for example, can hardly be considered ignorant men. In a word, no accidental, variable cause is proportionate to this universal effect. Therefore, its cause must be found in the invariable rational nature of man necessarily forming a judgment on a matter of utmost importance under the influence of objective evidence.

Nor are the *motives* of this judgment far to seek. The human mind, no matter how uncultivated, when confronted with the *order* of the inanimate world, with caused, contingent life and with caused, contingent *intellect* and *will,* spontaneously and necessarily infers, in virtue of the Principle of Causality, the existence of a living, intelligent First Cause distinct from and superior to all produced things. And these evidences from *without* derive a new force and interest from the natural capacity and longing for unlimited good, and the sense of duty, obligation and responsibility within.

Note (1).—What we assert in the present argument is that humanity is unanimous in affirming the *existence* of a Supramundane Personal Being who controls the world, and to whom man is accountable for his works. That their concept of the *nature* and *attributes* of this Being is, in many cases, very imperfect and even false, does not detract from the value of their testimony to the *existence* of such a Being as a fact.

(2).—The universality we claim is *moral,* not *physical* or *metaphysical.* The proposition "men hear and speak" is not falsified by the fact that there are some who are deaf and dumb.

(3.—Theoretical Buddhism has never been the religion of the *people* of India.

(4).—It is idle to seek to determine *priori* what were the primitive beliefs of mankind. This can only be known as all other positive facts of *history* are known. Now, the results of the most accurate historical investigations are thus summed up by Rawlinson in his "Religions of the Ancient World:" "The historic review which has here been made lends no support to the theory that there is a uniform growth and progress of religion from fetichism to polytheism, and from polytheism to monotheism. None of the religions here described shows any signs of having been developed out of fetichism. In most of them the *monotheistic* idea is most prominent *at the first,* and gradually becomes obscured and gives way befor a *polytheistic* corruption."

ARTICLE II.—NATURE AND ATTRIBUTES OF GOD.

II. **Self-existence** or *Aseity* may be said to be the fundamental element in our concept of God, inasmuch as (i) it is the first distinctive characteristic of God, absolutely incommunicable to creatures, at which we arrive in reasoning back from the existence of contingent Beings to their ultimate Sufficient Cause; and (ii) as from it, by a process of strict logical reasoning and analysis, we can attain to a distinct explicit knowledge of all the other attributes of the Godhead, knowable by our natural reason in our present state. For, it presents God to us as a Pure Necessary Act of Being, and thus at once shows us that no predicate of contingent Beings, however perfect they may be, can be applied univocally to God; since His perfection is independent and unreceived; theirs produced and dependent. On the other hand, as we have seen above a Pure Act of Being is inconceivable as limited in perfection, as composed of parts, as capable of intrinsic change, etc.; whence, we have the attributes of Infinity, Simplicity, Immutability, etc.

If, then, we are asked to define in our feeble human words what God is, we answer A Self-existent Being. A Pure Act of Being. All that unaided reason can know of God is contained *implicitly* in these few words, and can be gathered from them by analysis.

Note.—It is needless to call attention to the difference between Being as a transcendental predicate of all that is, or can be, and Being as the definition of God. The former prescinds from existence, the latter *is* "necessary existence." The former is the broadest of all predicates in extension, the least in comprehension; the latter is exactly the reverse. Embrace all the pure perfection to which the transcendental term Being can extend, in one most simple self-existent Actuality, and you are not far from our fundamental concept of God.

12. **The Infinity of God.**—The idea of the Infinite is the idea of the plentitude of all Being, of a Being who is all pure perfection without limit. This notion, as we have already said, is, as a matter of fact, conceived by us. We can form the concept of *actual Being,* of a *limit,* of a *negation.* Taking now the ideas *Being,* of *limit,* and of *negation,* we can combine them so as to form the complex idea Being Without Limits, i. e., Infinite Being. To illustrate: We are conscious of a power exercised by ourselves. We can conceive this power vastly increased. We can conceive an agent capable of moving 10,000 tons as easily as we move an ounce, and yet aware that the power of such an agent may be as rigidly limited as our own. But we are not compelled to stop here. We may conceive power without any limits at all. Here we should have the concept of infinite energy. In the same way we can form the concept of infinite intelligence, of infinite holiness, etc., and then, combining all these in one simple entity, we can conceive it as an omniponent, infinitely intelligent, all-holy, etc., Being. Such a concept is doubtless not as clear and distinct as it might be, but most certainly it is not purely negative. To conceive a perfection *without any limits* is not to destroy the positive perfection represented in the concept.

When, then, we say that God is an Infinite Act of Being we mean that He *is* unlimited, absolute perfection, containing in Himself all pure perfections without limit, to the exclusion of all imperfections, i. e., all non-entity. Hence, to speak of God as Infinite Knowledge, Power, Truth, Goodness, Beauty, Holiness, Lovableness, etc., is simply to unfold the contents of the two words, Infinite Being.

Note (1).—All *pure* perfections (Gen. Met. 7. Note) found in creatures, e. g., Life, Knowledge, Will, etc., are *formally* in God, i. e., He has, or rather is, all that these words stand for, apart from imperfection, or limitation, or dependence. The *mixed* perfections (ib.) of creatures are *eminently* and *virtually* in God, i. e., He has, or rather is all they are but in a nobler way; and is capable of producing them, and of doing all that they can do, in a more perfect manner.

(2).—Since the perfections of contingent things are of a wholly different order from those of God, no addition of the former to the latter, so as to form a sum total of perfection greater than that of God, is possible; any more than it is possible to increase the number of men in the world by adding to the actual men their photographs or shadows. Hence, God cannot be co-ordinated or classified with contingent Beings.

13. **The simplicity of God.**—All imperfection must be excluded from a Pure Infinite Act of Being, and consequently all composition, whether it be of essence and existence, of parts quantitative or essential, of substance and accident, etc.; since, as we have seen, every compound Being is necessarily dependent, contingent and finite. Hence, no real distinction is admissible in God between the manifold perfections which we attribute to Him. In Him they are all identified in the One unspeakable Simple Act of Being which is Himself.

Several distinct concepts of one and the same absolutely simple Infinite Being may and must be formed by the finite mind which gleans all its knowledge of such a Being from effects in which His perfection is variously and inadequately manifested. Creatures manifest partially, and, as it were, under various aspects, God's simple infinite perfection. All that all of them have of pure perfection, and infinitely more, is in Him, but in His own divinely simple way, not distinct and dispersed as it is found in creatures. Hence, when we affirm of God the various pure perfections, e. g., intelligence, volition, power, etc., which we find manifested in creatures, these do not imply any *real* distinction or composition in Him.

Yet, as our powers of thought cannot so conceive any of these perfections, that the concept of one explicitly and formally expresses them all, and as God is sovereignly equivalent to them all, we say that there is an Inadequate Virtual distinction between the Divine Nature and such attributes, and between the attributes themselves, as conceived by us (Gen. Met. 15). The perfection of the object and the imperfection of our powers of thought are our grounds for making the distinction, not any composition or real multiplicity in God.

14. **The unity of God.**—In virtue of His absolute perfection God necessarily stands *alone,* above and beyond all other Beings. The Infinity of His Essence excludes the possibility of its multiplication. He exhausts in Himself the plenitude of all perfect Being, so that no Being, who is not dependent on Him for all it has, can be conceived. Hence, the concept of a plurality of God's is self-destructive, for none of them would be infinite in Being, Power, Dominion, etc., and consequently none of them would be God. Again, in the hypothesis of many Gods, the Divine Nature would have to be considered as a universal, determinable by various individuations, and therefore as a potentiality.

Note (1).—Polytheism, as we have seen above, has never been a common belief of mankind. Even in the vast majority of the polytheistic systems known to us, One Being above the multitude of so-called gods and superior to them all, was clearly recognized, e. g., Amon Ra among the Egyptians, Brahma among the people of India, Ormuzd among the Persians, Zeus among the Greeks, Jupiter among the Romans, etc.

(2).—God is *indirectly* the First Cause of the *physical* evil in the universe, (a) inasmuch as it is a *consequence* of the co-ordination and subordination of the necessarily acting physical activities at work in the universe, i. e., of the order of the universe which He *directly* wills and produces (Gen.

Met. 26); and (b) inasmuch as this physical evil is a *means* for the attainment of some higher and more universal good which He directly wills, e. g., patience, charity, heroism, etc., in man.

As to *moral* evil, God is neither directly nor indirectly the cause of it. He indeed creates the free human will, but moral evil does not necessarily flow from it. The liberty by the exercise of which, in the few short years of mortal life, man determines his eternal destiny, is a grand though a dangerous gift. If he abuses it, he alone is the cause of the de-ordination in its physical act which constitutes sin.

Hence, there is no need of an absurd and self-contradictory Supreme Principle of Evil to account for the physical and moral evil in the universe.

(3).—The revealed Mystery of the Blessed Trinity does not contradict but asserts the unity of the Godhead. We believe without understanding how that one and the same Divine Entity subsists in three distinct Persons (Gen. Met. 48), i. e., is thrice self-possessed.

15. **The Immutability of God.**—All change implies composition, potentiality and imperfection in the subject capable of change (Cosm. 14, d). But God is an Infinite, Necessary, Simple, Pure Act of Being. Hence, He is incapable of change in Nature, Attributes and Life. All His judgments, decrees and purposes executed in time are as eternal as His nature. His decrees and purposes are formed in eternity, by an infinitely perfect Will in the light of infinitely perfect Intelligence. To suppose them ever to be changed would imply either error or defect of judgment, or fickleness and inconstancy of will. The heavenly bodies are in constant motion, the elements are ever at work, living things come into existence, increase and pass away, great men come and go, civilization advances and recedes, prayers are heard and answered, but the Divine "Fiat" which immediately co-operates in effecting it all is eternal and immutable, incapable of vicissitude

or shadow of change. The change is in the things affected, not in the First Cause of them. Hence, the realization in time of divine decrees eternally and freely made in full view of all the circumstances of each particular occasion, implies no change in God.

Note (1).—Capability to change a decision once freely taken is not essential to liberty. Freedom is not fickleness.

(2).—All man's free acts, prayers, etc., are eternally before the eyes of God and, as it were, condition His decrees.

(3).—God, in His immutable eternity, wills certain effects to be accomplished at certain times, and as His Will is omnipotent His decrees are, so to say, self-executive at the appointed time without any change in Him.

16. **The Eternity of God.**—Eternity means duration without possibility of beginning, end, or change (Cosm. 16). That it belongs to God is clear. For, beginning, end, and change can have place only in a produced contingent potential Being.

The duration of God is, therefore, absolutely and essentially indivisible: it admits of no past or future, but is a changeless, enduring *present* of all-perfect life. Hence, the Roman Senator defined eternity as "the possession, perfect and all at once, of eternal life." Without beginning, without possibility of end or succession, God possesses in an ever-present Now, infinite, unchangeable perfection of life intelligence and volition.

This ever-present duration of God is equivalent and more than equivalent to all possible successive duration or time, embracing in itself all the duration, without the imperfection of infinite time; just as the infinite simple Being of God embraces all the perfections without the imperfections of infinite finite Beings.

As the immovable centre might simultaneously correspond with and control every point of endlessly multiplied concentric circles moving around it, so God's immutable duration corresponds with, and controls, and embraces in its abiding *present every* point of the successive duration of all possible past and future time.

17. **The Immensity of God.**—As eternity means infinite duration without succession, Immensity means infinite presence without extension.   God as being a Pure Spirit is unextended: as being Infinite, His presence is uncircumscribed by any limits of actual or possible space.   Hence, God's simple spiritual substance eternally *is* wherever anything is or can be. Presence is a perfection; infinite presence, an infinite perfection; therefore, it is an attribute of God.   Again, an agent must be present where its immediate action is; but, the sphere of God's immediate action must be unlimited, else His power would be finite.   Hence, since God cannot change, He must actually be wherever anything could be created, i. e., everywhere.   "God is present everywhere, not only by His Power, but also by His substance; for power cannot subsist without substance."—Newton.

NOTE (1).—We must be careful to correct the imagination which would represent the Divine Immensity as a sort of infinite extension.   To do this, Cardinal Franzelin suggests, after St. Augustine, that we conceive God's presence everywhere as we conceive, *e. g.,* the truth, "twice two equal four" everywhere.   This truth is independent of all limitations of time and space.   It is whole and undivided everywhere. Without change it would be present to the minds of ten thousand new worlds, if they should be created at this moment. It would receive them into its presence rather than they it, and would be no more bounded by their limits than it was before.   Now, in place of this abstract ideal truth, say the same of the concrete substantial Truth, God, and you will have a true concept of His immensity.

CHAPTER II.

THE LIFE OF GOD.

18. In the preceding chapter we demonstrated the existence of God and studied the attributes of the Divine Nature which regard its own *mode of existence* and which are called the *quiescent* attributes of God. It remains for us to treat of the other attributes of God; those, namely, which refer to the *operations* of the Divine Nature; and hence are styled operative. We shall first consider the operations of the divine intelligence and will; for, immanent operations are primarily attributed to the nature possessed of them. Such, then, will be the subject matter of the present chapter, which will consist of two articles:

I. The Divine Intelligence.

II. The Divine Will.

It is to be noted, in addition, that to treat of the divine intelligence and will is the same as to treat of the divine life; for, to think and to will is the life of God (Psych., 42).

ARTICLE I.

THE DIVINE INTELLIGENCE.

19. **That God has intelligence** cannot be doubted. The visible universe with its evident *order* is an open book in which is written in characters bold and clear the sublime wisdom of its Maker. Besides, if man, the creature of God, is intelligent, what ought, then, to be affirmed of the Creator? Again, as knowledge and wisdom are pure perfections and as all pure perfections abide in God, He must, in consequence, be possessed of intelligence.

20. A word now, on **its chief prerogatives.** And, first, *its extreme simplicity.* God, who is a Pure Act, cannot contain within His Being any composition whatever. In the divine intelligence there are not, as in the case of created intelligences, distinct entities, as nature, faculty and operation. In God these are one and undivided save by a logical distinction. Neither is there in the divine intellect a multitude of thoughts, nor a "species intelligibilis," to fecundate it, as it were, and actuate it. Both the one and the other would give to the Being of God a composition most alien to its extreme simplicity.

Its infinite perfection. Since God is perfection itself, whatever, then, can be thought nobly (intensively or extensively) of the divine intelligence must be affirmed of it without limit or measure. Wherefore, it is clearness and distinctness and evidence itself; it is absolutely certain and infallible; it is comprehensive of truth in all its plentitude.

Its eternity. God, because of His eternity, excludes from His Being, as we have seen (16), beginning and end and change. Hence, God's knowledge is immutable: it is the same yesterday, today and forever: as it was for an eternity before the beginning of things, so it is forever after their creation: it is as if nothing thus far had been created, as if everything were yet to be created: as the glance of an eye beholds the actually present, so it regards the course and periods not only of actual centuries but even of all possible times.

Its immensity. This bespeaks the infinite multitude of objects which it covers, and signifies that there is nothing in any way knowable which is hidden from God. Hence, the saying that God is in all things by His presence.

21. Passing from the divine intelligence considered in itself to its objects, we affirm that **God knows and comprehends most perfectly both Himself and all things.**

Proof of 1st Part.—A characteristic of intelligence is self-consciousness; whence it was that in Rational Psychology (8) we argued from the fact of self-consciousness that man had a faculty distinct from sense, i. e., a faculty inorganic or spiritual, an intellect. Now, God's knowledge is evidently most intellectual. Hence, He is self-conscious; in other words, He knows Himself. Besides, this knowledge of Himself is most comprehensive. For God's power of self-consciousness on the one hand and on the other the full cognoscibility of His Being are equal; otherwise, He could not be the Pure Act that He is.

Proof of 2d Part.—St. Thomas, elegantly as he is wont to do, thus demonstrates it. God is the First Cause. His efficiency, therefore, extends to all things, i. e., there is nothing either actual or possible which does not depend on His agency. Now, whoever knows and comprehends the full virtue of an agent knows and comprehends all that it can effect. Since, therefore, God knows and comprehends His own self, and hence His own Agency, He, in consequence, knows and comprehends all things, whether actual or possible.

22. Does God know the evil of things? Most assuredly He does. Did He not, He would not know perfectly the good of which He is the Primary Author, for it must be held that whosoever knows a thing perfectly is aware of all that can happen to it. Now, it can well happen, as daily experience too plainly testifies, that what is good in things can be spoiled, nay even be destroyed, by what is bad in them. Whence, God would not know perfectly the good work of His hands were He not to know also what can mar it, i. e., evil.

NOTE (1).—As a thing is knowable so far as it is existible, and as, again, evil is but the privation of good, wherefore, from what God knows of goodness, He knows what is evil, just as from what He knows of light He knows what is darkness.

(2).—If idea be taken either in the sense of exemplar or model according to which an artificer fashions his work, or in the sense of a principle of cognition, in neither sense is there in the divine intelligence the idea of evil.

23. To complete what has been considered in the foregoing paragraph, it must be added that **the primary and immediate object of the divine intelligence can be only God Himself.**

Proof.—The quasi "species intelligibilis" of the divine intelligence is the divine essence. Now, an essence leads primarily and immediately to no other than that of which it is the essence. Therefore, the divine essence leads the divine intelligence primarily and immediately to the cognition of no other being than God Himself. Wherefore, God knows Himself primarily and immediately, and all other things secondarily and mediately.

24. A special difficulty is attached to God's knowledge of the future. At first sight, it seems to be irreconcilable with the freedom of human action. On this account we lay down the following theses:

God knows the future free actions of His creatures. This is clear from God's immutability. Whence, God knew yesterday what He knows today and will know tomorrow. But tomorrow He will know, *e. g.,* what I will do freely when I am doing it. Wherefore, God knew yesterday and knows today what tomorrow I will do freely; and so of any free action, mine or another's.

25. Moreover, **God not only knows the absolutely future free actions of His creatures, but the conditionally future as well.**

NOTE.—Future actions or events, when considered in their actual occurrence, are styled by many absolutely future; considered not thus, but before they occur as what would occur amid certain given circumstances, they fall under the conditionally future of futuribles. For example, if Cæsar had not died he would have assumed the royal purple is a futurible.

As in the present instance, the futurible oftentimes does not become the future, because the conditions are not actualized.

PROOF.—Who can deny that a free agent placed in such and such circumstances would act in one particular way or another? Certainly, he cannot simultaneously determine himself to two contradictory lines of conduct. Hence, the conditionally future lays claim to determinate truth. But God knows all truth. Therefore, etc. Besides, if God did not know the conditionally future, He could not govern with infallible wisdom. He might be disappointed, taken unawares by an unexpected free act of man or angel. He would, thus, be not Infinite Wisdom. Finally, all men acknowledge the same to be true by the prayers they address to the Deity. For they pray Him to grant them this or that favor in case He foresees that it would be profitable to them.

26. Lastly, **God's knowledge of the future free actions of His creatures is in no way derogatory to the freedom of their will.** Truth of thought, as we have seen in Logic (78), consists in the conformity of thought with thing. Now, conformity of thought with thing neither spoils nor destroys the nature of the thing; a mirror does not disfigure the features it faithfully images. Wherefore, God's perfectly true, and, therefore, infallible knowledge of the future free actions of His creatures neither spoils nor destroys the nature of them: it only faithfully mirrors them from afar, from all eternity.

NOTE.—God's knowledge, considered on the part *of its object,* is threefold; of pure intelligence, of vision, and Scientia Media. His knowledge of pure intelligence embraces His own essence as imitable in all possible creatures: His knowledge of vision comprises both His own actual essence in itself and whatever was, is, or ever will be: His Scientia Media regards what any creature would do under given circumstances. It is so called because the objects of it hold, as it were, a position *between* purely actual and purely possible things.

27. **Objections.**

(a)   God does not see the future; otherwise, a man would act before he existed.

Answer.—God does not see the future occurring from eternity, c.; occurring in time, n.   A man, otherwise, would act before he existed, d.; if God saw a man existing in time and acting from eternity, c.; if God from eternity saw a man existing and acting in time, n.   Things happen *as* God knows they will happen.   Hence, things that will happen in time He sees happening in time; still His knowledge of them is from eternity.

(b)   What God foresees cannot but happen.   Therefore, a free act of man foreseen by God, happens necessarily.

Answer.—Cannot but happen, i. e., infallibly happens, c.; necessarily happens, n.   Hence, n. concl.   God's knowledge does not change the nature of a free act.   The infallible divine foresight of a future event implies, indeed, a *certain* necessity; a *logical necessity* founded on the *real necessity* consequent to the most contingent occurrence, i. e., *after* an event occurs it *cannot be* that it did not occur.   But such a necessity is not the *antecedent necessity* with which an effect is produced by a necessary cause.

(c)   God's knowledge, then, is dependent on creatures.

Answer.—D.; if creatures were the motive as well as the object of God's knowledge, c.; were the object only, n.   In the field of knowledge motives are as causes in the world of reality; the former produce knowledge as the latter produce things. Hence, knowledge depends on its motives as things on their causes.   Now, God in no way depends on creatures.   Hence, they cannot be for Him motives of His knowledge.   On the other hand, the object of knowledge is what is known.   It is only ignorance, then, that is objectless.   Wherefore, creatures are the objects of divine knowledge; else, He would be ignorant of them.

NOTE (1).—*Idea* has various significations.   It more commonly signifies concept or simple apprehsion, as we have seen (Log., 6).   Taken in this sense, a multitude of divine ideas contradicts the divine simplicity and perfection.   It contradicts the divine perfection, because a concept is *inchoative* knowledge (Log., 81) ; it contradicts the divine simplicity, because God is and lives with one supremely simple act.   Another signification is that of archetype; the intellectual model according to which a rational agent works.   So taken, a multitude of ideas does not contradict the divine simplicity and perfection. Not the divine perfection, since it implies that the agent *intelligently* produces many things, which certainly is a perfection. Not the divine simplicity, since multitude does not here refer to the act, but to the objects of God's practical intelligence.

(2).—It is often said that nothing happens without the knowledge of God.   This must not be taken as meaning that the divine knowledge *of itself* is the cause of things, but that it is so *conjointly with the divine will.*   However, the same is not to be affirmed of the divine knowledge styled Vision For, an event will happen, not because God sees it, but contrarily.

ARTICLE II.

THE DIVINE WILL.

28. **There is a divine will** because there is a divine intelligence.   The one necessarily follows the other.   It is impossible that God, comprehending His own infinite goodness and sanctity, would not rejoice with an infinitely great joy in the blissful possession of attributes so divinely lovable.   Now, what else is joy in the possession of a good, if not an act of a will?   There is in God, then, a divine will.   Again, is there not a human free will?   *A fortiori,* there is a divine will; otherwise, the creature would be nobler than the Creator.

29.   Much of what has been affirmed of the nature of the divine intelligence is, mutatis mutandis, to be affirmed of the **nature of the divine will.** Wherefore, God's will is not ours, a *mere faculty.* His will is an ever-enduring *act.* The divine immutability vindicates for Him this high prerogative. Neither is there in Him a distinction of reality between the divine nature and will nor between the divine will and its operations. Both distinctions are repugnant to the divine simplicity. On this same account, the divine will is not exercised through a multitude of acts. Moreover, a multitude of *successive* acts would contravene the divine eternity. Hence, what God wills to be in time He willed from all eternity. Still, notwithstanding the simplicity and immutability of the divine will, human speech is not at fault when it speaks of the acts of the divine will as if they were many, *e. g.,* its liberality, its justice, and its mercy. For, as a strong man at one time can carry away as much as others at several, so the one eternal act of the divine will is *equivalently many,* efficaciously accomplishing more than all human and angelic wills could effect in common. Besides the transcendant perfection of the act of the divine will (formally one yet equivalently many) another ground for the distinctions given to it by the human mind is the diversity and the multiplicity of its objects.

30.   Whence, **theologians distinguish** between God's *antecedent* and His *consequent* will. The antecedent will supposes no condition. The consequent will regards certain conditions to be fulfilled by creatures. Thus, God wishes all to be saved and He damns many. He wishes, indeed, all to be saved and for that reason places at their disposal all necessary means. He does not intend, however, to confer on them the fruits of salvation, unles they on their part comply with prescribed conditions.

31.   To speak becomingly of the **emotions and feelings of the Deity,** one ought to remember that nothing imperfect

is predicable of God. Now, we have seen (Cosmo. 75), that there are concupiscible and irascible appetitions. The latter are hope and despair, courage and fear and anger. In their concept, these clearly involve imperfection, since the object of the irascible appetite is the *difficulty* to be overcome in attaining the good or avoiding the evil. Hence, they cannot with strict propriety of speech be affirmed of God. They are in God not formality, but eminently and virtually (12, Note 1). The same is to be said of sorrow. Besides sorrow, the concupiscible appetitions are love and hatred, desire, aversion and joy. These five abide in God formally for the contrary reason; all of them are predicable of the divine will in its relations to creatures, but only love and joy, in its reference to the Creator. Care, however, should be taken that they be affirmed of Him, not after the manner in which they are ordinarily used in human speech.

32. To conclude what we have to say on the nature of the divine will, we shall speak briefly on **moral attributes** so far as they are predicable of God. Ethics teaches that the human will is made perfect through moral virtue. Now, certain moral virtues, *e. g.*, 'liberality,' 'mercy,' do not imply in their concept any imperfection. Whence, like all other pure perfections, they are affirmed of God, not indeed precisely as habits, i. e., *additional* perfections, but substantially and illimitably.

33. Will, since it is intellectual appetite, is the power of loving, desiring and enjoying what is known by the intellect as good. This is its *object* (Psych. 12). Wherefore, the **object of the divine will** is whatever is known by the divine intelligence to be good. Now, Ontology teaches (22) that every being (Creator and creature) is good. Whence, God Himself and all other things are the objects of the divine will; but they are not so co-ordinately.

34. **God himself, i. e., Goodness Itself, is the primary object of the divine will: all others are its secondary objects.**

NOTE.—By the primary object of a will is meant what is loved, or desired or rejoiced in *for its own self* and *in reference to which* all others are loved or desired or taken pleasure in. These others are the will's secondary objects.

PROOF.—It is thus given by St. Thomas. All things about us in Nature have, as experience teaches, the inborn tendency not only to seek after what is good for them if they lack it, and to rest in the enjoyment of it if they possess it, but also to communicate it to others on attaining it. Man, naturally, not only seeks after knowledge, and is pleased on acquiring it, but having it, would share it with others who are without it. Now, if creatures are diffusive of the good they enjoy, how much more so is the Creator Who is Goodness Itself and Whose perfections are but dimly shadowed forth and faintly imaged in the actions of His creatures. Wherefore, God Himself and all things are objects of the divine will after this order: God Himself, Goodness Itself, is its *final,* i. e., its primary object; all others are its secondary objects, i. e., they are objects *in reference to God* inasmuch as it nobly becomes the Divine Goodness to bestow itself on others as far and as much as is possible.

35. But here arises a special question. **Can evil be the object of the divine will? and how?** It must be remembered, first, that there is physical and moral evil. Physical evil, as we have seen (Ontol., 24), is the privation, or that which effects the privation of some physical good, *e. g.,* 'blindness,' 'sickness.' It mars or destroys the good only of a creature, a finite good. Moral evil, on the contrary, militates against the Infinite Goodness. It is the privation or that which effects the privation of some moral good, i. e., the due

rectitude which ought to obtain between the free act of an intelligent agent and its right reason; and hence ultimately, which ought to obtain between its free act and the God of right reason.

Secondly, a will may regard its object in one of three ways. The object may be loved or desired *on its own account,* i. e., for itself—health. Thus regarded, it is an end. The object, again, may be desired not on its own account but *on account of something else* towards the attainment of which it is a help—medicine for the sake of health. Thus desired, it is a means. Thirdly, it may not be cared for at all, neither as an end nor as a means: it is only suffered, i. e., permitted. Strictly speaking, it is not the object of a will: it is involuntary. Moreover, that such permission be faultless two conditions are required: (1) what is permitted ought not to be the *necessary* consequence of that which is intended; (2) neither ought there to be any obligation to withstand it. Thus a man acts blamelessly when he does good to others, though he knows full surely that some ingrates among them will abuse his beneficence.

Now, God in no way wills moral evil: He permits it. He, however, wills physical evil not for itself, but in reference to some good connected with it.

PROOF.—No evil, not even physical, is *in itself* desirable. Only the good is desirable, and evil is the privation of good. Still, physical evil may be desirable *on account of some good connected with it.* That, in truth, some good may be connected with it follows from its *finiteness.* Physical evil does not vitiate the whole field, as it were, of goodness. Thus, a surgeon would amputate the arm or the leg of a patient, if thereby he could save the life of the sufferer. Similarly, God often wills physical evil for the good connected with it. He punishes a sinner severely for the vindication of the moral order: He wills the death of a horse killed by a falling tree on account of the greater physical good, the conservation of the laws of gravity so widely beneficial. Pope puts this latter point forcibly in his Essay on Man, when he asks the question,

"When the loose mountain trembles from on high,
Shall gravitation cease when you pass by?"

Moral evil, on the other hand, is in no way desired by God. It militates, as we concluded above, against Infinite Goodness, and God will never take up arms against Himself. Hence, since for a fact moral evil does exist, God merely permits it, and properly. It is not the necessary consequence of what He intends. It is the consequence of His gift of free will to an intelligent creature; a consequence which might have been avoided had it so pleased him who committed it. Again, God does not owe it to Himself to prevent it. He does not owe it to His sanctity; for He hates sin and forbids it. He does not owe it to His goodness; for He is not bound to effect the greater good. He does not owe it to His wisdom; because He knows how to draw good from evil. He can thus try man's virtue, make known His divine patience and mercy, and manifest His divine justice. Of course, the manifestation of His divine virtues are not the reason why God permits evil. To think so is to think Calvanistically. But moral evil committed, in consequence of it He intends such a manifestation. This entire paragraph renders groundless Manicheism, which contends that there are two First Causes, one of good, the other of evil.

36. Notes for the solution of objections.

The existence of evil is doubtless a mystery. It is impossible to offer a solution which completely clears up every difficulty attached to it. Let us, then, be resigned to remain with many of our Whys unanswered and be satisfied to show that in the world as we have it there is nothing *demonstrably incompatible* with belief in the power of goodness of its Maker.

The order which pervades the universe is as stern a fact as the existence of physical and moral evil. The former, indeed, is the predominant fact of the two, the latter being to it merely as a partial defect in a structure.

To allow one's eyes to rest on evil alone is *pessimism.*

The sum-total of the world's pain and suffering is after all not proportionately large, compared with the world's contentment and pleasure. Schopenhauer, it is true, pronounced the fact to be otherwise; but he did so falsely. A sound test for deciding this point is to interrogate the 'will to live.' Even Schopenhauer allowed this universality and persistency of the 'will to live,' but he declared it to be an infatuation implanted in us by the malevolence of Nature.

Were there no death to carry off the earlier generations, later generations, for want of room, could not experience the joy of living.

Death, again, is an *intrinsic* necessity.

Pain and suffering are not *pure* evils. Pain warns one of danger and stimulates to action. "I fail to see," justly remarks Professor Flint, "that the nearest approximation to the ideal of blissful life is the existence of a well-fed hog which does not need to exert itself, and is not destined for the slaughter." See (Month; July, 1905; pgs. 1-19).

37. God, then, has a free-will, the sphere of which, **its adequate object,** is as wide as that of His operation 'ad extra.' It cannot be doubted that the divine will is not vitiated with the liberty of contrariety (Psych. No. 16, Note a) ; for God is Holiness Itself, and such vitiation is not essential to liberty; rather it flows from the *weakness* of the finite will.

38. Here speaking of the free will of God, we meet with one of the greatest difficulties in all Theology, the **seeming opposition between the freedom of the divine will and the immutability of the divine being.** In a matter so far above human intelligence, we shall outline cautiously what may be given for its solution.

As the way in which God exists differs essentially from that in which we exist, so also the manner in which God acts, differs from that in which we act. *"Agere sequitar esse."* In this life, therefore, we cannot have a proper (in opposition to an analogical) knowledge of the one and the other divine object. For in this life the proportionate objects of our knowledge are the nature of material things, *their* mode of existing and acting. (Psych., 4 and 5.) Our knowledge, then, of divine things must, perforce, be analogical. From the faint shadow and the obscure image of the Creator in the creature, we rise to our knowledge of God, purifying created perfections of all potentiality and imperfection, and attributing them so negatively purified to the Creator.

Thus, we come to know first, that God's will must be free; for freedom bespeaks mastery and independence. Again, that it must be free in reference to all without Him; otherwise, God would not be the *sole Master* of the Universe, the *one supreme Lord* of heaven and earth. Now, freedom of will implies *indifference,* i. e., the absence of determination or fixation to one thing; the former is inconceivable without the latter. But in the instance of the divine freedom of will, the aforesaid indifference cannot be that of *fact,* i. e., the indifference of a faculty which may or may not be in a state of activity, which may be acting now one way, now another. Indifference like this includes imperfection, and consequently, cannot be affirmed of the divine will. The indifference, then, of the divine free will is that of *term or object.* In other words, the divine will, though ever enduring in one and the same act, may or may not regard this or that object. Carefully note that the perfection of power and independence involved in the concept of *one* infinite act accomplishing more than can be accomplished by a *multitude* of finite acts and accomplishing it all freely, is *God's intrinsically;* whereas the imperfection of mutability contained in the concept of an existing thing that once was not, is the *creature's intrinsically.*

CHAPTER III.

ACTION OF GOD IN THE UNIVERSE.

39. **Certain attributes of God are styled relative.** They are those that refer to existent things, *e. g.,* 'Creator,' 'Lord,' 'Ruler,' etc. Such attributes are affirmed of God not absolutely, but hypothetically. Thus, God is said *absolutely* to be wise and good, because He is so apart from all *supposition* of a created being, but He is said *hypothetically* to be Creator, *if* there exists a creature. Moreover, these attributes import no change in God, since the change they imply in their concept is not in God but in the creature. Whence, the relations which arise from God's action in the Universe are real not on the side of God, but on that of the creature. They are *non-mutual.* (Ontol., 56.) Whence again, the relative attributes of the Deity are affirmed of Him not *from all eternity* but *in time;* for it is in time that their foundations are put.

40. Now, three things can be chiefly considered in every existent creature: (1) its existence, (2) its activities or operations, and (3) its purposes or ends. In this chapter, then, we shall consider **the divine attributes that refer to these three main features of a created being.** And as God acts in the Universe, giving existence to it and all it contains, through the divine operation of *creation and conservation,* and as He acts with its powers and agents for the production of their every effect through the *divine concurrence,* and finally, as He leads all things to their appointed ends through His *divine Providence* over all, the present chapter will consist of the following three articles:

I. —The divine creation and conservation;
II. —The divine concurrence;
III.—The divine providence.

41. We shall first, however, refute **the false and im-**

pious hypothesis of certain philosophers who stupidly confound the material Universe of sight and touch with the
invisible and spiritual God, and thus destroy all concept of
divine creation, conservation and providence. These philosophers are called Pantheists, because they teach *all things* to be
God. Pythagoras before Christ and Scotus Erigena in the
Middle Ages taught that the Universe has come forth from
the Divine Substance by an *outward emanation,* by an out-
pouring or out-putting of the Divinity. The Jewish philosopher Spinoza held that there exists only one substance, infinite,
eternal, and endowed with extension and thought. Both
extension and thought, moreover, are, according to him, necessarily in constant activity, the evolution of the former producing material bodies, and the development of the latter beget-
ting human intelligences. This system of Pantheism is known
as *internal emanation.* Akin to it are the vagaries of the Pantheistic Idealists, of a Fichte, a Schelling, and a Hegel. With
all three a material universe is unreal, bodies with their varied
mechanical, physical, chemical and vital energies being ever-
changing phantasms, like those of a sick man's dream, errone-
ously supposed by simple-minded people to be objective
realities. Fichte, in place of the one infinite, eternal and indeterminate substance of Spinoza, assumes at first one eternal,
indefinite, cogitative subject which he styles TO EGO. This
EGO is not the *personal I* of ordinary speech; it is *individual
in general.* Since it is indeterminate in being, and has no
limits to its activity, it determines itself by conceiving and
knowing its objects; for, it so thinks of its objects that it
constitutes and places itself in diverse and definite states and
positions. Schelling, advancing farther along the line of
abstraction begun by Fichte, prescinds from all that differentiates TO EGO from TO NON-EGO (the subject thinking
from the object thought), and reaches what he names the
indifference of differences. With this he begins as the ABSO-
LUTE, the eternal and infinite reality. This reality pre-

supposed, all other realities follow as the transformations and the phenomena with which the ABSOLUTE whether under the form of object or that of subject extrinsically manifests itself. Hegel finally, attains the limit of German idealistic abstraction in the IDEA. Conceive Schelling's idea of the ABSOLUTE, cut out of it all that it represents and in the remaining empty logical framework you have Hegel's IDEA. He, too, calls his beginning of things absolute which evolves itself in the triple order (1) of the intelligible world of essences, (2) of the sensile world of bodies, and (3) of the internal world of mind. Hence, notions, nature and spirit. Pantheism, if not openly taught, is covertly conveyed in the speculations of many infidels of our day. Agnosticism, for instance, holds that for all we know to the contrary, the world's phenomena may be the sum total of actual being, the existence of God distinct from phenomena being classed among the unknowables.

42. **Now, Pantheism and Agnosticism are systems subversive of religion, of morality, and of society.** For, as Fr. Coppens clearly and sufficiently expresses it, "If Pantheism and Agnosticism were true, each of us would be, or at least might be for all we know, a part of the infinite substance; in fact, the worst men of the world would or might be self-existent, and therefore independent of a Maker and Supreme Master. If so, no one could or should worship a Superior Being; hence, no religion; no one need obey a higher law-giver; hence, no morality; without morality no restraint on man's selfishness, a mere struggle of might; whence, would soon result a mere state of barbarism, the destruction of society."

ARTICLE I.

The Divine Creation and Conservation.

A word first on divine power whence flow creation, conservation and the other divine actions.

i. *Divine Power.*

43. That God is powerful cannot be denied. Active power, for in no other sense can we speak of divine power, is an effective principle, i. e., a principle capable of producing something distinct from itself. Now to be possessed of such a principle is evidently to be possessed of a perfection. Therefore its possession is worthy of God. Following St. Thomas, we may define the power of God, either as a principle executing what the divine will decrees and the divine intelligence directs to be done, or as the very decree of the divine wisdom and good pleasure in so far as it is effective 'ad extra.' Its adequate object is everything besides God, which involves no contradiction. Wherefore, God is all powerful or omnipotent. That, what involves contradiction, *e. g.,* 'a square circle,' 'two mountains without a valley between,' does not lie within the field of divine omnipotence, is due to *no impotence* on the part of God's power, but to the *nothingness* of a verbal fiction. Wherefore speaking exactly, we ought not to say that God can not make a square circle, but rather that a square circle can not be made.

NOTE (1).—The active power of a creature is a quality, i. e., an accidental form distinct from its substance, and moreover, it is not in constant operation. Hence, in a creature all three (nature, power and operation) are really distinct from one another. On the contrary, in God all three are one.

(2).—Since every created agent effects its like it follows that there corresponds to the productive power of a creature a term or object of a determinate kind or particular species. Hence, active powers of a creature are limited or finite. It is not so with regard to the power of the Creator. Founded as it is on the infinite being of God, it too is infinite; and hence, it can effect whatever is existible.

(3).—A trite distinction is that of God's *absolute* and *ordered power.* This must not be taken in the false sense that God's absolute power signifies what He can do, His wisdom, goodness and other perfections not considered; whilst God's ordered power is what He can do, taken in conjunction with His perfections and tempered by them. For what God can do is the possible, and the possible is God's imitability, 'ad extra' which is in no way discordant with His attributes. The true sense of the distinction is twofold. (1) God's absolute power is the divine power considered *in itself,* i. e., by a logical antecedence, considered previously to the decree of the divine will predefining from eternity one order rather than another. In keeping with this, God's ordered power is the divine power considered as *carrying out the decree* of the divine will. (2) God's absolute power is what God can do *over and above the common laws* of grace and nature, as in the case of miracles; whereas God's ordered, or more correctly ordinary, power is what God does *according to the usual courses* of grace and nature.

ii. Creation.

44. We have demonstrated in a preceding paragraph that there is power in God, that this divine power is identified with its own act and the divine essence, and that in consequence it is infinite. Now an infinite power founded on the Self-Existent Being, and identified with its own action, is evidently independent of all outside of itself. Wherefore, the characteristic or special mark of its activity *is to presuppose nothing* of what it effects, i. e., activity is creative; for, **creation** is the production of something out of nothing.

45. Let us dwell a little on this divine operation. We have described it above as the production of something out of nothing. Now, the meaning of this is not, that nothing is made something, but that what is created is not created *out of any*

pre-existing material; or again, that what is created had *nothing of itself* existing previously to its creation.

46. Creation, therefore, is not strictly a *change;* for, the concept of change involves three elements : (1) a term *from* which, (2) a term *to* which, and (3) a *subject* which passes from the one to the other. But in creation there is neither the term from which nor the subject. Thus far we have described creation with respect to its term *from which.* As is plain, it may be defined with regard to its term *to* which and the mode of its efficiency. In the former case creation is the production of a thing in its entirety; in the latter case it is the production of a being, as such.

47. Creation can be considered either **on the part of God alone or on the part of the creature alone.** Creation, then, is either *active* or *passive.* Active creation is, as we have just seen, the *activity* with which God gives being to a creature, i. e., the divine action which is one with the divine essence in relation to creatures. To apprehend this distinctly, it must be remembered that there is immanent action, and there is transitive action. Immanent action *abides in* and perfects the *agent, e. g.,* 'feeling and thinking;' transitive action passes *over to* and perfects the *production, e. g.,* 'building a house.' Now, in God there is both immanent and transitive action. He thinks and wills, and He created the Universe. But with respect to the divine transitive action, it must be added that action predicated of the Creator and the creature is done so *analogically;* and hence, what is said of the operations and creatures and implies, imperfection cannot be affirmed *formally* of the divine operations which are in no way imperfect. Now the transitive action of finite agents is *specified* by what they effect; for, *omne agens agit sibi simile.* But external specification argues the imperfection of a sort of dependence. Therefore, transitive action as such, i. e., formally, cannot be affirmed of God. Creation, then, is *formally immanent* but virtually transitive; inasmuch as, like the transitive action of finite

agents it produces things distinct from itself though in a much nobler way.

48. **God alone can create;** for, creation is the efficiency of infinite power and all creatures have only finite powers.

Finally, the **term of creative action** is a subsistent thing, since existence, the formal object of such efficiency, belongs precisely to subsistent things. Hence, matter and form, accidents and such like are rather *concreated* than created.

49. **Passive creation,** i. e., creation considered on the part of the creature alone, is a *relation* of the creature to the Creator through the beginning of its existence. Since creation is not change in the strict sense of the word, it follows that it does not come under the category of passion, but that of relation. Moreover, it is, as has been said, a *non-mutual relation,* because it is *real* in the *creature* but *logical* in the *Creator.* The creature really depends on the Creator; but the Creator is not on an equal footing with the creature; much less is He dependent upon the creature.

50. Having premised these notions on creation, we affirm that **the Universe and the matter of which it is composed have been created by God.**

PROOF.—Either Creation, or Pantheism, or Dualism, or Aethism must be admitted. Either there is no necessary and infinite being—and we have Atheism; or, if this being exists, it is either really identical with or distinct from the Universe. If identical, we have Pantheism. If distinct, either the Universe is from itself or from the necessary and infinite Being. If from itself, then we have Dualism which admits the multiplication of the self-existent being. If the Universe is from the Infinite and necessary Being it is so either by emanation or by production. If the former, we again have Pantheism. If the latter, either the Infinite Being produces the Universe in its entirety, even the matter of which it is composed, or something real is presupposed to its production and out of which it is made. If the latter, we have Dualism a second time. If the former, we have Creation. The demonstration of creation in truth completes the demonstration of God's existence. There is no God unless there is a Being who is distinct from all other beings and upon whom all other beings *wholly* depend.

Note (1).—Hence Leucippus, Democritus and Epicurus erred in conceiving the Universe to have been evolved out of eternal, immutable, atomic matter. Hence, too, Plato and Anaxagoras erred in supposing the matter of the Universe to be self-existent, its form and order alone to be given by God.

(2).—God in creating the Universe did not act necessarily, since, as we have seen above, God is free in regard to all things about Him. Whether God has created the Universe from all eternity or in time is a question that cannot be solved on *purely rational* grounds. God, undoubtedly, has created the Universe *in time* but we know this from *divine revelation.* Could God if it had so pleased Him create from all eternity has been answered diversely by diverse writers. Some contend that He could not, because eternal creation is a manifest absurdity; others hold that He could, since creation passively considered demands only intrinsic possibility and actively considered is the divine power which is always in act. St. Thomas teaches that both sides are probable.

iii. God, the Exemplary Cause of the Universe.

51. **The creation of the heavens and the earth and all that they contain calls for a divine exemplar.** An exemplar, is a pattern or model which exists in the mind of an artificer and in accordance with which he fashions his work. It has the character of a cause inasmuch as the existence of the work depends on it; had the intelligent agent no knowledge of his work, he could not produce it. Hence, it is styled exemplary cause. Its action is as follows: the will commands the hands of the worker and the intellect guides them, presenting a model

intellectually expressive of the work intended. Now, God created the Universe in accordance with a divine model of it. For every effect that is neither the happening of chance nor the result of necessity, but the work of intelligence, calls for a model or pattern. But the creation of the Universe is the work of divine intelligence. Therefore, the creation of the Universe, of the heavens and the earth and all that they contain, calls for a divine model or exemplar.

52. This exemplar may be either *proximate* or *remote*. The proximate is the very *idea* which God had conceived of creation before He gave it being; the remote is the *source*, i. e., the divine essence whence God intellectually drew the divine concept of creation. That there is a remote exemplar as well as a proximate rests on the truth that the order of intelligence is ultimately founded on the order of reality: and that the divine remote exemplar is the divine essence, is the consequence of the primary objectiveness of this essence for the divine intelligence.

53. **Only intelligent creatures are made according to the image of God.** This proposition states a difference worthy of note between non-intelligent and intelligent creatures with respect to their resemblance to the Deity. All creatures in some way bear in themselves a *resemblance to the Divine Being,* but rational creatures alone rise to the dignity of His image. For, an image, argues St. Thomas, is a resemblance either in *specific likeness* or in the likeness at least of an accidental form *indicative* of what is specific, and chiefly, therefore, in the likeness of shape or figure, *e. g.,* 'the image of the Goddess of Liberty on a silver coin.' Now it is clear, that a specific similitude is had according to the *ultimate* difference of the species.

Whence, as intelligent creatures alone enjoy a resemblance to God so close that there cannot be a *closer,* it follows that they alone *differ the least* from God, and there-

fore, they alone are made to His image.   That intelligent
creatures resemble God far closer than all others do, is seen
from this that non-living creatures resemble Him in having
only existence; living, in having life and existence but intelligent in having intelligence and will as well as life and
existence.

iv.   God, the Final Cause of the Universe.

54.   God in virtue of His *power* is the *effective principle*
of the Universe; and by reason of His *wisdom* is its *Exemplar*.
On account of His *goodness,* it is to be added, He is also its
last end.   This triple relation of the Creator to His creatures,
completes their dependence on Him.   It likewise expresses the
admirable cycle according to which all things come *firstly* from
God and *lastly* return to Him.   We have spoken of God as the
First of efficient and exemplary causes: we shall now speak of
Him as the Last of final causes.

55.   A last end is simply and absolutely so, when all
others are ordained to it, and itself is ordained to none.   Wherefore, it is final not alone in *one order* of being, *e. g.,* "as heaven
is man's last end," but in *every order* of being; it is the *ultimate
end* of the *universal order* of creation.

56.   When it is said that one acts *for* an end, the term
"for" can be used to signify either a *cause* or a *sufficient
reason.*   Now, nothing can be a cause with respect to the divine
will.   Hence, it ought never to be said that God acts for an end
in the sense of His having a final cause for His action.   It is
equally true, on the other hand, that God always acts for a sufficient reason, since He always acts most wisely.   Wherefore
it is always to be said that God acts for an end, in this other
sense of the term.

57.   A will intent on some end looks both to the *good* it
wishes and to the *recipient* of the good.   Both objects taken
together make one adequate end.

58. **Goodness,** as the saying goes, is **diffusive of itself.**
Whence it happens that a noble and liberal soul, conscious to
itself of the possession of some great good, longs to have and
make others partakers in it. In such instances of beneficence,
he who would do good to another, regards himself as the *source*
of good. He is an object of his own will *because* he is good.
But he who has good done him by another is regarded by his
benefactor as the *recipient* of good. He is an object to the will
of his benefactor *in order that* he may participate in good.
Whence, it is plainly seen, that the *motive* for the love of
benevolence is not any good to be found in the beneficiary; nay,
more, such love is purest, when it does good to another in
whom there is nothing save demerit. This of goodness in
general.

59. **The divine goodness is the absolutely final end of
the Universe,** not for the *realization* or *enhancement* of the
divine goodness but in order that creatures may *participate in
it,* each in *its own measure.* That there is a final end for the
divine work of creation is plain enough. God does not; God
cannot work purposelessly 'That this final end is the divine
goodness itself, flows from the principle so often repeated in
this treatise: *all perfections belong to God.* Now, to be the
First of causes, whether efficient, exemplary or final, is a
perfection. Moreover, in the hierachy of causality, the final
cause enjoys the *primacy,* since it is the final cause that renders
the others, *causes in act.* Therefore, God, *i. e.,* the Divine
Goodness Itself is the final end of the Universe. Not in truth
because the divine goodness is as yet to be realized or enhanced
by means of creatures. For, argues the Angelic Doctor, God,
who is the First of agents, does not act as if He had anything to
gain, but only to bestow gifts on others. He who is Pure Act
is in potency to nothing but is the fountain of actuality for
everything. Add to this that *omne recipitur secundum modum
recipientis* and the thesis given at the beginning of this paragraph is made good in all its details.

NOTE (1).—Whence follows the nobler way in which intelligent creatures are ordained to fulfill the high purpose of the Universe. For, as intelligent creatures alone are made to the image of God in having intelligence and will, so they alone participate in the divine *beatitude* which consists in the knowledge and the love of the Supreme God.

(2).—As every creature partakes in the divine goodness, each in its own measure, it follows that every creature manifests the same in like manner. Still, such manifestation is *completed* only through the *intelligent creature*. For it is the *intellect* alone that can perceive the *divine perfections* reflected in the creature. Wherefore, man has been made the "Lord of Creation." "And let him have dominion over the fishes of the sea, and the birds of the air, and the beasts, and the whole earth, and every creeping creature that moveth on the earth." (Genesis: 1: 10). For, (1) they are all useful to him in forwarding his perfection; (2) he alone is capable of dominion, since he alone has intelligence and will; and (3) right order demands that the lower be subject to the higher.

60. **The Universe has been created for the Glory of God.** For what else is the glory of one save the knowledge, the praise of his great and good qualities—*"clara cum laude notitia."* But, as has been said, the Universe has been created to manifest the divine goodness, intelligent creatures effecting the same of themselves by means of the non-intelligent.

61. There is **a distinction of the divine glory** which ought not to be omitted. The divine glory is either *intrinsic or extrinsic.* The intrinsic glory of God is *God's own knowledge and praise* of the divine goodness, a knowledge and a praise worthy of it. The extrinsic glory of God is the *creature's knowledge and praise* of the divine goodness. It is *formally* given by the intelligent creature, but *instrumentally* procured through the non-intelligent.

Now, God's *intrinsic glory* is certainly the *ultimate* purpose of creation according to the manner set forth above. His *extrinsic glory* is the *very participation in the divine goodness* which He bestows on every creature, each participating in it in its own measure. From this, is easily seen the wide difference in meaning between the expression that God acts *for His glory* and the expression that He acts *for Himself*. God does not act as a rich lord would, who clothes his servants in the richest attire not for *their interest* and advantage, but in order to draw the admiration of all to himself.

62. This world cannot be said to be the *best* in an *absolute sense,* i. e., as if there could not be a better. Liebnitz made this mistake. For, the divine goodness is inexhaustible, and consequently, no creation could participate in it to such a degree as to render a higher degree impossible. However, it can be said to be the best in a *relative,* i. e., in a restricted sense; inasmuch as it is *wholly* capable of giving that degree of extrinsic glory which God has created the world to give. As to why He has preferred this degree of glory to another, I answer with St. Augustine, "because it had so pleased Him."

v. Divine Conservation.

63. It was said in the beginning of this article that the divine operation of conservation, as well as that of creation refer to finite existence. The truth is that **conservation is but continued creation.** To apprehend this distinctly, the difference between *direct* and *indirect* conservation must be noted. Indirect conservation *safeguards* the creature against what is *harmful* to its existence, or *procures* for it what is *beneficial*. It does not, therefore, *immediately* regard existence, and hence, it is styled indirect. Some have thought that it is *only* by indirect conservation that God keeps His creatures in being. As we shall see farther on, this is false. Direct conservation, on the contrary, *concerns itself immediately* with

existence. It preserves in duration the existence which the creature received through creation. Hence, it is said to be *continued* creation. As duration is the continuation of existence, so is conservation with respect to creation. How ridiculous, then, the conception of divine conservation by a certain thinker who imagined that it was a *constant re-creation,* the creature at every previous instant having been annihilated. The true conception is that as the creature needed God's action to *come into being,* so it continues to need God's action *to remain in being.* Wherefore, creation and conservation *actively considered* are one and the same divine action; *passively considered,* they differ in concept, inasmuch as the concept of creation contains the note, *beginning of existence,* not contained in that of conservation.

64. **That every creature needs the divine operation of direct conservation to remain in being is plainly evident.** There is the same need of the divine action that a creature remain in being as there is that it come into being. For, the creature is not changed in nature on coming into being; whilst existing, it is as contingent as before existing. Hence, it ever lacks the sufficient reason of its existence. Wherefore, it cannot keep itself in existence; it needs the divine support of conservation.

NOTE.—This truth does not contradict that of the immortality of the soul. Spiritual beings are, indeed, immortal by nature. But this does not mean that they are not also contingent by nature. Being immortal by nature, they are *so* contingent as *ever to call* for God's conservation.

ARTICLE II.

THE DIVINE CONCURRENCE.

65. Creatures, as we have seen, have received existence from the Creator in order to participate in the divine goodness

and thus give testimony to it. Now, creatures resemble the divine goodness in two respects: (1) they are good *in themselves,* i. e., absolutely good, and (2) they are good *for others,* i. e., relatively good (Ontol., *22*). Wherefore, (1) there is the divine action of creation and conservation which gives to creatures the good that is theirs and constantly preserves them in it. (2) There is the divine action of **concurrence** which constantly operates with them in the good they do others, i. e., it operates with them in their activities. We have just considered the divine action of conservation; it remains, then, to consider that of concurrence.

66. This divine action has been variously termed by St. Thomas, *e. g.,* 'the divine influence,' 'the action of God,' 'the divine motion,' 'the operation of God in the works of a creature.' Most modern writers style it, 'the divine concurrence.' The difference is, certainly, one of nomenclature. Still, it is worthy of note, that concurrence *taken literally,* conveys the idea of agents *acting co-ordinately* and having a part share in an effect, *e. g.,* two horses together pulling a wagon which neither could pull, if alone. Now, as is plain, the concurrence of God with the action of a creature cannot be such as that; and no scholastic writer thinks so. Everything not God is *subordinated* to God. Hence, in the case of divine concurrence the finite action of the creature is subordinated to the infinite action of the Creator. Moreover and in consequence, the Creator and the creature cannot be said to be part sharers in the production of anything. The truth is, that both the uncreated and the created agent, each in its own sphere produce the entire effect: the uncreated agent effecting it in the order of Universal Cause; the created, in the order of particular causes. We can borrow an illustration from Logic. The concept of a particular thing depends both on the transcendental notion of thing in general and the categorical notion of this thing in

particular. Without the former notion, the concept would be of *nothing at all;* without the latter it would be of everything in general but of *nothing in particular*.

67. **The commonly accepted use, then, of the term 'divine concurrence'** is that God *also* effects what the creature effects: (1) not, however, by doing part of the work, the creature doing the other part, but producing with the creature the *entire* effect; (2) and this is so effected by God on the one hand acting as the *Universal Cause;* the creature on the other, as a *particular cause;* (3) and moreover, as is seen from the illustration given above, the formal object of the divine activity being *existence and entity,* and the formal object of the created activity being that *particular phase* of existence and activity *specifically corresponding* to the nature of the created activity. Remark finally, that this last note of divine concurrence must not be conceived as signifying that God could not of Himself produce what the creature effects with His divine help. Herein the illustration and the illustrated part company. For the *abstract concept* of Being in general, *prescinding* as it does from every determination of Being cannot give of itself the notion of Being in particular. On the contrary, the *concrete reality* of Infinite Being *containing within Itself* either formally or eminently every reality of finite beings, can do of Itself whatever can be done by finite agencies. To repeat what has been said more than once, God bestows faculties and energies on His creatures and operates with them in their activities not because He stands in need of anything but for the beneficent reason that He would have them participants in His infinite goodness, each in its own measure.

68. Since, then, God operates in the work of His creatures as above stated, it follows that His concurrence is *immediate* as well as mediate. The divine concurrence is mediate because God gives existence to and conserves in being the creature's

nature with its faculties and energies, the effective principles of its operations. It is also immediate, since God as well as the creature is the *immediate effective principle* of the creature's action and effect.

Lastly, the divine concurrence is termed by many *general* and for three reasons: (1) it extends to *every natural* operation of *all* creatures; (2) it does not include the *special* concurrence of God with *some* of His creatures operating in the *supernatural* order; (3) it does not exclude the *determination* and the *specification* proceeding from the operation of the *particular* cause; for, as has been said, God in His divine concurrence acts as the *Universal* Cause, and produces the effect under the formal aspect of *existence and entity*. "It must be said," writes St. Thomas, "that although the First Cause inflows into the effect (as well as the secondary cause), still Its influence is *determined* and *specified* by the proximate cause." Hence, whatever there is of *deficiency physical or moral* in the act of the secondary agent, it must be attributed to the *particular*, and not to the *Universal* cause.

69. Having explained the notes of divine concurrence, we shall now prove that **God concurs immediately with the efficiency of every finite agent.** Every existent thing save God, whether an agent, or an act of an agent, or an effect, is contingent, and therefore has not in itself the sufficiency of its existence. Wherefore, every act or effect of an agent save God, as well as the agent itself, must have its inherent insufficiency for its existence made good by the action of God. Moreover, such insufficiency on the part of the effect or the act of the agent cannot be made good by the mediate action of God, i. e., through the medium of the agent by God *merely* giving existence to the agent and its energies, and conserving both the one and the other in existence. For the agent not having in itself the sufficiency of its own existence, cannot be the sufficient

reason for the existence of anything else. *Nemo dat quod non habet*. For the same reason, nay a fortiori, the act of the agent cannot be the sufficient reason for the existence of the effect. Hence, every act or effect of an agent save God as well as the agent itself must have its inherent insufficiency of its existence made good by the immediate action of God, i. e., God concurs immediately with the efficiency of every finite agent.

70. **The immediate divine concurrence with the free act of an agent does not destroy freedom of will.**

For God thus operates as a universal cause, leaving the determination and the specification of the act to the particular agent. Wherefore, if the act of the agent be naturally free, He allows it to be freely put. As Fr. Coppens vividly illustrates the truth, "the free act is man's and it is God's, but with a difference : as a boat is supported by the water, propelled and directed by the efforts of man, but by means of the water ; so human actions proceed truly from man, but with the concurrence of God." Thus far all scholastic writers are unanimous save Durandus, who held that the divine concurrence was only mediate. They are not in such perfect agreement in their subtle discussions concerning the intimate nature of the divine concurrence.

ARTICLE III.

THE DIVINE PROVIDENCE.

71. Speaking of the ultimate purpose of God's creation of the Universe, we have seen that it is His divine glory. For this, He has created the Universe, giving existence to the heavens and the earth and all they contain ; for this, He conserves all creatures in the existence He bestowed on them ; for this, He concurs with every created activity, thus "leading them to their appointed ends (common and particular) the

lowest by the middlemost and middlemost by the highest."
(St. Ignatius). The divine action by which the Supreme
Ruler of the Universe thus works out His purpose for creating
it, is divine government, or, as it is more commonly termed,
divine providence.

This will be the subject matter of the present article,
which will consist of two sections: one on the ordinary effects
of divine providence and the other on its extraordinary effects
or on miracles.

i. Divine Providence and Its Ordinary Effects.

72. *It is to be remarked first, that* **the providence and
the government of God taken strictly differ:** the former is
the *divine plan* according to which the Universe is to be led to
the end for which it has been created—*ratio ordinandorum ad
finem;* the latter is the execution of the plan. The one, therefore, is an *act of the intelligence* conceiving the end and the
proportionate means of attaining it; the other, an *act of the
will* putting it all into execution. For, providence (*procul
videntia*), is literally *seeing afar,* i. e., looking ahead. It is, says
St. Thomas, "the principal part of prudence to which the two
others are ordained, viz., the memory of the past and the intelligence of the present; inasmuch as, from what we remember of
the past and what we understand of the present, we conjecture
how we are to provide for the future. But it is the part of prudence to order things to an end, either for one's own interest, as
when it is said that he is a prudent man who orders his own
actions in keeping with the purposes of his life; or in the interest of others subject to him in a family, or a city, or a nation
* * * and it is only in this latter instance that prudence or
providence is predicable of God. For there is nothing in God to
be ordered to an end, since He Himself is the Ultimate End."
Wherefore providence, strictly speaking, is an act of the intelligence, as prudence is of which it is a part. Of course, it pre-

supposes the *wish* to accomplish some end, and for this reason it is often attributed to the will. However, as commonly used, providence has a much wider signification, signifying both the plan and the execution. This is the sense in which it is used in the present article.

73. **The object,** then, of divine Providence is twofold: (1) to determine the end of creatures, (2) to afford the means for its attainment. Now, these means are of two kinds. They may be either *intrinsic, e. g.,* 'inherent energies or faculties,' or they may be *extrinsic, e. g.,* 'opportunities and helps from without.' The end also may be twofold; either *universal* and *common* to all, or *particular* to and *proper* of each. The latter is subordinated to the former, as right order demands. We know (60), that the end common to all things is the Glory of God. We know, too (61), that this end is *principally obtained* through intelligent creatures and *instrumentally* through non-intelligent creatures. The end peculiar to each and every creature is not always known to *us;* an ignorance which evidently is no ground for the denial of such an end.

74. **God's providence extends to each and every creature and embraces each and every occurrence.** God, as He is infinitely wise, does nothing purposely. Now, whosoever wills the end wills also the means without which the end cannot be obtained. Therefore, God is provident in whatever He does. But God has created the Universe, conserves in being every creature in it, and concurs with every act performed in it. Therefore, God's providence extends to each and every creature, and embraces each and every occurrence. To an observer this providence becomes in great part palpably evident from the admirable order manifested in the world. The same is also a matter of observation in the conduct of men who pray to God for favors, and reverence Him as the rewarder of virtue and the avenger of vice.

74. **Divine providence regards man with a special care.**
For divine providence, since it is most orderly, cares for each
creature according to the nobility of its nature and the dignity
of its particular end. Now, man excels in nature all the other
creatures in the visible world and is for them their proximate
end, since they were all created *for* him, i. e., as means, to
enable him to know, love and serve God in this world and thus
attain his eternal beatitude in the next. Therefore, divine
providence regards man with a special care. Again, divine
providence regards with greater care a creature who is more
liable to fail in the attainment of the particular end for which
it has been created. But such is man gifted as he is with the
power of free will.

NOTE.—With respect to God, there are no such things as
chance, fortune and fate. Chance and fortune are said of what
occurs as no one expected it would occur; they differ in this,
that the former is an unexpected event in the physical order,
whilst the latter is unlooked for among what is done with a
purpose, i. e., chance happens among *physical* agents; fortune,
among *intelligent*. Now, nothing is unforeseen by God; nothing can take Him by surprise. He not only foresees, but fore-
plans all. Fate can be used in a true and a false sense. As
Boethius has said, fate has a true sense, if used to signify the
immutable disposition which God has made of His mutable
creatures, and according to which He holds them together,
each in its proper sphere. It has a false sense if used to
signify an *insuperable necessity* controlling all things, even the
power of God.

75. Divine providence, so far as it regards the ordination
of things is God's alone, but the order having been established it is **not executed without the agency of secondary
causes.** The reason of the latter is plain. God not only bestows on a creature, a participation in His divine being, but
also in His divine causality. It would be foolish, then, to expect God's help were we to make no effort on our part.

76. We have already seen that the existence of evil in this world is not incompatible with the divine goodness. We shall now see that **the distribution which God makes of the goods of this life and of its evils in no way militates against His divine providence.** A word first on the state of the question. With regard to the aforesaid distribution, we ought not to concede it to be such that the virtuous are always deprived of the good things of this life and the vicious alone are enjoying them. For, not to speak of a good conscience, which alone makes a man truly happy here below, and of a bad conscience, which renders him really miserable, it is not true that the virtuous are perpetually struggling with adverse fortune and the vicious are meeting with uninterrupted success. This is not the testimony of experience. Experience testifies simply to this, that the good many times meet with misfortune and the wicked with prosperity. Now, there are some who seem to have remembrance only for such instances. They never take notice of the misfortune which the wicked often fall into and the success which the good not seldom enjoy; for things then happen as they appear to be merited. But if the facts be broadly considered it will be seen that the good and the wicked are indiscriminately subjected to the ups and down of life. These few remarks having been premised, we shall now establish our thesis. And first it is to be noted that the goods of this life and its evils are rewards and punishments only *secondarily; primarily,* they are means for the attainment of the ultimate purpose of creation. Wherefore, if the distribution which God makes of them is not incompatible with the divine wisdom and goodness, they in no wise militate against divine providence. But the aforesaid distribution is not incompatible with the divine wisdom and goodness; for, through it both the moral order is advanced and the order of nature is conserved. Therefore, etc. Certainly, the moral order is advanced, since the human soul is thus lifted above this life and its perishable goods; since, too, it is thus urged to the constant practice of vir-

tue; the good are enabled to expiate their past offenses and their present faults into which even the very best often fall, and the wicked are drawn away from their evil ways. The *physical* order is also conserved; for this order requires that Nature be ruled by constant laws. Now, the laws of Nature would not be constant if for each and every offense punishment was given and for every act of virtue a reward was offered. Good and bad deeds are the acts of an ever-changing human will. The order of the Universe would, therefore, be in continual fluctuation if a due sanction were to be given on each and every occasion. Besides, free-will would lose much of its zest, since human prosperity and success depend not a little on human will. Finally, if to these be added the teachings of revealed religion, it will become more and more evident that the Supreme Ruler is not only wise and good in His providence, but most loving.

ii. Miracles.

77. **The notion of a miracle has been mistaken by many.** Spinoza, Hobbes and Locke held that the marvelousness of a miracle was due *only* to human ignorance. Their view has been well met by St. Thomas, who wrote centuries before them, "that which *nature* does through agencies unknown to mankind are not miracles, but wondrous works of nature." Houteville contended that a miracle was indeed an *uncommon* phenomenon, but still effected through the very same natural laws which effect the ordinary phenomena of the Universe. Bonnety taught that there were two series of natural laws framed by God; one according to which the ordinary phenomena were produced, the other according to which miracles were effected. It is evident that both hypotheses are gratuitous, and moreover they destroy the very notion of all *supernatural* work. Clark imagined that the laws and the forces of nature are nothing but the will of God, which at one time wills what is com-

mon and ordinary, at another what is uncommon and extraordinary. Such a position is nothing but *Occasionalism.*

78. **A miracle** is what is effected *out of and beyond the
order* of nature under which order lies every created agent.
It has in it these four elements: (1) It must be a phenomenon
of sense, otherwise it would fail of its end, which is to lead
men unto the knowledge of the supernatural. (2) It must
have reference to the natural order. Wherefore, creation and
the justification of the wicked, although they are effected by
God alone, are not miracles. (3) It cannot be produced by
natural causes. This inefficiency on the part of natural causes
may regard not only the very fact in itself, but also the order
and the manner in which it is produced. (4) There should
not exist any natural exigency for which God works it. Hence,
the creation of a soul is not a miracle.

79. **The division of miracles** is two-fold. The first is
the division into miracles (1) as to *substance,* (2) as to *subject,*
(3) and as to *mode.* A miracle as to substance, i. e., with respect to the very thing effected, is such, as from the very *nature*
of it, cannot be effected in *any way* by a natural agent, e. g.,
'the compenetration of bodies.' A miracle as to subject, i. e.,
with respect to that in which it is effected, is such as to exceed
any natural agency on account of the *condition of the subject*
in which it is worked, e. g., 'raising the dead to life.' A miracle as to mode, i. e., with respect to the way in which it is
effected, is such, as to baffle all natural powers not with regard
to the very thing effected, nor the subject in which it is produced, but *the way* in which it is done, e. g., 'a sick man cured
instantly.' Another division is that of miracles (1) *above*
nature, (2) *contrary* to nature, (3) and *not in line with* nature.
Those miracles are above nature which nature *can in no way
effect.* They are contrary to nature if there be in nature *dispo-
sitions contrary* to what is miraculously produced. They are,

finally, not in line with nature when nature can produce the effect itself, though not in the *manner* in which it has been effected.

80. **It cannot be denied that miracles are possible.** For if any impossibility existed, it should be either on the part of God or on the part of what is effected. But on neither hand can there be such an impossibility. Therefore, etc. The minor is thus proved. (a) There is no impossibility on the part of God. (1) For God is *omnipotent* and acts not *necessarily*, but *freely*. (2) His immutability is not thus called into question, since God has so established the order of nature as to reserve to Himself occasions wherein He Himself will work otherwise than the created agent. (3) Neither does any consequence follow contrary to His wisdom. God does not thus correct His work of creation. "The divine art of God," writes St. Thomas, "is not fully unfolded by what God has accomplished in the natural order. Hence, He can work otherwise than the course of nature. Hence, again, it does not follow that if God act contrary to the course of nature He thus acts contrary to His own divine art." (b) There exists no impossibility on the part of what is miraculously effected. This is clear from what we have said of the contingency of the laws of Nature (Cosmo., 23).

81. Some writers, as Rousseau, concede the possibility of miracles, but deny that they can be known when they are effected. Whence the following proposition: **Miracles can be recognized for certain.** It must be noted first, that there are wondrous works which, if they are regarded *absolutely*, i. e., as they are in themselves, they are not beyond angelic powers; but if they are regarded, as they ought to be, *relatively*, i. e., in relation to the order of the Universe, they cannot be effected by any agent placed under that order. An angel can make the earth stand still, and the devil might do so, were he

not held in check by the power of God. It must be noted also
that the end for which God acts miraculously is not the com-
pleting of the physical order. The physical order is in itself
complete, and, moreover, were a miracle its complement, a
miracle would not be a work *beyond* nature. Therefore, a
miracle regards the higher order of Providence. What this
higher order may be, is made evident *a posteriori.* "God,"
teaches St. Thomas, "works miracles for man's sake; either to
confirm some truth, or to demonstrate the sanctity of a person
whom He would propose as an example of virtue." A miracle
has then been fitly likened by the same holy doctor to the royal
seal which has been impressed on the message of a king.
Wherefore, since miracles are for a testimony of divine truth
or virtue, they are in no way connected with diabolic agency.
Having premised these few remarks on the purpose of a miracle. we shall now prove our proposition thus: That a miracle
be recognized to be such, it is sufficient to know *the fact* and
the *nature* of the fact, i. e., the work and its supernaturality.
Now, both can be known for certain. Therefore, etc. And
first as to the fact. It can be known for certain, since it is a
phenomenon of sense, and hence, can be known for certain by
those who properly use their senses, (Log. 108, 109). Secondly, as to the nature of the fact, it, too, can be known for
certain. This is clear in the cases of miracles *above* and *contrary* to nature, since they argue a cause that excels all natural
powers. It is clear also with regard to miracles which are
above nature *with respect to the way* in which the work has
been effected. For he alone can change a law who made it.
But God made the physical laws of nature. Therefore, He
alone, etc. But as the devil can most deftly, cunningly and
hiddenly manipulate the forces of nature, there seems to be
some difficulty in distinguishing his preternatural deeds from
some miracles of the above third class. Still supposing divine
providence, the distinction can be certainly made. For God will
not permit the devil to act save in those circumstances from

which it can be easily seen which is the true and which is the false miracle. Especially is this the case with respect to the *end* for which the work has been accomplished. The works of God are for the advancement of what is virtuous, and those of the devil for the destruction of the same. The *way* also in which the work has been carried on will clearly serve to mark the true from the false miracle. With this brief remarks on what has been termed the link between the natural and the supernatural orders, we shall bring to a close this little treatise on God, to Whom be glory for ever and ever.

INDEX.